The American Century in Europe

The American

Cornell University Press

Ithaca and London

Century in Europe

Edited by

R. LAURENCE MOORE

and

MAURIZIO VAUDAGNA

Cornell University Press acknowledges with gratitude financial support for this volume from the University of Turin and the Luigi Einaudi Foundation in Turin, Italy.

First published 2003 by Cornell University Press

Printed in the United States of America

Library of Congress Cataloging-in-Publication Data

The American century in Europe / edited by R. Laurence Moore and Maurizio Vaudagna.
    p. cm.
Includes bibliographical references and index.
  ISBN 0-8014-4075-0 (cloth : alk. paper)
  1. United States—Relations—Europe. 2. Europe—Relations—United States. I. Moore, R. Laurence (Robert Laurence), 1940– II. Vaudagna, Maurizio.
  D1065.U5 .A795 2003
  327.4073′09′04—dc21   2002012232

Cloth printing   10 9 8 7 6 5 4 3 2 1

Contents

PART TWO   CULTURAL RESPONSES

PART THREE   SOCIAL RESPONSES

Acknowledgments

We thank Hunter Rawlings III, president of Cornell University, and Rinaldo Bertolino, rector of the University of Turin, for funding an agreement of scholarly exchange between Cornell and Turin, the site of a conference on the subject of this book in May 2000. The Bairati Center for European American Studies and the Einaudi Foundation in Turin also sponsored the conference. We thank the University of Eastern Piedmont for generous help in making this book possible. Also, we owe a deep debt to the college of Lady Margaret Hall, University of Oxford, where Dr. Moore was the Starr Foundation Fellow during the final stages of the book.

Ithaca, New York   R. LAURENCE MOORE

Turin, Italy   MAURIZIO VAUDAGNA

The American Century in Europe

Introduction

R. LAURENCE MOORE AND MAURIZIO VAUDAGNA

When the world marched into a new millennium on January 1, 2001, the United States had just ended a decade of unprecedented economic prosperity. For a much longer period it had been the world's most powerful nation. In 1941 Henry Luce, in *Life*, his hugely popular magazine of photojournalism, heralded "The American Century." Luce expected the United States to play a crucial role in the global war it had not yet entered and to lead other nations into a better world once fascism was defeated.

Luce was certainly right to imagine that in the last half of the twentieth century, the United States would act self-consciously as a superpower. However, if more assertive in that role after World War II, the United States had seen itself as a great world power since the beginning of the twentieth century. Even before the Great War that began in 1914, a debate had begun in Europe and in other nations of the world, including the United States itself, as to whether American efforts to export its political and cultural values were good or bad. No one on the eve of the new millennium foresaw the events of September 11, 2001. Yet whatever changed on that day, the attacks on Washington and New York City did not mark the first time that the United States had confronted unpleasant consequences from anti-Americanism.

The authors of this volume have reviewed one century of American political, economic, and cultural power as it was felt in Europe. Disagreements among the authors will be clear. However, in one way or another, all of them accept at least this premise: the twentieth century has been profoundly affected by Woodrow Wilson's desire to make the world safe for democracy and for economic exchange between nations. American policy makers, whether or not they thought of themselves as Wilsonian, consistently sought a "new" world order to replace the one established by European-style imperialism. In place of that European system, Americans talked about an international system of autonomous states freed of colonialism but that operated, especially in trade relations, according to a common set of rules.

American dreams, which rested with impossible simultaneity on a theory of American exceptionalism and a wish to re-mold other countries in the American image, left room for irony, hypocrisy, and plain old deception. As Alan Brinkley notes in the opening chapter, American efforts to promote its own values as ones applicable everywhere seemed to much of the world a reflection of America's insularity, self-regard, and isolation from the legitimate concerns of many of the world's most populated nations. Through a long series of global interventions, many of them useful and some vital, American statesmen in the twentieth century misrepresented and possibly even misunderstood their own colonial designs. However, American influence was without doubt large throughout the world and loomed much larger than it would have because of a century of difficulties that beset Europe. Without Hitler and without Stalin, the United States could never have continued for so long to imagine itself a redeemer nation. And it could never with equal power have pressed American goals upon Europe.

As several authors in this volume argue, efforts by the United States to create a world in its own image reflected deep uneasiness about the ability of democracy to sell itself and even about the fragility of democracy within America's own boundaries. Nervousness led the United States on many occasions to seek a secure future for democracy by coming to the rescue of undemocratic regimes. It viewed friendly, stable, and authoritarian states as better in the short run than "rogue" democratic states. Yet at no point in the twentieth century was American power able to create an orderly world. It took two nations, two "superpowers," to impose a semblance of order among nations during the period of the Cold War. The United States and the Soviet Union and their respective allies and client states threatened one another with nuclear disaster. The potential horrors produced a stalemate because the two nations were not prepared to risk annihilation as long as their essential interests, however vilified by the other side, were acknowledged and let alone. From George

Kennan's "containment" policy emerged a set of rules that restrained the actions of both the United States and the Soviet Union. When the rules of the game were seriously broken, as when the United States sent spy planes over the Soviet Union or when the Soviet Union tried to introduce missiles into Cuba, the offending side backed off.

This is too romantic a reading of the Cold War. The two superpowers may not have fought each other, but in their rivalries they devastated other countries. Military ventures into Afghanistan and Southeast Asia produced disastrous results and left legacies that were to roil world politics far into the future. The Cold War only looked orderly compared with what followed. Some optimists greeted the collapse of the Soviet Union as an American victory. They suggested that American hegemony was complete and that the American Century, now called globalization, would extend well into the twentieth century. History had ended. That fact left many people far from sanguine. If the United States was now the world's only superpower, then what was going to check rash exercises of that power? What was going to blunt the force of American unilateralism, which, as Walter LeFeber notes, had guided American foreign policy in the twentieth century even when Americans ostensibly worked within the framework of NATO or the United Nations?

One answer to that question, of course, is a United Europe. As many of the chapters in this book argue, European states in the twentieth century were not powerless in responding to the American policies pressed upon them. Ronald Steel in particular shows how America's leadership role in NATO was in part thrust upon the United States by Europe, a Europe that wanted the security of American military might without having to pay the costs. French "independence" from American power carried too high a price tag for other nations that worried less about American supremacy than about the dangers posed to them if the United States really took its troops home. For all that, European states tried to guard their sovereignty and bowed to American leadership graciously only when it suited their purposes. A United Europe ought to do better. Perhaps Europe can emerge as something more formidable than the redundant "second pillar" that it has been for most of the post–World War II era. Countries in the Pacific Rim as well loom as potential checks on American power.

But with or without effective checks on the exercise of American power, there is much to worry about. The disintegration of old political boundaries that followed the breakup of the Soviet state spawned new conflicts that threatened to spin out of control. If the American-led coalition won a victory in the Gulf War, then we should be sobered by the understanding that such victories, even if the cause can be justified, bring more trouble. The Gulf War exacerbated old regional tensions and created new global ones that were even more ominous. Meanwhile, ethnic cleansing erupted in Africa, in Asia, and in the Balkans. No nation could halt it before it rang up enormous death tolls and left countless numbers of people homeless and without a stake in the prosperity promised by the new world economy.

Globalization, to the extent that it weakens nationalism, may also work to weaken old-fashioned diplomacy. Some states may collapse, unable to govern and unable to command the resources necessary to maintain an infrastructure. An opportunity opens to terrorists to lodge within weakened nations. These people, as the world has learned, can have agendas quite different from the sorts of considerations that guide diplomatic relations among states, even states hostile to one another. The events of September 2001 sounded a warning about what can happen when state diplomatic channels are bypassed and destructive weapons are up for sale to private groups. Ironically, the technology that launched the global economy was the same technology that made possible a worldwide al-Qaida network. Take away fax machines, cell phones, and the Internet, and they both collapse.

World capitalism, whether emanating from the United States, or Europe, or Asia, may have made everyone unsafe, though not for the reasons advanced by Karl Marx or by the protestors who disrupted world trade meetings in Seattle and Genoa. The disruption of politics as usual is one context for reading the chapters that follow, although they were written well before the attacks on Washington and New York City. Some of the authors revised their chapters in light of those events, although not so drastically as one might suppose. The relative lack of revision owes in part to the simple fact that no one knows how the so-called war against terrorism is going to turn out. Some imagine that at least in the short run the attacks will keep alive the idea of an American Century since the United States, with characteristic retention of decision-making power in a coalition of supposed equals, is the only nation able to mount an effective assault on world terror.

Perhaps more to the point, the triumphalism often associated with boosters of the American Century has played a role in provoking the terrorist threats that now stalk the globe. The sites of American financial power and of American military power were the carefully chosen targets of bin Laden. If most people around the world were profoundly shocked by the wantonness of a lethal assault, without warning, on innocent, ordinary people from many countries, large numbers of those same people thought that Americans could not escape blame for what had happened. More than one political commentator suggested with stupefying bluntness: "America had it coming." The evangelist Jerry Falwell said much the same thing, though for different reasons. The United States is not the cause of all the world's ills, but arrogance invites reprisal. So do global economic activities that advance primarily the interests of the United States and its richest trading partners.

Commentators have recorded the curious fact that the enthusiastic embrace of American culture by many peoples of the world has happened simultaneous with the eruption of anti-American sentiments. People on all continents protest the foreign policy of the United States while wearing American-designed baseball caps. They criticize American materialism yet flock to Hollywood films in which abundance is conspicuously displayed. They find fault with American individualism and dance to American music. Questions about the American Century stretch well beyond issues of international diplomacy. The chapters in this volume also give attention to issues of cultural influence as well as to values associated with the American social system. One general theme is relevant to the study of American influence anywhere in the world. Whatever that influence was, it was never total nor did it cross oceans in only one direction. The volume's title, *The American Century in Europe,* is meant to remind readers that the transmission of ideas and policies to another place always involves translation, not only in the most literal sense of going from one language into another but also in a more general sense of passing through selective cultural filters.

Alan Brinkley's opening chapter provides a historical overview of many of the issues that run through the rest of the volume. In part 1, five senior scholars who have spent their careers working on questions of international relations analyze the consequences of American diplomacy through the course of the twentieth century. While agreeing that the actions of the United States beyond its borders have been significant in shaping the twentieth century, they also show that the American Century cannot be analyzed without appreciating the ways in which Europe made it possible—either through the collapse of its own political institutions or by its calculated efforts to use the United States to further its own goals.

In part 2, four scholars direct their attention to the influence of American culture in Europe—high culture, popular culture, and religion. One important question is whether European attraction to an American style of life changed European national identities. To say that American movies and pop music are very popular in Europe and throughout the world is only to say that Americans are very good in these particular industries. It does not necessarily mean that they successfully sell American values, not without resistances and transformations, or destroy other national cultures. After all, Americans have read Dickens for years without becoming English.

The four chapters in part 3 underscore this point in a different way. In transport, medical service, education, social insurance, housing, and consumer habits, Europeans have not copied the American way. They have created a different sort of public sphere and different forms of social capital. The United States, with more visible poverty on its streets than anywhere in Europe, may be trying to learn from European social legislation. And Europe, saddled with social programs whose costs drive up unemployment, may be looking to the United States for effective forms of privatization. But this exchange is not marked by American dominance. In the section's final chapter, Richard Polenberg considers the future of America's global influence in the context of the wave of immigration into the United States over the past thirty years, mostly from Latin America and Asia. A republic of citizens who carry at least two passports may not solve the problems of globalization. However, a transnational model of citizenship may prove to be a significant means of restructuring relations between First and Third World nations.

The Concept of an American Century

ALAN BRINKLEY

The concept of an American Century has become a phrase usually used to describe a particular period in history: the emergence of the United States as the world's greatest power during and after World War II and its crusading internationalism during the Cold War. But such is the power of the idea that it has survived, in popular discourse, as a description of America's continuing image of itself as a nation that somehow sets the course of the world's history—a nation whose values and virtues continue to make it a model to other peoples. This chapter describes the origins of this idea during and immediately after World War II. But in the world of the early twenty-first century—a world seemingly defined by the catastrophic attack on the United States in September 2001 and by the new wave of nationalism that swept the country in its aftermath—the concept of an American Century suddenly seems alive again.

In many ways, of course, the idea of an American Century (if not the phrase) is as old as, indeed older than, the nation itself, and it is in the early origins of this idea that some part of the modern understanding of the concept can be found. Ever since the first Europeans set their eyes on the American continents, the idea that the New World would somehow transcend and redeem the Old became an article of faith among many people on both sides of the Atlantic. The European settlements in America were destined to be a "city on a hill," "the last best hope of man on earth," or—as Herman Melville wrote in the mid-nineteenth century—the "political messiah," who has come, he said, "in us . . . the pioneers of the world."

The seventeenth-, eighteenth-, and nineteenth-century proselytizers of American exceptionalism, and of the special role America was to play in history, saw the New World and the new nation as an example, a model, a light shining out to a wretched globe and inspiring it to lift itself up. It was a morally energized vision, but also a largely passive vision. Few people in those years supported active efforts to impose the American vision on other societies, or even to promote it abroad with any real fervor. It was a vision of the United States looking out across a decadent or uncivilized globe, vaguely disapprovingly, hoping its nations would choose to follow the American example and improve.

Another, different vision of America's role in the life of the world emerged late in the nineteenth century when a new and more muscular form of nationalism began to penetrate American thinking about the country's place in the international order. This new vision was inspired by, and was at times not very different from, the European imperial visions of the time, as Henry Watterson, the editor of the *Louisville Courier-Journal,* suggested when he wrote around the time of the Spanish-American War and the American acquisition of the Philippines and other colonies:

From a nation of shopkeepers we become a nation of warriors. We escape the menace and peril of socialism and agrarianism, as England has escaped them, by a policy of colonization and conquest. From a provincial huddle of petty sovereignties held together by a rope of sand we rise to the dignity and prowess of an imperial republic incomparably greater than Rome.

Theodore Roosevelt, similarly, told a California audience in 1903 that all nations pass away but that "the great expanding nations" of history leave behind "indelibly their impress on the centuries. . . . I ask that this people rise level to the greatness of its opportunities. I don't ask that it seek the easiest path."[1]

The more powerful expression of this new sense of America's global role, however, was not a conventionally imperialist one. It was the vision articulated by, among others, Henry Cabot Lodge, the Massachusetts senator who became the most powerful obstacle to Woodrow Wilson's dream of a new world order. Lodge saw no contradiction between his fervent opposition to the League of Nations and his equally fervent commitment to the idea of America as a global power. But he did place boundaries around that idea. "We are a great moral asset of Christian civilization," he said in 1919, during the debate over the league:

How did we get there? By our own efforts. Nobody led us, nobody guided us, nobody controlled us. . . . I would keep America as she has been—not isolated, not prevent her from joining other nations for . . . great purposes—but I wish her to be master of her own fate.[2]

The cluster of ideas that such statements represent marked an important departure in America's relationship to the world but also a sharply bounded one. America would take its place among the great world powers, the early champions of empire insisted, but it would not tie its fortunes to those of any other nation. It would make no alliances and acquire no colonies (other than the ones it had somewhat hesitantly absorbed after the Spanish-American War). The United States, unlike European colonial powers, would not seek new opportunities to remake other societies in the Western image. It would, rather, act unilaterally to promote its interests and to preserve an "open door" for American trade.

THE vision of an American Century that emerged during and after World War II was a fusion of these two related, but until the 1940s mostly separate, visions. The critical ingredient that now set the United States on its new path—born of the nation's experience in World War II—was the determination of many Americans to use the nation's great power actively and often very aggressively to spread the American model to other nations, at times through relatively benign encouragement, at other times through pressure and coercion, but almost always with a fervent and active intent.

Many prominent Americans worked to promote this new and more expansive vision of America's global destiny, which for a time in the 1940s had relatively little broad public support. But the man whose name is most clearly linked to the idea of an American Century is undoubtedly Henry R. Luce, the founder and crusading editor/publisher of *Time, Fortune,* and *Life* magazines and as early as 1940 one of the nation's most outspoken internationalists. He believed strongly that the United States must assist Britain and its allies in their war against Germany, and he also believed, earlier than most supporters of Britain, that eventually America itself must become a combatant. In 1940 he joined a group of influential internationalists to pressure the Roosevelt administration to find new ways to help the imperiled British war effort. Known as the Century Group, after the elite New York men's club in which they held their meetings, they played an important role in persuading the president to create the Lend-Lease program in March 1941. A few weeks before that, on February 17, 1941, Luce published a celebrated and controversial essay in *Life* magazine called "The American Century," whose title—although not original to Luce—he helped make a part of the nation's public language.[3]

Luce's vision of an American Century was rooted in part in his own experiences. He was born and spent his entire childhood in China, the son of a Presbyterian minister and missionary who taught in a small college for Chinese converts to Christianity. His first sustained experience with America came when he entered prep school in Connecticut in 1913. In China, Luce lived with his family inside walled missionary compounds, where he encountered virtually no Chinese people (except domestic servants) and instead spent his youth almost entirely in the company of like-minded missionary families from America and England. Outside the compounds were the fetid villages and ravaged countryside of a desperately poor nation. Inside were the pleasant houses, carefully tended gardens, and stable communities of the Victorian Anglo-American bourgeois world.[4]

The contrast between the ordered world of the missionary compound and the harsh social and physical landscape outside it reinforced the assumptions driving the Protestant missionary project in China: the unquestioned belief in the moral superiority of Christianity and in the cultural superiority of American (and Western) culture; and the commitment to showing the way not just to the love of Christ, but to a modern, scientific social order based on the American model. Luce as a child knew relatively little about America other than the idealized image of it that his father and other missionaries created to justify their own work. America to him began not as a physical place, not as a diverse and contentious culture, but as an abstraction—an ideal and a model. And even though he spent over half a century living in the United States after 1913, he never really abandoned his youthful attachment to a carefully constructed myth about America's history and its place in the world. Decades later, the ebullient, moralistic, paternalistic language of "The American Century" echoed in many ways the missionary credo that Luce—and the many other missionary children who went on to play influential roles in America's late-twentieth-century global missions—must have heard every day as a child.[5]

But "The American Century" was also an impassioned piece of propaganda written for a particular historical moment—an essay designed to rouse Americans out of what Luce considered their slothful indifference and inspire them to undertake a great mission on behalf of what he considered the nation's core values. It was an effort to force his fellow citizens to confront the reality of the war and America's obligation to play a forceful role in both ending it and building a better world in its aftermath; it was an effort to persuade them of the importance of saving Great Britain and defeating fascism. As part of that effort, he sketched a bold picture of the nation's destiny that exaggerated only slightly what would by the late 1940s be a widely shared and increasingly powerful view—a vision in which American abundance and American idealism seamlessly merged.

The American Century, Luce wrote,

must be a sharing with all people of our Bill of Rights, our Declaration of Independence, our Constitution, our magnificent industrial products, our technical skills. . . . we have that indefinable, unmistakable sign of leadership: prestige. And unlike the prestige of Rome or Genghis Khan or 19th century England, American prestige throughout the world is [the result of] faith in the good intentions as well as in the ultimate intelligence and strength of the whole of the American people.[6]

How, Luce wondered, could a nation that embodied such important and potentially universal values, a nation with such unparalleled wealth and power, remain on the sidelines in the battle for the future of the world? All America's hopes for its future would fail, he insisted,

unless our vision of America as a world power includes a passionate devotion to great American ideals . . . a love of freedom, a feeling for the equality of opportunity, a tradition of self reliance and independence, and also of cooperation. . . . we are the inheritors of all the great principles of Western civilization—above all Justice, the love of Truth, the ideal of charity. . . . It now becomes our time to be the powerhouse from which the ideals spread throughout the world and do their mysterious work of lifting the life of mankind from the level of the beasts to what the Psalmist called a little lower than the angels.[7]

Something of the same moralistic, evangelical language appeared in another powerful call for a new American role in the world, a speech delivered a little more than a year later, on May 8, 1942, by Vice President Henry A. Wallace and widely known as "The Century of the Common

Man" (although its original title was "The Price of Free World Victory"). Wallace would later become a controversial, even reviled figure for his leadership of dissenting leftists in the early years of the Cold War, for his bitter criticisms of what he considered America's excessive militarism and aggression, and for his perhaps unwitting alliance with communists in the 1948 campaign. But he gave his speech at a high watermark in his political career. A little more than a year into his vice presidency, he had a reputation—soon to be shattered—as the second most important figure in government, as the "assistant president," as Roosevelt's likely heir. His 1942 speech was not the work of the later, embittered and ostracized Wallace. It was the work of a prominent, mainstream Democrat—an important and influential figure in the Roosevelt administration—attempting to rouse the public behind a war that the nation was not yet clearly winning.[8]

Wallace was implicitly critical of what he considered the imperialistic rhetoric of Luce's 1941 essay, and he was careful to distance himself from any notion that the United States could unilaterally impose its values and institutions on the world. But he too presented a vision of the future that included a central role for the United States in both inspiring and shaping a new age of democracy. "This is a fight between a slave world and a free world," he said. "Just as the United States in 1862 could not remain half slave and half free, so in 1942 the world must make its decision for a complete victory one way or the other." Naturally, Wallace expected the "freedom-loving people"—who were not Americans alone, but among whom Americans stood preeminent—to answer that question and to shape the postwar world. The shape of their answer, he said, was embodied in the Four Freedoms that Franklin Roosevelt had proclaimed in January 1941, freedoms that "are at the very core of the revolution for which the United Nations have taken their stand." And just as Luce's vision of an American Century included a vision of exporting Western industrial abundance to the world, so Wallace insisted that "the peace must mean a better standard of living for the common man, not merely in the United States and England, but also in India, Russia, China, and Latin America—not merely in the United Nations [as the Western alliance then called itself], but also in Germany and Italy and Japan."[9]

"Some have spoken of the 'American Century,'" Wallace added, in an obvious effort to distance himself from Luce. "I say the century on which we are entering . . . can be and must be the century of the common man." In the years to come, as Wallace's own vision (and political fortunes) changed, he came increasingly to see his speech as a full-throated rejoinder to what he considered Luce's more imperialist vision. At the time, however, both Wallace and Luce spoke generally kindly about each other's remarks and seemed to agree that they were, on the whole, fighting the same battle. ("I do not happen to remember anything that you have written descriptive of your concepts of 'the American Century' of which I disapprove," Wallace wrote to Luce shortly after he delivered his speech. Luce's description, he added, "is almost precisely parallel to what I was trying to say in my talk.") In his vision of a world modeled on American notions of freedom, in his commitment to spreading the fruits of economic growth to the world, in his insistence that "older nations will have the privilege to help younger nations get started on the path to industrialization," and perhaps most of all in the extravagant rhetoric with which he presented these ideas, Wallace's speech was less an alternative to Luce's essay than a variation on it. "There are no half measures," he concluded. "No compromise with Satan is possible. . . . We shall fight for a complete peace and a complete victory. The people's revolution is on the march, and the devil and all his angels cannot prevail against it. They cannot prevail for on the side of the people is the Lord."[10]

"The American Century" and "The Price of Free World Victory" were major documents of their time. Both Luce and Wallace arranged to have them repeatedly reprinted, and they circulated widely throughout the United States and the world. But they are of interest today not mainly because they had great influence on the public conversation of their time; their influence was, in fact, relatively modest in the end. They are of interest because they are among the most visible symbols of a growing movement among American leaders, and eventually among many others, to redefine the nation's relationship to the world and, in the process, to redefine America's sense of itself. They make clear that the idea of an American Century was not a product of the Cold War, that the idea preceded and helped to define the Cold War—just as the Cold War eventually helped to redefine it. And they suggest something of the crusading power that idea came to assume among influential Americans across a wide swath of the political and ideological spectrum.[11]

THE idea of an American Century found concrete expression in many ways. It helped support the aggressive internationalism of American foreign policy after World War II and throughout the Cold War. It helped inspire the Marshall Plan and the larger postwar system of foreign aid.

It helped sustain America's vast military establishment and justify the nation's increasing covert interventions in other nations. It helped bind the United States to the United Nations, the World Bank, and the International Monetary Fund, and to legitimize the complex system of alliances that the nation created in the 1940s and beyond.

Another compelling expression of that idea came in efforts to refurbish, and even redefine, the idea of the American nation itself in the years after World War II. For in the aftermath of that terrible struggle, it no longer seemed possible to take for granted the moral and practical claims of democracy and freedom. To many Americans, the great task after the war—a task that came to seem even more urgent several years later as the Cold War cast its shadow across the nation's cultural landscape— was to define American identity, to tie it firmly to a belief in the nation's great moral power, to mobilize the American public to embrace it, and then to export it to the world. This was the great cultural project of the 1940s and 1950s, a project fully compatible (and often synonymous) with the nation's geopolitical goals. And it mobilized in its service not just the state but a large community of intellectuals, academics, writers, philanthropists, business and labor leaders, clergy, journalists, and many others.

One of the earliest and most celebrated efforts to arouse popular enthusiasm for the idea of an American Century, to reinforce Americans' commitments to the particular virtues of the national project, was the Freedom Train—an exhibit of more than a hundred important documents and artifacts from American history, which between 1947 and 1949 traveled across the nation behind a red, white, and blue locomotive. Among the items in the train's exhibit were the Mayflower Compact, the Bill of Rights, a manuscript copy of "The Star-Spangled Banner," the Gettysburg Address, the Emancipation Proclamation, a draft of the Declaration of Independence edited by Jefferson, a copy of the Constitution annotated by Washington, one of Woodrow Wilson's drafts of the Covenant of the League of Nations, the flag that had flown at Iwo Jima, and much more. Upon leaving the train, visitors were invited to add their names to a Freedom Scroll and to take a pledge rededicating themselves to the American creed. More than 3.5 million Americans visited the train during its two-year journey.[12]

The Freedom Train represented not only the urgency behind the effort to promote American identity but the wide array of forces committed to furthering that promotion. The idea emerged out of the federal government. William Coblenz, who worked in the public information office of the Justice Department, proposed a traveling exhibition after being inspired by a lunchtime visit to the National Archives. "It seemed to me incredible that a display of such topical interest was not being brought to all the American people," Coblenz later wrote. He enlisted the support of the attorney general and eventually the president behind the idea. By allowing these great documents to travel across the nation, Attorney General Tom Clark argued, it might be possible to reverse the "cynicism, disillusionment and lawlessness" that the end of the war had produced. "Indoctrination in democracy is the essential catalytic agent needed to blend our varying groups into one American family," he claimed. "Without it, we could not sustain the continuity of our way of life." Funding for the train came from major American banks and corporations, funneled through the American Heritage Foundation, which was created to organize the train and "to remind people that freedom is a continuing struggle." The design of its exhibits was supervised by Hollywood studio executives. Its progress across the country was eagerly chronicled by the national press and publicized through an elaborate campaign designed by the advertising industry. The Freedom Train was one of many efforts by such private/public alliances to promote American values and cement the idea of the American Century in the first years after the war.[13]

The promotion of the American Century was not simply a product of government and of defenders of free enterprise, however. It was a major project of the academic and intellectual worlds as well and became most clearly visible in the growth of the American Studies movement. Before the war, there had been about a dozen such programs scattered among a few elite northeastern colleges and universities and mostly devoted to interdisciplinary work in history and literature with no particular ideological foundation. After the war, both the number and the character of such programs rapidly changed. By 1947, there were more than sixty programs, spread through almost all regions of the country, and more than a dozen graduate programs training scholars to keep the movement alive. And out of the American Studies movement—out of the formal American Studies programs but also out of the even more widespread scholarly ethos that the movement created—came an extraordinary outpouring of scholarship devoted to exploring American national identity, the "American character," and the nature of American democracy. "Somewhere back of the American Studies ideas," Leo Marx wrote in 1979, "there once lurked an amorphous conception of the United States as the embodiment of a social ideal." This scholarship was not uniformly, or even primarily, celebratory; indeed some of it provided some extraordinarily harsh critiques of American culture and politics. But there was an essential unity within the movement in the belief that there was such a thing as a national character and identity; that it was important for the nation to examine, strengthen, and improve its culture; and that there were lessons in this effort both for Americans themselves and for much of the rest of the world.[14]

Many of the early founders of American Studies became deeply involved in the Congress for Cultural Freedom, funded (unbeknown to some of them at the time) by the CIA, whose goal was to trumpet the superior virtues of American culture to a world tempted by communism. Some helped create the Fulbright program, which for half a century now has sent American scholars overseas to help other peoples understand the United States. And others helped create the Salzburg Seminar, a summer program in Europe—conceived by three Harvard students in 1947, taught by leading American scholars of American Studies, and specifically designed to help European students understand the United States and use its history and culture to rebuild their own. Most of the faculty—led by F. O. Matthieson of the American Civilization program at Harvard—were people of the liberal left, determined to present a critical view of the United States and to illustrate its long and painful struggle against its own demons. Hence Matthieson's passionate belief that the central document of American Studies was Melville's *Moby Dick*. "No more penetrating scrutiny has yet been made of the defects of individualism," he wrote of it. And hence Richard Hofstadter's insistence that "we Americans came with no intention of acting . . . as national apologists." But they also had, as Matthieson told the first group of students, who came from all over Europe, "a strong conviction of the value of American democracy" and of its suitability for other societies. "Heretofore Americans have come to Europe as students," Matthieson told the participants. "But now we come, not to study your culture, but bringing our own." The Salzburg Seminar (which still survives) attracted funding from the Ford Foundation and many other proselytizing American philanthropies, and the support of the State Department.[15]

In 1944 the British historian Denis Brogan published a book titled *The American Problem* (later published in the United States under the title *The American Character*). In it he wrote of the challenges facing the United States after the war in dealing with a world destined to become more and more interconnected. The American problem, he wrote, was a double one:

the problem of making intelligible to the American people the nature of the changes in the modern world which they can lead, or which they can resist, but which they can't ignore. That is a problem for Americans. There is the second problem: the problem of making intelligible the normal American's view of the world, of his own history and destiny.

Americans, he concluded, "have much to give, materially and spiritually: a well-founded optimism about their own possibilities; a well-founded belief that some of the problems of unity . . . have been solved in the American Experience." The American Studies movement embraced the challenges and, at times, expressed the faith that Brogan described.[16]

So did Henry Luce, who had helped popularize the idea of an American Century in 1941, and who devoted much of his postwar energy to making his magazines effective champions of that idea both at home and abroad, both in promoting the aims of American foreign policy and in leading a highly public search to define the "national purpose." To Matthieson and many other academics and intellectuals, the Luce publications were crude purveyors of a simplistic, hegemonic vision of the American Century. In fact, Luce's magazines were far from uniformly celebratory, and Luce himself sought constantly to persuade leading intellectuals (including some of the most dyspeptically critical) to contribute essays to *Life* and *Fortune*. But Luce's magazines did include a large dose of exuberant nationalism—particularly in the overseas editions that were becoming an increasingly important part of the company's activities. Luce believed that by illustrating the brilliance and variety of American culture, business, religion, and politics, his publications could help arouse Americans to commit themselves to the larger purposes he believed they must accept, and also inspire the peoples of other countries to recognize the value of the American model. Most of all, his magazines could inspire the world to emulate the core value of the American people.

The "postwar *Time*," Luce once explained to his editors, will have to do "plenty of explaining" to the new readers it hoped to attract around the globe. It would have to explain itself, certainly, but it would also "have to explain about America." There was much about America that needed explaining to the world, not all of it attractive, Luce argued. "But if we had to choose one word out of the whole vocabulary of human experience to associate with America—surely it would not be hard to choose the word. For surely the word is Freedom. . . . Without Freedom,

America is untranslatable." And that, then, was the postwar mission of his magazines. "Despite all confusions by which we have been confused and may have confused others, I think we have achieved some intellectual right to say that we of Time Inc. have fought, are fighting and will fight . . . 'For the Freedom of All Peoples.' . . . We believe that the relation of the people of the U.S. with the other peoples of the world must be based on the principles of Freedom. (This can be endlessly celebrated.)"[17]

THE idea of an American Century, and the widespread efforts to promote and solidify that idea, reflected a vision of the nation that even in the 1940s many Americans feared was unstable. How else can we explain their fevered efforts to promote and solidify that vision among a public they suspected had a weak attachment to it. Even the proselytizers themselves offered very different versions of what America was and what an American Century would mean. Yet in the end, almost everyone involved in this great, sprawling project seemed to agree that it was possible to define the meaning of America in terms that would be broadly acceptable; that there was such a thing as an American creed and an American character; that the idea of an American Century rested on something more than a realistic appraisal of American power; that it had a basis in the values and culture of the American people.

In the end, though, the American Century theorists were never able to produce a definition of an American character or an American creed that adequately represented their own time, let alone ours. The Freedom Train is one of many examples of the great difficulties inherent in defining the American ethos. It was the product of awkward compromises that belied its message of a universal American commitment to a set of national symbols. There was a vigorous debate over whether to include the National Labor Relations Act of 1935 as one of the central documents of American freedom, a debate the defenders of including the act lost. Even the Fourteenth and Fifteenth Amendments to the Constitution—guaranteeing African Americans "equal protection of the laws" and the right to vote—were, the organizers feared, too controversial to add to the train's picture of the American creed. There was a prolonged struggle over how the train should deal with the racial norms in the South and elsewhere, and a bitter debate among the organizers about the appropriate stance to take. Ultimately, the organizers forbade segregated viewing of the train and cancelled visits to several cities (including Memphis and Birmingham) that balked at that requirement, but they also made concessions to segregationists. In some cities, they permitted separate lines for black and white visitors and admitted them in alternating groups of twenty-five. They permitted an extra car containing the Confederate constitution to accompany the train through Georgia. Despite the huge popular interest the train provoked, the admittedly scanty evidence suggests that few African Americans, and indeed few people of color of any kind, visited it—perhaps a reflection of their view that freedom, for many Americans, remained an empty ideal. "I want freedom itself," Paul Robeson said at the time, "not a freedom train."[18]

Those who announced the dawn of the American Century, and the much larger group of people who attempted to promote it as a projection of American values and morality into a crippled and beckoning world, were able to sustain their image of a vital American creed only with considerable difficulty—and only by ignoring, suppressing, or marginalizing the considerable conflict and diversity and injustice that lay beneath the bright, shining surface of American life; by flattening out their vision of America and the world and creating a Manichaean image of the globe. Their enthusiasm was understandable. They were acting in the shadow of the greatest war in human history that produced some of the greatest crimes against humanity the world has ever seen. And they were acting, too, in the midst of a new conflict—more difficult to understand, sometimes vague in its aims, subject to no easily foreseeable resolution—that they considered equally momentous and that they believed required a firm commitment from the American people and from the nation's allies, a commitment they knew would not be easy to sustain. Similar efforts have followed the terrible events of September 2001, as leaders from many areas of American life have mobilized themselves to fortify and inspire the nation in a new and difficult struggle against a shadowy and elusive foe. The example of the comparable efforts of a half century ago, therefore, can be seen both as an inspiration and a warning.

For in embracing the idea of an American Century in the 1940s, a generation of internationalists—determined to overcome the nation's long tradition of isolation and autonomy in the world—were in fact inventing a national image, sometimes wittingly, sometimes not, that they believed would be helpful to that goal.. And in creating this carefully constructed artifice and projecting it so energetically into the world, they were not only contributing to the creation of the kind of American Century so many predicted—a century in which they hoped America would be not just all-powerful but widely emulated and admired. They were also sustaining the nation's insular self-regard and isolation, which their project was allegedly designed to destroy.

NOTES

1. Watterson as quoted in Robert Dallek, *The American Style of Foreign Policy: Cultural Politics and Foreign Affairs* (New York: Alfred A. Knopf, 1983), 27; "Message to Congress," December 6, 1904, in *The Works of Theodore Roosevelt,* ed. Herman Hagedorn (New York: Scribner's, 1925), 255–56; John Milton Cooper, *The Warrior and the Priest: Woodrow Wilson and Theodore Roosevelt* (Cambridge: Harvard University Press, 1983), 71, 75.
2. William Widenor, *Henry Cabot Lodge and the Search for an American Foreign Policy* (Berkeley: University of California Press, 1980), 318.
3. Robert E. Herzstein, *Henry R. Luce: A Political Portrait of the Man Who Created the American Century* (New York: Scribner's, 1994), 1–23.
4. Jessie Gregory Lutz, *China and the Christian Colleges, 1850–1950* (Ithaca: Cornell University Press, 1971), 12–24; Jane Hunter, *The Gospel of Gentility: American Women Missionaries in Turn-of-the-Century China* (New Haven: Yale University Press, 1984), 128–73; Elizabeth Root Moore, oral history.
5. Henry R. Luce to Elisabeth R. Luce, July 7, 1912; Henry R. Luce to Henry W. and Elisabeth R. Luce, December 24, 1916; both in Henry R. Luce MSS, Time Inc. Archives.
6. Henry R. Luce, *The American Century* (New York: Farrar and Rinehart, 1941), 32–34.
7. Ibid., 38–39.
8. John C. Culver and John Hyde, *American Dreamer: A Life of Henry Wallace* (New York: Norton, 2000), 275–80; Edward L. Schapsmeier and Frederick H. Schapsmeier, *Prophet in Politics: Henry A. Wallace and the War Years, 1940–1945* (Ames: Iowa State University Press, 1970), 29–33.
9. Henry A. Wallace, "The Price of Free World Victory," in Wendell Willkie et al., *Prefaces to Peace* (New York: Cooperatively published by Simon and Schuster, Doubleday, Doran, Reynal and Hitchcock, and Columbia University Press, 1943), 369–75.
10. Ibid., 373, 375; Henry A. Wallace to Henry R. Luce, May 16, 1942, diaries of Henry A. Wallace, University of Iowa Library, vol. 10, 1575.
11. Richard J. Walton, *Henry Wallace, Harry Truman, and the Cold War* (New York: Viking Press, 1976), 10–14.
12. "The Freedom Train," *New Republic,* September 20, 1948, 7; Stuart J. Little, "The Freedom Train: Citizenship and Postwar American Culture, 1946–1949," *American Studies* 34 (1993): 35–36; Eric Foner, *The Story of American Freedom* (New York: Norton, 1998), 249–52; Wendy Lynn Wall, "The Idea of America: Democracy and the Dilemmas of Difference" (Ph.D. diss., Stanford University, 1998), 212–50; Frank Monaghan, *Heritage of Freedom: The History and Significance of the Basic Documents of American Liberty* (Princeton: Princeton University Press, 1947). Monaghan, one of the organizers of the Freedom Train exhibition, described this as a "book presenting and explaining the documents on the Freedom Train . . . the finest collection of original documents on American history ever assembled for exhibition purposes." It provides the texts of the documents on the train along with prefatory notes by the author.
13. William A. Coblenz, "The Freedom Train, and the Story of Its Origin: Our Civil Liberties on Wheels," *Manuscripts* 10 (winter 1958): 31–33; "Why They Throng to the

Freedom Train," *New York Times Magazine,* January 25, 1948, 18–19, 52, 54; "The Freedom Train," *Tide: The News Magazine of Advertising, Marketing, and Public Relations,* April 30, 1948, 24–32; Robert Griffith, "The Selling of America: The Advertising Council and American Politics, 1942–1960," *Business History Review* 52 (1983): 397–99; Little, "Freedom Train," 42–43, 49–51; James Gregory Bradsher, "Taking America's Heritage to the People: The Freedom Train Story," *Prologue* 17 (winter 1985): 229–34.

14. Leo Marx, "Thoughts on the Origin and Character of the American Studies Movement," *American Quarterly* 31 (1979): 398–401; Tremaine McDowell, *American Studies* (Minneapolis: University of Minnesota Press, 1948), 26–28; Wall, "Idea of America," 251–53.

15. Richard T. Arndt, "American Cultural Diplomacy: The U.S. Government Role," in *Exporting America: Essays on American Studies Abroad,* ed. Richard P. Horwitz (New York: Garland, 1993), 16–22; F. O. Matthiessen, *From the Heart of Europe* (New York: Oxford University Press, 1948), 15–66; Richard Hofstadter, "The Salzburg Seminar, Fourth Year," *The Nation,* October 28, 1950, 391–92; Henry Nash Smith, "The Salzburg Seminar," *American Quarterly* 1 (1949): 30–37; Wall, "Idea of America," 304–45.

16. Denis W. Brogan, *The American Character* (New York: Alfred A. Knopf, 1950), xx, 169.

17. Henry R. Luce, "The Practice of Freedom," memorandum to *Time* magazine staff, August 1943, Time Inc. Archives.

18. Foner, *Story of American Freedom,* 250–52; *New York Times,* December 25, 1947; Michael K. Honey, *Southern Labor and Black Civil Rights: Organizing Memphis Workers* (Urbana: University of Illinois Press, 1993), 246, 249.

PART ONE

DIPLOMATIC RESPONSES

The United States and Europe in an Age of American Unilateralism

WALTER LAFEBER

At the center of U.S. foreign policy during the so-called American Century have been the problems thrown up by the contradictions between Americans' belief in their exceptionalism and the faith that their principles (or most of them) are universal. This contradiction has directly shaped several centuries of the nation's foreign relations, most notably development of Americans' supposed isolationism, which can more accurately be termed unilateralism. The country never followed a policy of being isolated (especially economically), but it has consistently tried to bridge the huge gap between thinking of itself as simultaneously exceptional and universal with the overarching faith that the exceptional can use various types of force to make its values comfortably universal.[1] Until the twentieth century, Americans had the necessary power to impress those values on much of the North American continent, and in the past one hundred years they have enjoyed the power to extend and protect their values around large parts of the globe. The terrorist attacks of September 11, 2001, changed important parts of the world scene, but as noted briefly below, they—contrary to popular perception—did little or nothing to limit the centuries-old American unilateralism.

This chapter argues that both U.S. exceptionalism and universalism were applied mostly to the North American continent until the 1890s, when a group of intellectuals and politicians—driven by the overwhelming success of the nation's economy during the second industrial revolution—began to formulate American exceptionalist principles for the world. Woodrow Wilson became the symbol and spokesman for the application of these principles. Then, when Wilson at a crucial moment lacked the power and insight necessary to overrule European and Japanese objections to his agenda, the American crusade took other forms until Harry Truman revived unilateralism successfully and in a quite different context during the late 1940s. Americans began to believe in a rough formula: exceptionalism plus sufficient power equaled unilateralism. The 1940s, moreover, marked the maturation of a U.S. power that could begin to translate American exceptionalism into American universalism through, especially, the use of unilateralism. That unilateralism can, in the context of American history, be so easily interchanged with isolationism, in the root sense of being isolated, should give pause to those who advocate unilateralist approaches.

Europe became a testing ground of this translation, which is appropriate because it was a European who provided one of the first, and best, definitions of American exceptionalism. "The position of the Americans is therefore quite exceptional," Alexis de Tocqueville wrote, "and it may be believed that no democratic people will ever be placed in a similar one." Tocqueville emphasized Americans' "strictly Puritanical origin, their exclusively commercial habits, even the country they inhabit" as shaping their exceptionalism.[2] A modern and more succinct definition that better fits into a discussion of U.S. foreign relations is that "'American exceptionalism,' summarized, is the notion that the United States was created differently, developed differently, and thus has to be *understood differently*—essentially on its own terms and within its own context."[3] The somewhat contradictory idea that Americans, while exceptional, are blazing the way for admirable and needed universal values also comes in part from Tocqueville, but in part as well from other sources, including the Declaration of Independence. Thomas Bender has summarized the idea of universalism (without using that exact phrase) by noting that "The U.S. has been, as Alexis de Tocqueville proposed, a site for the study of historical phenomena that have a significance beyond itself." Bender and the study group he led emphasized the "transnational significance" of certain American exceptionalist beliefs, including democracy, religious pluralism, modernization, racial hierarchy, migration, environmental change, capitalism, technology, slavery and freedom, and empire and colonialism, among others.[4] The "transnational significance" of such traits may be useful for a comparative cultural study, but this approach reveals much less about how U.S. foreign policy and its power shaped an American Century.

Reconciling these forms of exceptionalism and universalism has preoccupied Americans in the post-1890 era. They have spent that time assuming their exceptionalism while—out of a necessity forced on them by their expanding economy and a cultural imperialism that is driven by a quest for profit, verification, and justification—they have gone abroad to bring the world under an American canopy. Although (or because) the assumption and reasons for moving abroad tend to be contradictory, Americans have necessarily used force, claims of superior morality, and direct antiforeignism to be able to hold fast to exceptionalist beliefs while professing to practice universalism.

This problem that has so haunted both U.S. domestic and foreign policies over several centuries can be stated another way. American self-identification has been shaped by a belief in being a God-chosen "city on a hill" (to use John Winthrop's original phrase that Ronald Reagan did so much to popularize) and a further belief in being children of a unique, continually moving frontier. At the same time, over these centuries Americans have fought wars often aimed at groups who denied the city-on-the-hill idea—whether they were those (such as Mexicans, Hawaiians, Filipinos, British/Canadians, and Vietnamese) who disliked the reality that the population of that city came down off the hill to seize and annex their lands, or others (such as Germans, Japanese, Russians, and Chinese) who insisted on the worth of their own missions. Many of these wars, of course, especially those in the twentieth century, were about age-old problems of national interest and the survival of a way of life; that is, they were about problems that were hardly unique to the United States. But Americans did not usually view them that way.

The first American Century, as publisher Henry Luce styled it in 1941, was thus erected (as Luce did not note) on the Revolutionary War against Great Britain and a series of bloody wars to expand the American continental dominion against Indians, Mexicans, British/Canadians, Spaniards, and Southerners. After the 1890s, the American Century built on the ruins of the Spanish Empire, the self-immolation of Europe between 1914 and 1918, and the success with which Americans exploited the second industrial revolution's technologies that appeared in the late nineteenth century. All of these developments could be (and were) interpreted by Americans as sound evidence for believing in their own exceptionalism. But that century also rested on deeper roots: a historic political economy whose motto was, to paraphrase Robert Cooper, "Thou shalt be free to make deals," and a foreign policy that reconciled its belief in American exceptionalism with its belief in an American mission by acting on the principle "We shalt be free to act unilaterally."[5]

Europeans were a primary target of U.S. expansion across the American continent until the 1890s, when continental conquest was complete, but also in the post-1890 era. The European powers were targeted in part because their own global reach and historical circumstance established colonies or protectorates in areas coveted by the United States. But Europeans were also viewed as the villains because Americans grew to fear, and committed themselves to destroying, Europe's policies of closed empires, colonization, arbitrary (rather than self-determined) political borders, and government-protected marketplaces. All of these were to be replaced with American-style openness so that deals could be struck. In the economic realm (which most American policy makers insisted could not be separated from the political in what Secretary of State Dean Acheson dismissed as the diplomatic equivalent of a cream separator), the United States insisted on building an international system based primarily on its own evolving domestic principles, not on the more exclusive and closed policies of, say, the British imperial preference system, or German or French statism (or Japanese *keiretsu* networks).

In the political-diplomatic arenas, U.S. officials have generally insisted (not always successfully), on the freedom to act unilaterally, and when they have not so insisted, Congress has frequently rejected their handiwork—as in the first Hay-Pauncefote treaty in 1900 that gave the United States vast rights to build an isthmian canal but required military cooperation with the British in defending the canal, or in the environmental and human rights treaties a century later that seem to fit in well with American values but not American interests. The United States has tended to work with international organizations when it could control the organizations (such as the United Nations in 1950–51 as opposed to the UN of the 1970s and 1980s) and when the organizations protected the freedom to make deals while not unduly limiting the United States's right to act unilaterally outside the organization (as in Vietnam and Kosovo). Europeans have begun calling such actions "parallel unilateralism," that is, "a willingness to go along with international accords, but only so far as they suit America, which is prepared to conduct policy outside their constraints."[6]

This kind of deal making and this type of unilateralism were two sides of the same coin throughout the twentieth century. From McKinley in 1898 to Wilson in 1917, Roosevelt in the late 1930s and 1940s, Truman at the outset of the Cold War, and Reagan in the 1980s, the proper kind of deal making in the marketplace required commitment—unilaterally (or, as Wilson would have it, "associated" and not "allied"), if necessary—on the battlefield. As British historian Geoffrey Perret has generalized about the process, "America's wars have been like rungs on a ladder by which it rose to greatness."[7]

A war that formed one of the lower rungs became both the founding conflict of the American nation and powerful instruction about how American exceptionalism, if it had to engage in international diplomacy, moved inexorably toward unilateralism once it had sufficient maneuvering room. While Americans argued in early 1776 over whether to declare independence, possibly the most influential pamphlet in the nation's history appeared. In *Common Sense*, Thomas Paine argued that the colonies had to embark on the hard road to independence because "the cause of America is in a great measure the cause of all mankind." Several months later, Thomas Jefferson further explored the universal meaning of this "cause" by expanding on the assumption that "all men are created equal." Another section of Paine's pamphlet, however, generated more controversy. The author declared that because Europeans were dependent on American goods (at least "while eating is the custom in Europe"), no political alliances were necessary. "It is the true interest of America to steer clear of European contentions," he announced. In perhaps the first significant argument made on behalf of an independent American unilateralism, however, Paine turned out to be terribly wrong. And Americans were quick to learn the appropriate lessons.[8]

To save themselves and their dream of a large, independent empire, U.S. leaders decided after agonizing deliberations that they had to form an alliance with France. The partnership proved to be traumatic for the Americans. Within months the French minister used his power to influence the U.S. Congress not only to accept guidance from Paris but to settle for a constricted territorial deal with the British (so, in part, the new United States would not threaten French interests to the south and west). The Americans circumvented France's pressure by dealing directly with London and obtaining a vast expanse of territory that stretched to the Mississippi River. But the alliance, which was to last "forever," remained in force when the French Revolution turned into a European war and threatened to suck Americans into the growing bloodshed. Vigorous, sometimes violent debates over whether the alliance was to be honored split political parties and personal friendships. The French alliance threatened to divide the twenty-year-old nation. In 1800, during a temporary lull in the European conflict, U.S. officials finally freed themselves of the 1778 commitments. Americans would not again enter into such an alliance for a century and a half—that is, until they were in a position to control the North Atlantic Treaty Organization (NATO), which became the backbone of the West's military structure during the Cold War. During that century and a half, and after, Americans frequently viewed Europeans as not only dangerous opponents of American freedom of action but possessors of a value system (colonialism, statist economic arrangements, nondemocratic regimes) that directly challenged the principles of American exceptionalism.

Europeans were, in a word, enemies—not only those who (as the Monroe Doctrine warned in 1823) were committed to keeping the United States restricted to a small area surrounded by threatening European colonies, but also those who (as American politicians and business representatives warned in a crescendo after the 1880s) were committed to preventing U.S. goods from carrying out what the Europeans called an "American invasion" of Europe. Not all Europeans, however, were seen as enemies. By the 1890s, the British, long the most hated and feared of all Europeans, were, through a series of circumstances, becoming sympathetic to and cooperative with the United States. For their own purposes, the British especially agreed to get out of the way after 1895 as the United States extended its reach into the Caribbean–Latin American region. An informal Anglo-American partnership developed that shaped events in Asia, Europe, and Africa as well as in the Western Hemisphere. Americans entered the partnership not only because it was informal but also because it was understood—especially by such political and intellectual leaders as Theodore Roosevelt, John Hay, Elihu Root, and Henry Adams—that given the way international affairs were evolving, the United States, not Great Britain, would soon become the senior partner. With the right junior partner, partnership could enhance, not diminish, U.S. power to act unilaterally.

The historic turn in American relations with Europe was not the only benchmark in the relationship during the 1890s. During that decade a consensus also arose among U.S. political, business, and academic leaders that the success of the American economic machine and (if the Civil War and its causes were ignored) political system proved that certain values had shown themselves superior. These values included the importance of a small state whose powers were restricted to ensuring that the marketplace acted fairly and on legitimate (that is, generally agreed upon) principles; a marketplace that explicitly accepted and acted upon American capitalist assumptions, including individual freedom to make deals; a marketplace that was free of politically imposed restrictions that unfairly inhibited trade and investment or, in the words of Secretary of State John Hay, violated the American belief in an economic "fair field and no favor"; and the principle that such an open and free marketplace was the best protection against, if not a preventative for, the European practice of linking political commitments to economic arrangements and thus infecting both.

The belief that free, or at least freer, trade in the marketplace was a prerequisite for political freedoms became a fixed tenet of U.S. officials. Moving from this belief, moreover, these officials could conclude that as American economic practices and assumptions spread, American political practices and freedoms would move with them. Rising economies, free from European (or Japanese) statism, not only provided the foundation for abolishing poverty but for abolishing nonrepresentative governments. American exceptionalism could thus become increasingly universal—but only if the political restrictions were subordinated and finally dissolved by economic development. Then people elsewhere, as those in the United States, could be free and have the economic wherewithal to act politically on their own. Until the world reached that level of enlightenment and economic development, however, Americans had, under this set of beliefs, not only the right but the obligation to act unilaterally if necessary. Finally, exercising such a right and obligation became increasingly possible after the 1890s because by the end of that decade, U.S. economic and military (especially naval) power finally gave Americans the necessary means both to act unilaterally, if it were necessary, and to police the important parts of the international marketplace so they would be open, free from undue political pressure (at least any undue non-American pressure that might smack of mercantilism), peaceful, and generally accepted as legitimate.[9]

Such a definition of the way the world should work pushed Americans closer to the British, who increasingly accepted some of these principles and who understood it was in their interest to try to co-opt rather than confront the United States. Meanwhile, a statist France, an imperial and militarily aggressive Germany, and, above all, Russia (seen by Americans as a corrupt monarchical system aiming at colonizing and monopolizing potentially rich areas of northeast Asia and Central Asia) were viewed as the leading enemies. By 1900, moreover, the second industrial revolution and a resulting globalization process—a process that by measurements of the percentage of domestic national product devoted to international investment defined the world as more integrated and globalized in 1900 than in 2000—had begun to create an Atlantic village in which Americans and Europeans were pulled ever closer together. The question for U.S. officials by 1915, therefore, was not whether they would have to involve their nation in the growing European conflagration but under what kind of terms they would necessarily become involved.

Economic ties and common fears of German militarism finally brought Americans in on the Allies' side, but for President Woodrow Wilson it was a long (three-year) and painful decision. He knew that the British, French, and Russians had met behind closed doors in Paris during 1916 to plan for a postwar world that would resemble their statist economic systems, not an American open-door policy. These same allies had also brought Japan and Italy into their coalition by, in part, promising them control of former German colonies or lands once claimed by Germany's ally, Austria-Hungary. Wilson understood that even for the British, not to mention the French, Russians, and Italians, the postwar world was to look more like their nineteenth-century systems than the world the Americans, especially Wilson, hoped to make. For this reason, perhaps above all others, the president determined to enter the war so he would be assured a place at the peace table. He explicitly went into the conflict not as an "allied" power but as an "associated" partner because, as he told advisers, the United States had no real allies. The careful word choice also revealed how painstakingly Wilson tried to preserve his ability to act unilaterally and without obligations to the nations with which he now pledged to fight history's bloodiest war. Given the French, Russian, and even British objectives, American exceptionalist principles could become universal only if the United States could act on its own and not be compromised by a world that was considered old in more ways than one.

When Wilson outlined his competing vision for the postwar world, most notably in his "peace without victory" speech of 1917 and his Fourteen Points declaration of 1918, he explicitly announced that he was advocating American principles and values because they could best reorder a world ruined by European principles and values. Thus the president proposed that "the nations should with one accord adopt the doctrine of President Monroe as the doctrine of the world: that no nation should seek to extend its polity over another nation or people." The Monroe Doctrine was not popular in Europe or Latin America; it had been used as a weapon to replace European interests with American in the Southern Hemisphere. The doctrine's principles had even evolved into a policy in the Caribbean–Central America–Mexico region that made Wilson the greatest military interventionist in the area in United States history.

But the president was more concerned with making a case before the world for the power of American exceptionalism and the necessity of American unilateralism than he was with coming to terms with the history of his own foreign policy. He therefore demanded that "all nations henceforth avoid entangling alliances which would draw them into competition of power. . . . These are American principles, American policies. We could stand for no others." Then came the universalism: "And they are also the principles and policies of forward looking men and women everywhere, of every modern nation, of every enlightened community. They are the principles of mankind and must prevail."[10] As Wilson increasingly recognized by his insistence on the term *associated,* the exceptionalism would be transformed into the universal only if American unilateral freedom of action could somehow be preserved—and if the United States possessed the necessary military power to pull off the transformation. Thus the president insisted throughout the years of 1916–19 that the United States build the world's greatest navy so it could leap ahead of British power and Americans could, as Wilson phrased it, do as they pleased.

But neither U.S. economic nor military power, as immense as they were, proved sufficient to give Wilson what he wanted at the Versailles peace conference. Or, at least, he could not figure out how to use this power unilaterally to bring European conservatives (as the French), liberals (as the British government), and revolutionaries (as Lenin's new regime in Russia) over to his way of thinking. In truth, squaring such a political circle was impossible. He tried to deal with Lenin initially by defining an alternate worldview (the Fourteen Points address of 1918) and then moving to exclude the Bolsheviks from any part in the peace conference. He attempted to bring the French and British into his own device of a League of Nations but did so only after some of his important principles (such as freedom of the seas) had to be compromised.

Most notably, he tried to deal with the overriding question of the disintegrating European empires and, by proclaiming the principle of self-determination (an idea based on Wilson's definition of the American experience), to stop Lenin's attempt to turn those pieces of former empires into communist states. His conservative secretary of state, Robert Lansing, shared Wilson's admiration for American history but doubted its universal applicability. He knew, moreover, that the president had brewed potent phrases but had not done the necessary homework to understand their implications. "When the President talks of 'self-determination' what unit has he in mind?" Lansing wrote in one memorandum. "Does he mean a race, a territorial area, or a community. Without a definite unit which is practical, application of this principle is dangerous to peace and stability." Or, again, in a later memo, the secretary of state feared placing such an idea "into the minds of certain races. . . . What effect," he shuddered to think, "will it have on the Irish, the Indians, the Egyptians?" He might have also questioned its impact on the Serbians, Czechs, Slovaks, Bosnians, and other groups in the former Austro-Hungarian Empire. "Will it," Lansing asked, "not breed discontent, disorder, and rebellion . . . ? The phrase is simply loaded with dynamite. It will raise hopes which can never be realized."[11] Lansing certainly did not mind using force unilaterally, but he feared brandishing it for quixotic, ill-thought-out ideas that were rooted in American exceptionalist thought rather than in European realities.

A valuable insight into what went wrong for Wilson at the peace conference was provided by one of the youngest and most perceptive of the Wilsonians to accompany the president to Paris. When he offered the insight in 1943, Walter Lippmann was a distinguished American journalist and the United States was again involved in a world war. In trying to draw the appropriate lesson from Wilson's bitter experience for the post–World War II peace settlement, Lippmann concluded that the president failed because he "was trying to establish collective security without forming an alliance. He wanted the omelet. He rejected the idea of cooking the eggs." So with Wilson's principles compromised and, as it turned out, American unilateral actions unable to rectify the compromises, the U.S. Congress rejected the president's handiwork. Or, as Lippmann phrased it, "The people, agreeing that an alliance was abhorrent, proceeded by intuitive common sense to the conviction that without an alliance, the League was unworkable and unpredictably dangerous."[12] It was apparently better to avoid such a league than to compromise either American exceptionalist beliefs or the freedom to act unilaterally outside of any alliance. In any case, even what was perhaps the ultimate statement of American exceptionalism—Wilson's remark, while he was en route to Paris, that "If I didn't feel that I was the personal instrument of God, I couldn't carry on"—proved to be irrelevant, given his inability to figure out how to use his various kinds of power to force the Allies to accept his postwar plans.[13]

In American foreign policy, the 1920s were marked by intensified economic deal-making, especially with Japan, Germany, and Great Britain.

This approach moved from dual assumptions: that the United States controlled the dominant economic power in the world, and that healthy global politics could only be based on American economic principles. Washington's policies also involved unilateral political activities outside the League of Nations. As events turned out, it made little difference that the United States never joined the league. Americans, at this point in their supposed century, would have acted ahistorically if they had joined a league they could not control. Once aware of their lack of control, they would have moved to make the organization less potent and less relevant to their own plans. The league, moreover, was indeed largely irrelevant to the growing economic imbalances, and, in important areas, corruption, that gradually undermined the global political superstructure between 1919 and 1933. U.S. economic deal-making did not prevent the catastrophe of the post-1929 years because it was a major cause of that catastrophe.[14]

The unilateralism and belief in American exceptionalism that led to the U.S. rejection of cooperation in 1919–20, and then to postwar disillusionment, led as inevitably to the unilateralism and abstention from political deal-making in the late 1930s. Secretary of State Cordell Hull was one of the best examples in American history of the official who believed that because politics followed economics, it was imperative that the economic system follow U.S. principles. In 1934 he pushed legislation through Congress that set up a trade policy based on reciprocal trading principles. The measure aimed at battering down such obstacles to American trade as the newly built British imperial preference system that made the Commonwealth market (including Canada and Australia) highly difficult for U.S. traders and investors to penetrate. Hull's legislation became the foundation for American trade policy throughout the rest of the twentieth century. But more immediately, his approach had less and less relevancy in a world of Nazism, communism, and Japanese militarism. Indeed, his kind of deal making—that is, the faith that private economic transactions could, without cooperative international political action, create a rapidly developing but stable and interdependent world—was reaching the end of its own history.

Henry Luce, a founder of the *Time, Life,* and *Fortune* magazine empire, was perhaps the most publicized of those who announced early in World War II that history was about to make a major turn. But it was not to be a turn away from American exceptionalism or unilateralism. To the contrary. In his 1941 volume of essays *The American Century,* Luce gave the common name to the era of U.S. dominance precisely by restating both the exceptionalism and the unilateralism. He began by laying down the maxim that if Americans hoped to regain their pre-1929 prosperity, they had to act on a global basis because the pre-1939 New Deal efforts to rescue the economy on a merely national basis had miserably failed. To act on a global basis economically, Luce added, required Americans to go to war militarily. After a long period of failed deal making in the private marketplace, no alternative now existed to its failure but to enter the world war. Only then could the requisite economic system be put into place and, as an integrated part of that system, an international "moral order" installed.

Luce wanted nothing to do with the traditional national-interest argument that would later dominate U.S. diplomatic debates. "We are not in a war to defend American territory," he wrote. "We are in a war to defend and even to promote, encourage, and incite so-called democratic principles throughout the world." The publisher asked condescendingly, "Are we going to fight for dear old Danzig or dear old Dong Dang?" Obviously Americans were above such ambitions. They would join the war as "the most powerful and vital" people in the world so they could act as "the dynamic center of ever-widening spheres of enterprise . . . , the training center of the skillful servants of mankind . . . , the Good Samaritan." Luce carefully noted that this did not mean demanding democratic systems from "all mankind including the Dalai Lama and the good shepherds of Tibet." But as it turned out, he did pretty much mean just that: the entire "world environment" had to be made congenial to U.S. principles if the globe was to work properly. "It must be an internationalism of the people, by the people and for the people."[15]

Luce's small book has made a large impact in shaping American thinking over more than a half century because he identified and brought together the two elements that have shaped U.S. policy, and many of the most important events, in the world arena since 1941: the traditional American belief that the United States is a nation set apart, an exception from the usual run of history; and the realization that by the early 1940s, U.S. officials commanded such tremendous military and economic power, especially relative to that of other major nations being bled or decimated by the war, that these officials could reach objectives only dreamed of by Woodrow Wilson. Many peoples see themselves as having exceptional histories and characteristics, as indeed they have. But it was the United States whose power could now both validate and carry out long-held beliefs in American exceptionalism so that the supposed exceptional could become increasingly universal. Whether Americans were truly exceptional or, more than they knew, part of long, global historical trends shared by many civilizations was a question that could be debated (although little doubted within the United States). What was not debatable, by Americans or people abroad, was who controlled—and, as in the destruction of Hiroshima and Nagasaki demonstrated, who was willing to use—the dominant military and economic power. Even the other postwar superpower, the Soviet Union, never had the military power to match, globally, American force. For a short time in the late 1950s and early 1960s, when some believed that the Soviets were going to replace Americans as the leading economic power, this scenario was viewed as a future, not present, danger.

The United States thus helped win the world war, as Luce predicted, and also the Cold War that followed. But his American Century was not one of unfettered or—more to the point—unhelped American individualism working political wonders through economic arrangements. Luce's vision required governmental institutions on the national level (such as the Export-Import Bank, or the Federal Reserve system), and, on the international level, multilateral institutions (such as the International Monetary Fund and the World Bank), to shape the postwar world—or, as it turned out after 1945 given the communist empires, a half-world—in which individuals could make deals. U.S. military power maintained order in areas where communism threatened the marketplaces (as in Central Europe) or where new nationalisms posed threats (as in Latin America). Dependable allies cooperated with and often improved U.S. policies, especially in Europe, where many of the American assumptions were more easily accepted. When the policies were not accepted (when, for example, France and other Europeans objected to Washington's determination to rebuild Germany rapidly and even militarily), the United States had the power to impose the policies anyway. Europeans no longer dealt with a United States that put its faith in the Dawes Plan, the Lamont-Kajiwara banking deal, and other largely private enterprise arrangements that aimed at informal political objectives with little formal governmental involvement. Such approaches had been sent to history's ash heap by the economic depression and rise of Nazism in the 1930s. In their place were formal military alliances controlled by the United States, along with government-formulated and supervised economic deals (such as the Marshall Plan and an expanding, targeted foreign aid program), that laid out guidelines and limits for the private dealmakers.

With these arrangements as a base, and an economic culture that could adapt to a rapidly changing technology as its central weapon, the United States and its allies won the Cold War. The triumphalism that followed, symbolized by President George Bush's 1992 proclamation that "By the grace of God America won the Cold War," beautifully captured the confidence in American exceptionalism that the end of the Cold War created.[16] But such confidence both lacked historical evidence and hid important lessons about Luce's American Century. The most obvious lesson was that the United States did not, for all its unilateralist tradition, win the Cold War on its own. Europeans contributed considerably more than did the United States in rebuilding their own economies, creating viable political systems out of the rubble of World War II, undertaking the pivotal Willy Brandt initiatives toward the Eastern Communist bloc, and demonstrating faith in what turned out to be the explosive (for the Communist system) human rights basket at Helsinki in 1975. To their misfortune, U.S. officials placed greater trust in American exceptionalist thought and less in European advice on such issues as dealing with the new Soviet leadership in 1953–54, formulating policy toward Vietnam during the 1960s, and handling Central America in the 1980s. We now know how self-defeating, and at times tragic, were U.S. policies in Korea after September 1950, Iran after June 1953, Guatemala after June 1954, and Latin America and Vietnam in the 1960s and after. These failures are not listed to deny that the good people won the Cold War but to indicate that good people in their egotism of power (to paraphrase Reinhold Niebuhr) too often made major mistakes for which millions of people paid with their lives.

The problem with believing that one is exceptional, and then possessing the power to try to spread the exceptional values and ways of life to others who may have doubts about them, is that the exceptional can be so powerful that it is difficult to stop them. And because the exceptionalists believe themselves so virtuous, they cannot stop themselves. Some thoughtful observers have begun to consider what this might mean for a continuing American Century. Coral Bell, with her perspective from Australia, notes that since the end of the Cold War, "the United States has mostly tiptoed through the current unipolar structure of the society of states with a sort of ponderous tact, like a benign Ferdinand-type bull making its way delicately around a China shop of unknown value." Bell believes that "History is not much help" in understanding this creature, "for no equal degree of unipolarity has existed since the high point of the Roman world almost two millennia ago." She argues that the life of this unipolarity will not be brief: "It will last at least another four decades or so, and possibly a great deal longer, though that will depend on Washington's choice of strategies." China is often seen as the next great rival to U.S. dominance, but "China's shadow is often greater than even its very real substance warrants."[17]

"Europe," Bell concludes, remains the only feasible rival for the United States "in the next three or four decades." The Europeans possess the economy, technologies, potential military forces, and vibrant culture that could go far in offsetting U.S. power. "Europe's only real deficit . . . is its low capacity for decision-making, particularly in times of crisis." While, however, Europe works through the problem of finding a decisive voice, Russians and Chinese, aided by some Islamic nations, will try to check unipolarism. She doubts they will have much success. "The new norms are, in effect, Wilsonian rather than Westphalian. Eighty years after his disastrous defeat in 1920, the ghost of Woodrow Wilson bestrides the world," especially "his maxim 'Every people is entitled to choose the sovereignty under which it shall live.'" This is "the principle (whether they know it or not) behind every separatist insurgency from the Kosovars and the Kurds to the East Timorese and the Irian Jayans"—even of "Scottish nationalists and Quebecois." Bell believes U.S. supremacy, with European and Japanese cooperation, along with Wilsonian principles, will highly benefit the "world's future."[18]

Perhaps. But the history of the first American Century is more relevant to such predictions than Bell is willing to admit, and that history offers alternate perspectives that are not as optimistic as she appears to be. Wilsonian self-determination, as Lansing noted, easily destabilizes rather than reorders. When some took this Wilsonian tenet seriously, moreover, and when, in the president's eyes, corrupt outside forces tried to take advantage of the resulting disruption, he became the greatest armed interventionist in his nation's history. Teaching Latin Americans to "elect good men" (as Wilson phrased it to a British diplomat) as part of their quest for choosing their sovereign turned out too often to climax with U.S. military commitments. If Wilson's version of American exceptionalism "bestrides the world," as Bell believes, the American Century's history indicates that the ghost might not at all be an agent of stabilization and peaceful aid.

Two scholars, Michael Hardt and Antonio Negri, agree with Bell that another American Century has begun, but they define its form, substance, and authority differently. The two go well beyond Bell by directly calling the new U.S.–constituted configuration nothing less than an empire. The secret to American power, the authors believe, is the American constitution, by which they mean both the "formal constitution" and the "material constitution, that is, the continuous formation and reformation of the composition of social forces." Such an approach leads Heldt and Negri to a provocative insight into the American Century: the post-1890 "U.S. constitutional project" is built not on Jefferson's idea of an "extensive [landed] empire" but "on the model of rearticulating incessantly diverse and singular relations in networks across an unbounded terrain." In other words, "The contemporary idea of Empire is born through the global expansion of the internal U.S. constitutional project."[19]

With this statement the authors explain (1) the deep historical, and especially ideological, roots of a belief in an American Century, resting on principles of American exceptionalism, that, as Martin Sklar especially has noted, coalesced in the 1890s, at the same moment the United States became one of the leading world military powers; (2) how Americans think more systematically and imperially than they often prefer to think they do; (3) why Americans can easily move from supposed Jeffersonian "open spaces," as Hardt and Negri define the presumed American frontier, to supposed "open spaces" on the global frontiers of technology and investment after 1900; (4) why Americans assume it is a positive right to follow the U.S. method of "reinventing incessantly diverse and singular relations" or, to use the earlier phrase, to enjoy the freedom to make deals; (5) and why, given the constitutional tradition that allowed Americans to act unilaterally across a continent for several centuries, they can easily transfer the unilateralist approach across the globe while justifying it with their successful constitutional (and social, and—above all—economic) model.

In this interpretation, it is an American Century with few internal restraints, formal or informal. Hardt and Negri know that in its earlier form, the U.S. Constitution and its implicit assumption about the existence and virtue of "open spaces" (that is, the supposed open frontier that has formed a crucial part of exceptionalist thought) could hide "ingeniously a brutal form of subordination" by ruthlessly warring against Native Americans on the grounds they were outside constitutional processes because they were "subhuman." They also occupied lands, or "open spaces," desired by whites. African Americans were enslaved within that Constitution.[20] Taken alone, therefore, the Constitution did not necessarily allow only benign "relations" in those "open spaces." It took mass economic and political movements to protect the rights of minorities within that system, a system that lasted well into the first American Century.

The question, raised but only partially analyzed by Bell, is whether such balances and countervailing forces will emerge in what she and others see as a new American Century. To rephrase, will other nations or groups of nations be able to mass enough power to check U.S. attempts to universalize parts of its exceptionalist faith? Some respected observers believe the dominance of U.S. technology, business management practices, and their cultural payoffs are already destroying "Europe's social model." *The Economist* phrased it in the baldest terms: "Democracy loses and borderless capitalism wins." Although Europeans have shown "a distaste for and distrust of American might in business, diplomacy, and arms," it nevertheless is the case that "in economics and economic policy, the European model . . . is giving way to none other than the American kind." The "leftist parties" in Europe increasingly resemble "America's New Democrats," while hitherto national markets in Europe merge "into a truly global (that is American-dominated) common market, forgive the expression. Put it this way: what is the point of 'Europe,' if 'Europe' is turning out to be just another United States?" Given that it is *The Economist,* the next line is inescapable: "In certain obvious ways, of course, that is a fate devoutly to be wished."[21]

It is not only that in the mid-1990s there were more American banks in London than in New York City. Nor was it only that U.S. high-tech companies poured $95 billion into international investments in 1998 (up 86 percent in five years) while exporting $181 billion in goods and accounting for a significant portion of the U.S. trade deficit by sending $40 billion of their overseas companies' products into the United States. Nor was it only that foreign investors sent $68 billion into the United States in 1998 (even while Americans spent more for amusing themselves and falling behind other developed nations in education and spending on research as a percentage of total economic output).[22] A larger question is whether its friends (much as those friends acted as checks during a few crucial moments in the Cold War) can slow down the strides (as Bell phrased it) of Wilson's ghost of American exceptionalism across the globe, when the direction, speed, and purpose of those strides are unilaterally determined.

A snapshot of how important parts of the world appear at the start of a new millennium might provide hints to deal with this question. According to a United Nations study of March 2000, the U.S. population will grow from 260 million to 350 million in 2050, while the European Union's will drop from 375 million to 330 million. The median age in Italy will rise from 42 to 53 (as Italy loses 28 percent of its population), with other European nations and Japan following that trend. The United States median age will move in the opposite direction because of its openness to immigrants—an openness that has brought a million of them into the country each year since 1990.[23] Such demographics at least raise doubts about Bell's belief that it might be Europeans checking the power of expanding American exceptionalism.

R. W. Apple of the *New York Times* observed on New Year's Day 2000 that "Today America bestrides the world. . . . We have come to see this as the culmination of a naturally occurring process, not unlike the Marxists who saw the rise of communism as the preordained consequence of a scientific process." This seemed to be the view of the George W. Bush administration, which came to power a year later. During its first months in office, it reaffirmed its determination to build a missile defense system, despite strong objections from many nations, including its closest European allies, and although creating such a system without Russian agreement could effectively destroy the 1972 anti-ballistic missile treaty that had been a cornerstone of arms control. The new administration also pulled out of the Kyoto accords that were written (and signed by the United States) to protect the environment and warned that an important biological weapons protocol was probably going to be discarded. European opposition to such unilateralism, contrary to Coral Bell's hope, could apparently be ignored. An early draft of a Pentagon planning statement for the next generation of U.S. military strategy rested on the assumption that the Pacific Ocean would be the most likely theater of future major U.S. military operations, because China, not Russia, posed the greatest danger. Such a policy would reorient a U.S. defense policy that since World War II has given primacy to European stability and containing Russian ambitions. Pentagon planners also asked for the creation of "long-range power projection" that would emphasize U.S. airlift capacity and other means for moving the country's firepower quickly and effectively, and, obviously, make American force projection much less dependent on cooperation from allies.[24]

The Bush administration's classic unilateralist approach changed little after the horrors of September 11, 2001. In response to the terrorist attacks in New York City and Washington, D.C., the president prepared a military assault on Afghanistan, where the terrorist headquarters were apparently located. He asked for little military help or advice from allies. Under the leadership of Secretary of State Colin Powell, a coalition was quickly pieced together, and support for the United States came from all parts of the globe (with the exception of a few Islamic nations, although other Islamic countries, led by Pakistan, provided crucial help). Great Britain's prime minister, Tony Blair, was as outspoken as President Bush in condemning the terrorism and went beyond the president in laying out the case—especially important for influencing Islamic opinion—that Osama bin Laden's terrorist network was responsible for the killing of some three thousand Americans. But the United States wanted little help from even the British. When Blair planned to send troops to help protect aid agencies dispensing desperately needed relief in Afghanistan, the British accused Washington of blocking their effort. As *The Economist* commented, despite Blair's strenuous efforts, "the stark truth is that if Britain did not exist, the history of Afghanistan after September 11th would probably have been no different."[25] The coalition was useful in rounding up terrorists overseas, cutting off financial aid to terrorist groups, and acting as a support group for the U.S. effort, but the war in Afghanistan, resembling the Korean War, was a wholly American-run effort behind a coalition the United States controlled.

How long the September 11th attacks will be the prime shaper of world affairs depends in part on U.S. actions. If the war in Afghanistan could be completed on Washington's terms, the Osama bin Laden terrorist network broken up, and other terrorist cells put on the defensive, and if President Bush took no further significant steps against states he believed supported terrorism, the American deployment of power would be tolerated, at least for some time. If, however, the United States, defying the warnings of Europeans and others, attacked states suspected of harboring terrorists and/or developing weapons of mass destruction (Iraq would be the prime target), European and Islamic governments could well turn against the American action, unless the United States won quickly, conclusively, and established a well-regarded and effective government to replace the overthrown regime—a large order. Europeans might well return to developing their plan for a 60,000-troop rapid deployment force, planned in response to the U.S. intervention in the Balkans during the 1990s—an intervention taken at times against European wishes. This force could provide some independence from fifty years of Washington's control of European military decision-making.

Even Henry Kissinger, whose toleration of foreign (especially European) critics while he was secretary of state was limited, warned that insensitive, unilateral globalization of American culture and economics (what he termed the "global adoption of the American model") could "evolve into a two-tiered system in which globalized elites are linked by shared values and technologies while the populations at large, being excluded, seek refuge in nationalism and ethnicity." Kissinger feared these larger groups would work "to become free of what they perceive as American hegemony. In such an atmosphere, attacks on globalization can evolve into a radical chic, especially where the governing elites are small, and the gap between rich and poor is vast and growing." He warned that "no economic system can be sustained without a political base."[26] The same warning could be given about a long-term military system or political alliance. But unilateral expansion of policies based on American exceptionalist principles is not the best method for creating the needed political bases, even after the horrors inflicted on the United States in September 2001.

When he was the U.S. ambassador to France in the late 1990s, Felix G. Rohatyn feared that if the American Century continued as it had evolved during the post–Cold War era, the misunderstandings and differences between Americans and Europeans would widen. "Now I sense a feeling that the very existence of the United States, and our enormous weight in the world, are causing a threat to their [Europeans'] identity," Rohatyn declared in 1999, "making it absolutely necessary from their point of view to counter what they see as a menace to their culture and their society."[27] Given the apparent acceleration of U.S. unilateralism, the most significant challenges to the continuation of the American Century may—if Rohatyn and Bell are correct—lie within, not between, civilizations.

NOTES

1. The "incompatibility of the exceptionalist claim with political messianism, of singularity with universalism" is well noted by a French scholar who provides a useful perspective on two centuries of U.S. foreign policy: Serge Ricard, "The Exceptionalist Syndrome in U.S. Continental and Overseas Expansionism," in *Reflections on American Exceptionalism,* ed. David K. Adams and Cornelis A. van Minnen (Staffordshire, U.K.: Ryburn, 1994), 73–82. *Isolationism* has long been a term of opprobrium in American politics, especially when self-styled internationalists use it to attack their opponents. These internationalists, for the most part, are reluctant to use the more accurate term *unilateralism,* perhaps in part because it would on close examination reveal that these internationalists are not significantly different from their opponents in approaching foreign affairs. A brief, useful demolition of *isolationism* as an appropriate term to describe the history of U.S. foreign relations abroad is Paul Johnson, "The Myth of American Isolationism: Reinterpreting the Past," *Foreign Affairs* 74 (May/June 1995): 159–64.

2. Alexis de Tocqueville, *Democracy in America,* 2 vols. (New York: Knopf, 1948), 2:36–38.

3. Byron E. Shafer, ed., *Is America Different? A New Look at American Exceptionalism* (Oxford: Oxford University Press, 1991), v.

4. Thomas Bender, *La Pietra Report: Project on Internationalizing the Study of American History, a Report to the Profession* (New York: Organization of American Historians, New York University, 2000), 7–8. This report, summarizing three summers of conference deliberations by distinguished groups of international scholars, tends to play down American exceptionalism by insisting that the American experience be compared with, and placed inside of, transnational and other international developments over the past several centuries. It is possible to wonder, however, whether the emphasis on the transnational context and the need for multicultural approaches underestimates the various types of power employed by the United States in the early twenty-first century to shape that transnational context, and consequently makes the report less relevant to a meaningful national debate because the report neglects the importance of using history directly to shape political debate within the United States itself. The report is interesting for discussing cross-cultural influences, but it has little to say about the more important subject of how Americans used power to formulate and extend (or refuse to extend) their interests across cultures, including American cultural interests.

5. Cooper's phrase is "Thou shalt make deals," as he outlines what post-1989 Europe has learned from Americans. But the "be free" addition seems necessary to separate the twentieth century from earlier economies. See Robert Cooper, "The Meaning of 1989," *Prospect* (December 1999): 29.

6. *The Economist,* March 31, 2001, 24.

7. Geoffrey Perret, *A Country Made by War* (New York: Random House, 1989), 1.

8. Thomas Paine, *Common Sense* (New York: Wiley, 1942), 23, 26–27, 31–32.

9. This assessment of the 1890s rests in large part on the pioneering work of Martin Sklar, who has developed these ideas in essays and books. Especially important for the purposes of this chapter is his "The Open Door, Imperialism, and Postimperialism: Origins of U.S. Twentieth-Century Foreign Relations, circa 1900," in *Postimperialism and World Politics,* ed. David G. Becker and Richard L. Sklar (Westport, Conn.: Greenwood Press, 1999), 317–35.

10. Quoted and given a pro-Wilson interpretation by Wilson's leading biographer, Arthur S. Link, in Link's *Wilson the Diplomatist* (Baltimore: John Hopkins Press, 1957), 96–97.

11. Robert Lansing, *The Peace Negotiations, a Personal Narrative* (Boston: Houghton Mifflin, 1921), 96–97.

12. Walter Lippmann, *U.S. Foreign Policy: Shield of the Republic* (Boston: Little, Brown, 1943), 76.

13. Felix Frankfurter, *Felix Frankfurter Reminisces,* as recorded in talks with Harlan B. Philips (New York: Reynal, 1960), 161.

14. An important analysis of this process, especially the relationship between the primacy of U.S. economic deal-making and American exceptionalism, is Frank Costigliola, *Awkward Dominion* (Ithaca: Cornell University Press, 1983).

15. Henry R. Luce, *The American Century* (New York: Farrar, Rinehart, 1941), 9–11, 13, 20–25, 35–40.

16. *New York Times,* January 29, 1991, A16.

17. Coral Bell, "American Ascendancy and the Pretense of Concert," *National Interest* (fall 1999): 55–56.

18. Ibid., 58–61.

19. Michael Hardt and Antonio Negri, *Empire* (Cambridge: Harvard University Press, 2000), xiv, 182.

20. Ibid., 169–70.
21. *The Economist,* February 12, 2000, 15.
22. *Washington Post,* March 13, 2000, A2.
23. *Washington Post,* March 22, 2000, A28.
24. *Washington Post,* March 23, 2001, A9.
25. *The Economist,* November 24, 2001, 55.
26. *Washington Post,* December 20, 1999, A33.
27. *New York Times,* December 2, 1999, A12.

Democracy and Power: The Interactive Nature of the American Century

FEDERICO ROMERO

If one looks for a constant, unifying theme in U.S. world vision throughout the twentieth century, there can be little doubt of the central place occupied by the concept of democracy. From Woodrow Wilson's most famous slogan—"to make the world safe for democracy"—all the way to the "enlargement of democracy" that synthesized American foreign policy doctrine during the 1990s, it stands out as the most recurrent keyword.

In declaratory and prescriptive terms, *democracy* was, and is, ever present. Less visible, though perhaps no less crucial, was its importance as an interpretative concept and analytical tool. Its prominence might have varied according to the specific context in which the United States happened to be interacting with other actors and cultures. And surely it was not the sole and only keyword. *Liberty, free trade,* and above all *national security* were no less relevant in many periods, but they always complemented *democracy* rather than replaced it. No one, however, would deny its prominence as a much-proclaimed principle and a persistent public catchword. Many scholars would also argue that it was the main matrix through which several American statesmen scrutinized the future of the international system, weighed the chances for peace and stability, outlined their mental maps of world affairs, and organized their priorities.[1]

Its very ubiquity, however, calls for an effort to circumscribe and refine the multiple, variable meanings that *democracy* incorporates and particularly to set them against the background of diverse historical con-

47

texts. This is not merely the standard task that professional historians
are supposed to perform; it appears to be especially consequential in
view of two distinct factors. The first might be highly contingent, but it
is rather conspicuous and quite relevant to present-day reconsiderations
of the so-called American Century. The current, predominant public narrative of the twentieth century as an epic, protracted, and ultimately successful struggle between democracy and totalitarianism in its various
forms—a struggle that entailed also the reshaping of the modes and rules
of international coexistence—is certainly not new. It was, after all, the
specific ideology that sustained the West throughout the Cold War and
defined the political culture that anchored Western Europe to U.S. leadership in the 1940s, thus erecting the central pillar in the architecture of
the American Century.

It was only in the 1990s, though, that such a view acquired its full-
fledged triumphalist overtones, permeated scholarly and policy analyses, informed many historical reconstructions, and became the publicly
held, "common sense" view of the past. After all, it is today—not one
or two generations ago—that we reckon to be living in a Wilsonian
world of globalized democracy and free trade, and therefore read the
twentieth century backward as a long voyage initiated and oriented by
Wilson's inspiration to "make the world safe for democracy." It took the
end of the Cold War to prompt George F. Kennan—perhaps the most
penetrating and influential anti-Wilsonian realist—to declare: "I was
long skeptical about Wilson's vision, but I begin today in the light of just
what has happened in the last few years to think that Wilson was way
ahead of his time."[2] And it is in the 1990s' most relevant and canonical
survey of the history of U.S. foreign relations that Wilson is credited with
establishing "a new American agenda for world affairs."[3]

The second factor pertains to the analysis of the term, of its history
and specificity. As historians we might not always be exempt from the
inducements of reading backward, but when we consider American international thinking we should be highly wary, indeed skeptical, of any
attempt to associate the protagonists of the century's crises, and the architects of the responses that were devised, with an optimistic, triumphalist view of the historical course of democracy. In normative terms
the call for democracy as the foundation for peace and stability, and its
elevation to foreign policy's guiding principle, is obviously central not
only in Wilson's thought but systematically in that of all American leaders, from Franklin D. Roosevelt's "quarantine" speech of 1937 to Ronald Reagan's damnation of the "evil empire" in 1983. In between these

two dates is inscribed the fully dichotomic representation of a world divided along antagonistic, irreconcilable principles, with the ensuing glorification of democracy as emblem, identity, and strategy. In the trying times of antifascist total war, and then of anticommunist containment, the exaltation of democracy took on a crusading tone and became a narrative of heroism and hope, although it was in these very circumstances that the United States was also propelled by security considerations and power dynamics to restrict, violate, or undermine democracy in various parts of the world.

Those public and institutional mobilizations of America were not, however, at all rooted in a triumphalist, or even optimistic, analysis of the chances of democracy worldwide but rather in pessimistic fears about history's motion away from the advancement of democracy and perhaps toward its gradual suffocation. This is all too obvious in 1939–41, but such an assessment pertains to the Cold War period as well. Between the idealist public pronouncements of the Truman Doctrine or the New Frontier, and the sober realism of George F. Kennan or Henry Kissinger, there runs a wide difference of opinion about the vitality of American democracy, about its actual and potential influence in the international context, and especially about the wisdom of the results its decision-making process can lead to. But most, if not all, the engineers and managers of containment—from Paul Nitze to Zbigniew Brzezinski—shared not only a keen awareness of America's powerful resources but also, to various degrees, a gnawing, persistent pessimism about the strength of democracy, and at times an outright fear of history's movement away from it.[4]

The nightmarish vision that democracy could regress and possibly be defeated, that its fabric could unravel and its solidity dissolve, that its enemies could be more implacably enduring, was always just under the surface of the optimistic appeal to its values and promise. The strategy and public discourse of "making the world safe for democracy" were voiced in a positive, progressive narrative of democracy's bright future, but they cannot really be disconnected from an enduring apprehension. There was a fear, first of all, that the American experiment might turn out to be not a promise of universal validity but rather a prolonged delusion that could not be replicated elsewhere and perhaps could not even be defended at home without altering its very nature in militarist, statist, and ultimately antidemocratic ways. Above all, there was a subtle, obstinate anxiety about the relationship between democracy and modernity. The fear was that the twentieth century's great and defining transformations—industrialism and rationalization, nationalism and mass politics, decolonization and multiple demands for social inclusion— could not really be channeled within an international order capable of safeguarding the democracies and building its own stability on the extension of their procedures.

TRIUMPHALISM and fear, then; a promise of regeneration and a vision of collapse. It is this deep, persistent ambivalence (which inhabited both the intuitive and the analytical realms) that can give us the key to disentangle the logic of Wilsonianism and focus on the most crucial factors of continuity in American international thinking in the twentieth century.

This deep-seated ambivalence can be dated from the years 1914–17, because in the previous decades the internationalism of the American elites had rested on a basic confidence in the stabilizing thrust of industrialism, trade, and modernity: up to that point, progress had been an unscathed faith. At the turn of the century, those elites had contemplated a world in which the connections between states, peoples, markets, and cultures were for the first time truly global—a world in which the United States, as the rising economic power, could easily envision the expansion of its values and interests, usually seen as coterminous with modernity itself. As it was taking on the status and role of a great power, the United States could now transcend these elites' traditional conception of the Western Hemisphere as inherently different and separate from Europe. Instead, it increasingly came to see itself—as Herbert Croly pointed out—as an organic component, if not the very epicenter, of a world that was being unified around the precepts of a liberal and industrial civilization.[5]

William McKinley and Theodore Roosevelt laid the geopolitical foundations of this emerging centrality by establishing U.S. hegemony in the Caribbean area, where the United States played its specific, active part in a larger, universal "civilizing mission" toward the nations (the races) that Euro-American culture deemed premodern if not primitive.[6] Meanwhile, the "open door" doctrine, "dollar diplomacy," and the Taft administration's proposals for international arbitration sketched out the contours of a code of collaboration between great powers. Positing a basic commonality of values, interests, and connections, those proposals assumed that antagonism could be replaced with cooperation and international conflicts turned into judicial disputes.

This overall optimistic view about a growing international liberal and industrial civilization was tempered by darker concerns—expressed, for instance, by Brooks Adams and entertained even by Theodore Roosevelt—about the potential threats embodied in Russian despotism or in imperial Germany's assertive mercantilism. These apprehensions, however, could not really dispel the larger notion of great-power peace as a congenital outgrowth of modernity, and the threats these apprehensions evoked often appeared more as a residue of the past than an intrinsic characteristic of an ongoing trend toward what today we would call globalization.[7]

Beginning in August 1914, all this obviously faded—and more radically so as the war grew into a total, unstoppable slaughter with devastating social and cultural consequences—and President Woodrow Wilson started out on his path toward Wilsonianism. For a lot of good motives—strategic, political, economic, and cultural—neutrality was the natural choice for the United States, but the policy soon acquired a complex dimension. On the one hand, it embodied a defense of the nation's main interests, in itself no less "selfish" than the policies pursued by each of the belligerents. On the other hand, it was amplified to include—and signify—the "rights" of noncombatants worldwide. From the narrow representation of the legitimate claims of American shippers and exporters, neutrality was rapidly conflated into a principled assertion of the human and political rights of violated Belgium and, by extension, of every other subject who did not willingly partake in the European carnage.

In its American rendition, neutrality primarily came to mean utter differentiation from the belligerents' destructive logic. It symbolized a superior, peaceful, progressive modernity that strove to assert itself in spite of, and against, the European powers' proclivity for war. As such, it anticipated the distinct systemic view that in 1916 brought President Wilson to step forward as the self-appointed mediator for a "peace without victory." Woodrow Wilson was undoubtedly urged in such a direction by his personal messianic zeal, but far more consequential were the considerations he was maturing on the nature of an international system in the era of interdependence.

In January 1917, Wilson publicly proscribed any notion of a balance of power and linked instead the prospects for lasting peace to the idea of a "community of power," defined by the language of democracy and rooted in its principles and procedures. "No peace can last, or ought to last, which does not recognize and accept the principle that governments derive all their just powers from the consent of the governed." In his view, this was not simply the idealistic, ambitious principle for a just peace but the only realistic basis for a sustainable peace: "Any peace that does not recognize and accept this principle will inevitably be upset."[8]

In early 1917, already stalemated by the generalized rejection of his inadequate effort at mediation, Wilson saw his options drastically narrowed by Germany's decision for unrestrained, all-out submarine warfare in the Atlantic, and in April he called the nation to a war to "make the world safe for democracy." American power was now to be fully employed in order to prevent a German victory and to lay down the lines of the peace to come. Perhaps equally important was the way in which the nation's power was going to be used, because the debate on war strategy contributed to define what later came to be known as Wilsonianism.

The combined events of summer and fall 1917—German victories, multiple signs of unrest and fatigue on the domestic fronts of the Entente, and the unfurling of revolution in Russia—conjured up ominous scenarios. It was now possible to predict an impending German victory. In public culture as well as in the private imagination of most American leaders, Germany had become the epitome of despotic, militarist statism. Were it to conquer Continental hegemony by military means, it could then proceed to extend its harsh rule around Europe and impose its presence the world over. The traditional threat of an expanding Continental power—outlined in the previous decades in the Anglo-Saxon, maritime geopolitics of Halford J. Mackinder and Alfred T. Mahan—was being blended with progressive anxieties about democracy, free trade, and liberalism.[9] From such a mix emerged the first contours of the specter that would occupy the center of the American worldview in the central decades of the twentieth century: the menacing race to world conquest by an alien, powerful, intractable enemy, which could not be reconciled with the norms of freedom, sovereignty, and interdependence.

A second scenario, less precisely focused but perhaps no less disturbing, revolved around the fear of revolution and, more broadly, of the spreading social unrest that was rapidly growing out of the war's devastation and dislocation. If it is disputed how much Wilson specifically feared the Bolshevik Revolution—which he loathed but also deemed probably short-lived—it is clear he was deeply concerned about the disorder that engendered revolution and the destructive forces that the war had let loose in European societies.[10]

It is also for this reason that he considered the balance-of-power concept not so much unjust as historically inadequate. If a small local crisis in the Balkans could grow into a European war of unlimited violence, and then into an unstoppable world conflict that endangered liberal civilization, it followed that the traditional balancing mechanisms were worn out and tragically obsolete.

The very destructiveness of the war, its swift expansion, and the catastrophic vastness of its consequences were interpreted by Wilson as manifestations of "new cascade dynamics" in international affairs, of potentially unstoppable spiraling trends that represented the dismal underside of interdependence and modernity.[11] To quote Frank Ninkovich, author of one of the most stimulating analyses of Wilsonianism:

The very forces that made progress possible—technology, trade, a global division of labor, and interdependence—also made possible the system's destruction if pushed in the wrong direction and not checked. The greater the degree of integration, the more explosive would be the disintegration produced by runaway modernity. Thus Wilson recognized one of modernity's most prominent and paradoxical features: as the world became more industrialized and integrated, it became more orderly and predictable; at the same time, breakdowns in the system, though perhaps less frequent, were more calamitous.[12]

Wilson thus perceived more lucidly than others the fragility and vulnerability of interdependence in the face of competing hegemons (which would segment it in separate and potentially antagonistic areas), of revolutions, and of the incipient nationalist upsurge of "uncivilized," premodern peoples who did not see its benefits and did not want to shoulder its costs. Interdependence could metamorphose from opportunity to risk, and perhaps utter disaster, if those destabilizing and fragmenting pressures that threatened it were not confronted, restrained, and conquered. But this effort required entirely new ways and tools, adequate to the radical novelties that characterized the twentieth century.

Thus at the roots of Wilsonian internationalism there is not so much the missionary utopianism of his Presbyterian background as a gloomy perception of an unprecedented danger, and therefore of a necessity. International relations, and more broadly international life, must be reorganized in light not of the old threats (those that had prescribed the nineteenth-century republican tradition of anti-European American isolation) but of the new and emerging ones. Wilson stated in March 1919: "In my opinion, to try to stop a revolutionary movement is like using a broom to sweep back a spring tide. . . . The sole means of countering Bolshevism is to make its causes disappear."[13]

To his European counterparts, he no longer imputed a conservative political philosophy that democratic America despised and rejected but rather the dangerous obsolescence of their conceptual and analytical tools:

The conservatives do not realize what forces are loose in the world at the present time. . . . Liberalism is the only thing that can save civilization from chaos. . . . Liberalism must be more liberal than ever before, it must be even more radical, if civilization is to escape the typhoon.[14]

Wilson's solutions to these dilemmas can perhaps best be understood by analogy with the top-down social engineering recipe that progressive thinking applied to the domestic tensions brought into American society by the second industrial revolution: market regulations negotiated with the main interest groups, guaranteed by unobtrusive but authoritative government controls, and sanctioned by electoral consent in the first mass politics system. Just as supply and demand could no longer perpetuate their smooth interaction without public regulations, so the logic of the balance of power had grown incapable of providing its balancing outcome and therefore had to be replaced with "an organized and rationally directed community of power" legitimized by public consent: "Organized democratic world opinion, institutionalized in a League of Nations, would have to take the place of the Invisible Hand."[15]

In this light, democracy was a principle and a faith that voters' instincts were more pacific than those of their rulers. But it was primarily a procedure to conciliate diverse interests by means of formalized rules, in accordance with the needs of a more specialized and interdependent world. And it could also be a vehicle for inclusion, as long as this was cautiously controlled and channeled from above. Last, but most crucial, democracy was not intended as the disavowal of power but rather as the proper seat and method for the organization of a superior—indeed overwhelming—power legitimized by public opinion.[16]

This aspect was often overlooked or ignored by Wilson's realist critics, who focused on his most cathartic, idealist statements in order to indict his policies in view of the subsequent failure of a League of Nations made powerless by the absence of the United States, or of the persistent, paralyzing Anglo-French disagreement on the treatment of Germany.[17] But it is nonetheless a key aspect of Wilsonianism, and especially of its legacy in American international thinking. The nexus between power and democracy, although hardly the focus of his conceptual elaboration, had a key place in Wilson's strategies. From Mexico to Siberia, President Wilson used American power more often and widely than any of his predecessors. The 1917 decision for war, his choice for the status of associate rather than allied power, and the deployment of a large, autonomous expeditionary force to coerce Germany into surrender and then dictate the peace terms: all these are the components of a strategy that does not dilute power in an idealized notion of democracy but rather revolves on power as its unmistakable axis. After all, the League of Nations itself was conceived as the mechanism for mustering and organizing the deterrent function of the democracies' power, and especially America's. And in 1919, in spite of all the principled rhetoric about collective security, Wilson did not preclude the option of an American security guarantee to France.

Wilsonianism, then, does not substitute democracy for a logic of power but strives to integrate both terms in a unified approach originating from the verified perilousness of an interdependence that is positive, indeed indispensable, only insofar as it can be structured, regulated, and defended. Because the tensions inherent in modern interdependence cannot be confined in a corner nor allowed to fester all the way up to generalized, highly destructive wars, they have to be preempted, defused, and—whenever necessary—restrained and halted by force. A positive confidence in the global reach of modernity is thus intertwined with a keen perception of its fragility, and therefore with a globalist notion of American security, interest, and prosperity. They cannot be upheld and preserved within a national dimension; they have to be anchored to a dynamic but controlled transformation of the entire international framework.[18]

A world that is not safe for democracy, safe for free-market capitalism, and safe for a peaceful coexistence of the great powers is not only detrimental to America or ethically objectionable; in the twentieth century it is inherently unstable and dangerous. As on a bicycle, one either moves forward or collapses. In the Wilsonian view, stability cannot exist unless it is conceived as a continuous forward dynamic of modernity. And modernity—incarnated primarily in America but comprehensive of most phenomena of advanced industrial civilization—must be truly global or is immediately threatened and ultimately nullified.

EVER since Wilson, this defense of global modernity is a key intellectual (and instinctual) subtext of the American approach to international relations, as it emerged in transparent form with the Atlantic Charter of

1941 and the Bretton Woods agreements of 1944. Obviously the intervening twenty years, and especially the late 1930s crisis, nurtured a deeper and more urgent appreciation of the direct role of American power as pivot and guarantor of such a dynamic global order. Wilson may not have theorized about such a role, although he certainly practiced it; Franklin D. Roosevelt elevated it to an explicit, undisputed assumption.

The keyword here is *national security,* that ever-present concept that first arose in 1938–41, when the bellicose expansionism of militarist and dictatorial regimes conjured up not so much a direct threat to the material security of U.S. territory and population as an intolerable transformation of the world scenario.[19] In the ascending geopolitical language of the time, the threat came to be seen in the guise of a potential domination of Eurasia's vast resources by great hostile powers;[20] in the more established language of principles and political ideas, what the perceived threat amounted to was the step-by-step suffocation of democracy. In either of these codes—and they grew inextricably mingled—the danger was the end of the world upon which America had predicated the historical fulfillment of its own experiment and promise: a world of interdependence, of shared legal procedures, of unfettered access to markets and resources, of democratic sovereignty as a universal principle.

The national security that was perceived under threat was actually a vision of the future—a pure concept rather than a real context—posited on the international projection of America's democratic, free-market, and liberal experience as the only sound and dependable basis for sustained peace. The very antithesis of such a view—then and ever since labeled as totalitarianism—was not so much an adversary to be checked and counterbalanced, in accordance with a classical balance of power approach, but a mortal enemy that could not be tolerated.

The Rooseveltian logic of unconditional surrender inaugurated, on the American side, that absolute delegitimization of the enemy that would later define the Cold War.[21] The nexus between power and an international order favorable to the democracies became not only explicit but truly crucial, with the unabashedly hegemonic reframing of the international organization—now the United Nations—around the Rooseveltian "four policemen," among which the United States was to be the superior, ultimate arbiter and guarantor of the system.[22] In the postwar years, when American elites became convinced that integrating the USSR in such a democratic and hegemonic order was impossible, or at any rate too dangerous, the very same concept of national security provided the matrix for identifying a Soviet threat and countering it with a strategy of containment.

Until late 1949, the nature of the Soviet threat was not primarily defined in military terms. America's foremost postwar apprehensions resided in the multiple, converging factors of economic frailty and political instability in Europe. Great Britain's financial exhaustion, the power void that had taken the place of Germany, France's and Italy's precarious recovery, the dollar gap—these and other factors sketched a scenario of prolonged instability replete with opportunities for the Soviets. As George Kennan and other analysts repeatedly stated, the extension of Soviet influence could simply take place by default, that is, by the inaction of the United States and the passive drifting of the West.[23] As on a tilting plane, new subjects and areas could gradually, inexorably lean toward the Soviets. If unchecked, such a dynamic could ultimately realize the geopolitical nightmare conceived in 1940: the domination of a hostile power over the whole of Eurasia.

It was on the basis of this feared chain of potentially unfurling events that the Truman administration devised a strategy conceived as a "response" and articulated in the division of Germany, the economic reorganization of Western Europe, and an Atlantic Pact primarily intended as political and psychological reassurance. The common thread was the consolidation of Western-oriented industrial democracies as bulwarks of containment, with the United States as leader, defender, and guarantor of this new Western European and Atlantic order.[24]

It was in 1950—with the Soviet A-bomb, the Chinese Revolution, and the Korean War—that bipolar antagonism rapidly became militarized and the American national security doctrine turned to a markedly strategic and military language geared to the notions of superiority and deterrence. Its basic rationality, however, remained rooted in the original traits. Its overarching goal still resided in the defense of the vital interconnections between the various components of what had by now become known as the West (although inclusive of Japan as well), and increasingly also between this West and its colonial or postcolonial "periphery." It was a national security that revolved around promoting (quasi) global interdependence, reaffirming and consolidating a world in which democracies, free markets, and liberal values could prosper and expand; if not, they would deteriorate and perish.

Many historians have exposed the analytical shortcomings and punctured the gross analogies that were at the basis of this repetitive American view centered on the recurrence of a similar menace—simultaneously ideological and geopolitical—embodied first in Nazi Germany, then in postwar Stalin's Russia, and, to a minor extent, in Mao's China throughout the 1950s and 1960s.[25] There is no need here to review the long debate on the analytical validity, or lack thereof, of the concept of totalitarianism, but it is worth pointing out that this recurrent view of an analogous threat—however defective it was on each specific occasion—derived to a large extent from an enduring perception of systemic frailty.

From the point of view of American strategy-making (which is not one and the same with public propaganda, and whose epistemological and practical priorities do not coincide with those of scholarly analysis), the crux of the matter was not the different natures of Nazism and communism, or the degree of similarity between them. The real issue was the viability of the fabric of democratic and capitalist interdependence, or rather its recurrent vulnerability, which those two antagonists so crudely exposed. Throughout the Cold War, the United States did not merely defend the system of Western interdependence from its external foe with a rebalancing and deterrent strength. The United States protected it and glued it together with a preponderant power—economic and cultural power, no less than strategic—precisely because they always thought that such a system, although inherently multilateral, required the indispensable guarantee of American power for its solidity and durability.

It is for this reason that the credibility of American power was considered such a sine qua non for Washington's international strategy; it was supposed to be the keystone of a complex, multiple system whose cohesion was deemed ultimately to rest on American might and resolve. For President Lyndon B. Johnson, the costs and perils of defending the South Vietnamese regime were justified not simply by a principle, by pressing domestic reasons, or by the ambitious desire to lift the rural Mekong out of poverty as the New Deal had done for his Texas. Those costs and perils seemed congruous, and virtually inevitable, in order "to avoid a humiliating U.S. defeat (to our reputation as a guarantor)."[26] It is also this conceptual junction between democracy, hegemony, and credibility that explains the manifest contradiction between the numerous American violations of democracy (in Iran, Guatemala, Chile, South Africa, and elsewhere) and a strategic logic that rationalized those interventions as necessary to the stability of the international system of democracies.[27]

EVEN when seen in this light—not as a principle of political philosophy but as a code word for a hegemonic, multilateral system of liberal, free-market, industrial nations—democracy is a term that remains fraught with contradictions and internal tensions. The most obvious and widely discussed concerns the relationship between democracy and capitalism. The most radical, robust, and recurrent scholarly criticism of American international attitudes has come from historians who argue that U.S. power was (and is) used to make the world safe for capitalism, and specifically American capitalism, and that this has often hindered, limited, or distorted democracy in various areas of the world as well as in the United States.[28] For the sake of my argument, it is not necessary to delve into this discussion. Suffice it to say that in the vast range of theoretical assumptions that run from the incompatibility between democracy and capitalism to their utter inseparability, American internationalist thinking has clearly embraced the latter and always maintained it as a key element of its strategies.

What I'd like to emphasize here is the interactive nature of this nexus between democracy and American power. In the current processes of globalization—as well as in the comparable ones of a century ago—the multiplication of commercial and financial flows, and the dissemination of norms and cultures from capitalism's metropolitan centers (and especially from America), generate growth and interdependence as well as tensions, instability, and actual or potential fragmentation in the international fabric. They induce transformations and upheavals that foster local defensive responses and can activate radical reactions in diverse nations, societies, or parts thereof. It is often at this point that U.S. power actively intervenes abroad.[29]

The transformative effects of global modernization were (and are) deep, continuous, and unsettling. They induce a vast array of adjustments and responses in the societies involved, and they in turn can propel an expansion of democracy as well as its most radical suppression. Throughout the twentieth century, Europe has experienced virtually the whole range of possible responses, and the consolidation of democracy it eventually achieved was directly and manifestly associated with the projection of American power during and after World War II. An almost equally broad range of political adjustments or reactions to the tides of global change took place in Asia and Latin America.

The premises of Wilsonianism rest precisely on the assumption of this ambivalent dynamic as the fundamental challenge that the international system must deal with. But Wilsonianism (and even more broadly America's twentieth-century internationalism) is not a formalized, rigid, immovable doctrine. As a body of ideas and cultural assumptions, it took shape over a century that threw successive, different, particular challenges to the United States. It is only through these specific emergencies and contingencies that Wilsonianism grew into a project, a set of strategies, and, above all, a widespread and deep-rooted culture.

When talking of an American Century, we usually refer to its historical sources in the cultural assumptions, economic recipes, social relations, and political settlements that grew out of the United States's own national experience. But the processes that amalgamated these various elements, and then translated them in a peculiar international vision and strategy, cannot be explained in purely American terms. The external historical contexts, the shifting scenarios of challenges and opportunities designed by other actors, were equally crucial in reordering the priorities and connections that forged the American concept of international relations.[30]

The image of an American Century can be used with a variety of meanings, but when it is set in the international context, the only way to make sense of it is as an interactive process. The notion of the twentieth century as an American Century is literally inconceivable if we do not weigh in the other aspects and actors of international life that gave shape to it. There is no American Century without the century of Germany, of Europe's self-destruction, of Soviet Communism, of postcolonial liberation and re-organization, of the rise of East Asia, and so on. These actors and transformative processes had agency in their own right, and their luminous or hideous protagonism must be taken into account—if for no other reason at least because the threats and opportunities they embodied constantly reshaped America's own approach to the world, its recipes and solutions, and to a considerable extent even its own identity.

This is particularly relevant when we focus on the American reading of the relationship between democracy and power, because the latter evolved incrementally in relation to multiple, mutable challenges and possibilities. At least ever since F. D. Roosevelt, the Wilsonian concept was spelled out as a deliberately hegemonic effort to consolidate liberal industrial regimes in selective areas of crucial importance. Even though the UN adopted a (strongly tempered) one nation–one vote principle, the gist of U.S. strategy was not the attempt to establish a worldwide system of majority-based democracy institutionalized in an organization of legal peers. It rather aimed at connecting those selected areas in a framework of economic and political interdependence anchored to, and by, America's preponderant power.

In this context, American power functioned as the ultimate defender of this Western subsystem from external pressures as well as its internal ordering principle, so as to mediate its tensions, prioritize its efforts, assure its cohesion. This cohesion—it is well worth emphasizing—was constantly rearranged by negotiation, but America never entrusted it to the uncontrollable vagaries of a loose, unbound, and unrestrained multilateralism. The main, incremental lesson Washington had drawn from the dangers faced in World War I and in the 1930s was that democracy and interdependence could decline and perish if left not only without a shield but especially without a strong connecting glue.

American leadership stems from economic superiority, cultural universalism, and military might, but it is fully activated and brought to bear upon friends and foes when it comes to be seen as the prerequisite for the survival and viability of multilateralism. It might well be worth wondering, for instance, if that strategy's masterpiece—the integrative solution to the German problem via the incorporation of a democratic West Germany in a European economy and an Atlantic alliance, but in a structurally subordinate position—would have equally taken place in the absence of a perceived Soviet "threat." The State Department might well have concocted something along the lines of the Marshall Plan anyway. But at the very least we have reasons to doubt that Congress would have financed it or that France would have reconciled itself to an independent Federal Republic next door. I am not so fond of counterfactuals as to argue that Stalin actually prevented another Wilsonian failure in the second postwar period, but even this simple hypothesis shows that the making of the American Century cannot be ascribed solely to America.

This brings me to my conclusions concerning the issue of European-American relations in the present and presumably in the foreseeable future. A historical reading of the predicaments of interdependence in the twentieth century has fastened American international thinking to the notion that the stability, prosperity, and—in the last resort—survival of democracies require a variable but robust dose of American hegemony and leadership.[31] This is the assumption behind the recent expansion of NATO and the preference accorded to it (rather than to broader organizations such as the UN or OSCE) as peacemaker and peacekeeper. It is the assumption that makes for the ambivalent attitude that America maintains toward Europe's admittedly hesitant attempts at a unified, larger role in the international arena. (It is also, by the way, the source of the endemic, unresolved attrition with those states, such as China or Russia, that only reluctantly submit to the unipolarity of the current world scenario.)

The issue that was featured throughout the previous century has thus acquired a new shape and relevance, and it is worth venturing into another hypothetical question. Was there in the twentieth century, and is there today, *any* kind of hegemony in Europe that America would deem safe enough to live with? In other words, was it the militarist, statist, self-enclosed, and totalitarian nature of German and Soviet hegemonic threats that made them utterly unacceptable? In historical terms the answer is obvious, and we Europeans especially are fortunate that the ugly face of totalitarianism mobilized America, but the question is still worth asking if we want to unravel the mechanisms that made the American Century. After all, the kind of Europe that inhabited recurrent French dreams—an assertive Europe led by Paris, perhaps protectionist and too fond of managed trade but surely democratic—was discarded by Washington not only as a shaky and unreliable proposition in the context of bipolar antagonism but clearly as an undesirable one as well, as the current polemics on the relationship between NATO and a European defense project make clear.

To what extent then could a more cohesive, self-assured, and autonomous Europe find a place in America's vision of global interdependence? In theory the degree of attrition inherent in such a hypothesis could be minimal, because it would depend on Europe's continuing attachment to and compliance with a consolidated set of economic and political interdependencies. Freedom of trade and cooperation in NATO appear as the basic parameters upon which America would evaluate the development of a more independent and assertive Europe.

But twentieth-century history has rooted an axiom in U.S. international conceptions, the deeply held persuasion that the stability of the international system of democracies rests on a benign but firm American hegemony. In relation to Europe, this means a leading role within, and by means of, NATO. In the post–Cold War period, the wars in the former Yugoslavia further confirmed the apparent immutability of this axiom in American eyes. To envision a more balanced cooperation between the United States and a unified and assertive Europe, one obviously needs first of all to imagine the solution to many intra-European dilemmas. If those hurdles are overcome, however, that legacy from the twentieth century will have to be reckoned with. A self-reliant Europe capable of effective action in defense of its own stability as well as that of its immediate periphery would begin to loosen the established nexus between democracy and American power.

Only at that moment—if it ever materializes—will the American concept of international order be truly tested, because it will for the first time be disjoined from the crucial corollary of unipolarity (a virtual one in the Cold War and an actual one thereafter) that has so far intertwined democracy with hegemony. Were this to happen, the twentieth-century equation that conjoined democratic interdependence with the preponderance of America's "indispensable" power would fade into history.

Notes

1. See, for instance, Tony Smith, *America's Mission* (Princeton: Princeton University Press, 1994).

2. George F. Kennan's statement at the hearings of the U.S. Senate Foreign Relations Committee, 1989, as quoted in Daniel P. Moynihan, *On the Law of Nations* (Cambridge: Harvard University Press, 1990), 151.

3. Akira Iriye, *The Globalizing of America, 1913–1945*, vol. 3 of *Cambridge History of American Foreign Relations*, ed. Warren I. Cohen (New York: Cambridge University Press, 1993), 18.

4. Particularly in respect of Western Europe, see the considerations of Dana H. Allin, *Cold War Illusions: America, Europe and Soviet Power, 1969–1989* (New York: St. Martin's, 1994).

5. Herbert Croly, *The Promise of American Life* (1909; reprint, New York: Dutton, 1963).

6. See Thomas D. Schoonover, *The United States in Central America, 1860–1911* (Durham, N.C.: Duke University Press, 1991); Anders Stephanson, *Manifest Destiny: American Expansionism and the Empire of Right* (New York: Hill and Wang, 1995).

7. See Akira Iriye, *From Nationalism to Internationalism: U.S. Foreign Policy to 1914* (London: Routledge, 1977).

8. Woodrow Wilson, "Address to the Senate," January 22, 1917, in *Public Papers of Woodrow Wilson*, ed. Arthur Link (Princeton: Princeton University Press, 1966–93), 40:535–37.

9. See Halford John Mackinder, *Democratic Ideals and Reality: With Additional Papers* (1919; reprint, New York: Norton, 1962); Alfred T. Mahan, *The Interest of America in Sea Power* (New York: Harper Bros., 1897).

10. Among the most recent literature, see Betty Miller Unterberger, *The United States, Revolutionary Russia, and the Rise of Czechoslovakia* (Chapel Hill: University of North Carolina Press, 1989); Georg Schild, *Between Ideology and Realpolitik: Woodrow Wilson and the Russian Revolution, 1917–1921* (Westport, Conn.: Greenwood Press, 1995); and David S. Fogelsong, *America's Secret War against Bolshevism: U.S. Intervention in the Russian Civil War, 1917–1920* (Chapel Hill: University of North Carolina Press, 1995).

11. Frank Ninkovich, *The Wilsonian Century: U.S. Foreign Policy since 1900* (Chicago: University of Chicago Press, 1999), 65.

12. Ibid., 66–67.

13. Woodrow Wilson at the peace conference, March 1919, quoted in Paul Mantoux, *The Deliberations of the Council of Four (March 24–June 28, 1919)* (Princeton: Princeton University Press, 1992), 1:47.

14. Woodrow Wilson, January 1919, quoted in Lloyd Gardner, *The Anglo-American Response to Revolution, 1913–1923* (Oxford: Oxford University Press, 1984), 1.

15. Ninkovitch, *Wilsonian Century,* 67.

16. See Tony Smith, *America's Mission* (Princeton: Princeton University Press, 1994), chap. 4; and Thomas J. Knock, *To End All Wars: Woodrow Wilson and the Quest for a New World Order* (New York: Oxford University Press, 1992).

17. A good example is Henry A. Kissinger, *Diplomacy* (New York: Simon and Schuster, 1994).

18. See the recent discussions by Tony Smith, "Making the World Safe for Democracy in the American Century," *Diplomatic History* 23, 2 (spring 1999): 173–88; and Ross A. Kennedy, "Woodrow Wilson, World War I, and an American Conception of National Security," *Diplomatic History* 25, 1 (winter 2001): 1–31.

19. On the origins and history of the term itself, see Emily Rosenberg, "Commentary: The Cold War and the Discourse of National Security," *Diplomatic History* 17, 2 (spring 1993): 277–84.

20 See Melvyn P. Leffler, *A Preponderance of Power: National Security, the Truman Administration, and the Cold War* (Stanford: Stanford University Press, 1992).

21. See Anders Stephanson, "Fourteen Notes on the Very Concept of the Cold War," in *Rethinking Geopolitics,* ed. Gearoid O'Tuathail and Simon Dalby (London: Routledge, 1998), 16–38. On the intellectual history of the concept of totalitarianism, see Abbott Gleason, *Totalitarianism: The Inner History of the Cold War* (New York: Oxford University Press, 1995).

22. See John L. Harper, *American Visions of Europe* (Cambridge: Cambridge University Press, 1994), chap. 3.

23. See Memorandum from the Director of the Policy Planning Staff (Kennan), May 16, 1947, in *Foreign Relations of the United States, 1947,* vol. 3 (Washington, D.C.: U. S. Government Printing Office, 1963), 220–23.

24. See Carolyn Eisenberg, *Drawing the Line: The American Decision to Divide Germany, 1944–1949* (New York: Cambridge University Press, 1996); John L. Gaddis, *Strategies of Containment: A Critical Appraisal of Postwar American National Security Policy* (New York: Columbia University Press, 1982); Charles S. Maier, ed., *The Marshall Plan and Germany* (New York: Berg, 1991); Michael Hogan, *The Marshall Plan: America, Britain and the Reconstruction of Western Europe, 1947–1952* (Cambridge: Cambridge University Press, 1987).

25. A good example is Ernest R. May, *"Lessons" of the Past: The Use and Misuse of History in American Foreign Policy* (Oxford: Oxford University Press, 1973).

26. Memorandum by John McNaughton (assistant secretary for defense) to Robert McNamara, March 14, 1965, quoted in Lloyd C. Gardner and Ted Gittinger, eds., *International Perspectives on Vietnam* (College Station: Texas A&M University Press, 2000), 10. See also Lloyd C. Gardner, *Pay Any Price: Lyndon Johnson and the Wars for Vietnam* (Chicago: Dee, 1995).

27. See David F. Schmitz, *Thank God They're on Our Side: The United States and Right-Wing Dictatorships, 1921–1965* (Chapel Hill: University of North Carolina Press, 1999).

28. When approaching these "revisionist" arguments, it is always worth starting from their initiator, William A. Williams, *The Tragedy of American Diplomacy* (1959; reprint, New York: Norton, 1988). For a recent, focused, and synthetic discussion, see Walter LaFeber, "The Tension between Democracy and Capitalism during the American Century," *Diplomatic History* 23, 2 (spring 1999): 263–84.

29. This is an argument persuasively advanced, in the context of late-nineteenth-century U.S. expansion in Central America, by Walter LaFeber, *The American Search for Opportunity, 1865–1913,* vol. 2 of the *Cambridge History of American Foreign Relations,* ed. Warren I. Cohen (New York: Cambridge University Press, 1993). He has more recently generalized it to encompass U.S. foreign policy in the twentieth century: "Wilsonian self-

determination . . . could be a maxim so full of dynamite that it could further destabilize, rather than reorder the world"; see chap. 2.

30. An interesting discussion, in this and other respects, is in Robert Latham, *The Liberal Moment: Modernity, Security, and the Making of the Postwar International Order* (New York: Columbia University Press, 1997). See also Geir Lundestad, "How (Not) to Study the Origins of the Cold War," in *Reviewing the Cold War: Approaches, Interpretations, Theory,* ed. Odd Arne Westad (London: Frank Cass, 2000), 64–80.

31. For a current, peremptory reaffirmation of the axiom that predicates a favorable world situation (*balance* would be an inappropriate term in this case) upon American preponderance, see Donald Kagan and Frederick W. Kagan, *While America Sleeps* (New York: St. Martin's, 2000).

Europe: The Phantom Pillar

RONALD STEEL

The Atlantic alliance, that hardy survivor of the Cold War, came into being as a result of European fears, American ambition, and Soviet opportunism. A product of the Cold War, it remains today, despite dramatically changed conditions, its most enduring monument. The political and ideological division of Europe has passed, and so has the Soviet Union, yet NATO retains a remarkable vitality.

On the surface this is surprising, because military alliances usually come into being to deal with specific dangers and wither once those dangers have passed. Yet NATO, we can now see, is a very different kind of alliance. Its inner structure and logic mask its outward appearance. Its initial raison d'être was the Soviet threat. But it survives because of what Europe is and how it relates to the United States.

Although it is dominated by the United States, NATO is in part a European invention. In the late 1940s, Europeans in the West, weak and demoralized by war, feared that the victorious United States might revert to its prewar isolationism, leaving to them the task not only of rebuilding their economies but of blocking the expansion of socialism from within and communism from without. This fear turned out to be unfounded. But it did not seem unreasonable at the time, when the United States had only just begun its psychological adjustment to its new status as the world's preeminent military and economic power.

American internationalists were still traumatized by the economic collapse of the 1930s. Fearful of another depression and of closed trading blocs harmful to the American economy, they felt it essential to bring economic as well as political stability to Europe. For this reason they saw American security guarantees as instrumental rather than as an end in themselves. These guarantees would allow the Europeans to focus on rebuilding their economies rather than on rearmament. Reconstruction was essential to the global trade and economic integration that, the Americans were convinced, held the key to their own prosperity.

Of course economics was far from being the only factor. There is no persuasive monocausal explanation for the Cold War. What degenerated into an East–West divide had political, psychological, and historic roots as well as military ones. But there were many in Western Europe as well as in the United States who believed that the Soviets would be tempted to expand their control if they could do so with relative impunity. The Soviets cooperated in forging the new consensus by imposing brutal dictatorships on the countries they occupied.

During the period 1947–48, when tensions between East and West reached a critical point, European leaders launched a major campaign to involve the United States formally in a transatlantic security system. They sought to seal any pact with a promise by the United States to keep a sizable number of troops on the Continent. These "hostages" would, they believed, fortify deterrence by automatically involving the United States in any conflict. The Europeans pledged that as their economies grew stronger, they would build a European "pillar" of military strength to complement the American one.

George Kennan, then in the State Department, later wrote that he "regarded the anxieties of the Europeans as a little silly" and did not "see any reason why the development of military strength on our side . . . was required."[1] He did, however, strongly support the economic and political objectives that the military program was designed to facilitate. But there were many in Congress and in positions of influence who had not been persuaded. They viewed such an intimate military and economic involvement with Europe with considerable suspicion. To gain approval of the treaty, Secretary of State Dean Acheson made assurances that there would be no permanent deployment of United States forces on the Continent. This imprudent pledge soon had to be broken in the wake of mounting East–West tensions culminating in the Korean War (1950–53).[2]

Of course it is easy to overdo the "empire by invitation" explanation for America's dominant role in European affairs. United States officials did not see themselves primarily as good Samaritans. They believed that they had, in a real sense, inherited the world. They had compelling reasons for wanting to reconstruct Europe's political, economic, and military structure within a tight American framework. They were convinced that American prosperity and also American security depended on it. They saw the trade wars and rivalries of the 1930s as having been a major cause of the Great Depression and the rise of totalitarianism. And they believed, with some reason, that Europeans had been inadequate guardians of their own destinies.

European elites had compelling reasons of their own to seek membership in the American "empire." While they may have been less concerned than America about the expansion of communism, they very much wanted American assistance in rebuilding their economies and in containing communist labor and political influence within their own societies. America's appeal, as Melvin Leffler has observed, "inhered not so much in the attractiveness of its political economy, which was veering toward the center while most of the world was heading toward the left, but in America's wealth and strength, that is, in its ability to offer aid, arms, and military guarantees."[3]

Even before the end of World War II, American officials orchestrated the Bretton Woods monetary agreements (1944) meant to facilitate free trade and investment. They financed the European Recovery Program (Marshall Plan, 1947) to break down trade barriers and self-contained blocs within Europe. They insisted on an early restoration of German and Japanese industrial production and the integration of those economies into a global free-enterprise system. NATO became central to this policy. It was the constabulary arm of the Marshall Plan.

A key part of the program was the involvement of a restored Germany in a wider European democratic structure. This would be done through both NATO and the Marshall Plan. But the restoration of Germany, so soon after its war of aggression, required both persuasion and hard guarantees. Such a restoration would be made palatable by ensuring that German power would be confined within an American-dominated security structure. The Atlantic alliance was thus designed to offer reassurance not only against the reality of Soviet armed might but to Germany's World War II victims against the uncertain future ambitions of a restored Germany.

The democratic society that is today's Germany is in considerable part a result of the policies of inclusion, restoration, and reassurance that were pursued by the United States and Germany's western neighbors. The European Union itself is, in this sense, in significant part a product of the insurance policy that the United States has provided to Germany's neighbors through its dominance of the alliance. However much Europeans may at times have strained under an unofficial American guardianship, it nonetheless provided a zone of security in which the work of European reconciliation and unification could proceed.

This structure remained solidly in place during the forty-odd years of the Cold War. It managed to survive a series of severe strains, such as the Suez crisis of 1956, the Gaullist challenges of the 1960s, the American obsession with Vietnam, and the dispute over missile strategy in the early 1980s. Even the end of the Cold War did not threaten the cohesion of the alliance or the balance of forces within it.

For all the architectural analogies about twin pillars and the rhetoric of formal equality, the structure of the alliance remains conceptually what it was during the early days of the Cold War. It is an alliance in which the controlling levers are operated by the United States. At various times over the years, Americans and Europeans have expressed impatience with this structure. Europeans have perennially sought a stronger voice in decision making, while Americans have asked for greater "burden sharing" by their partners in what is viewed as a common defense.

Both sides have a point. Americans still call all the shots. The final decisions on all matters continue to be made in Washington. In this the Europeans have a fair complaint. It is also true, however, that the United States carries the greater part of the load. From Washington's perspective the Europeans should do more. On the surface this may sound eminently reasonable. But there is a flaw in the logic.

Although the United States has urged its allies to build up their military strength, it has shown no interest in loosening its own reins of control over NATO. It has never suggested that the Europeans might act independently on matters that directly concern, or even interest, the United States. It wants Europe to be unified, but not so unified as to oppose the United States on critical matters of economics or diplomacy (or even on minor matters like trade with Cuba). It says it desires a strong Europe. But it is clearly not interested in one strong enough to challenge the United States's direction of the alliance. As Henry Kissinger, who has often enough scolded the Europeans for their foibles, has correctly observed, United States policy toward Europe "has always been extremely ambivalent: it has urged European unity while recoiling before its consequences."[4]

Over the years United States officials have made various attempts to address this problem by proposing one version or another of Atlantic "partnership." During John F. Kennedy's presidency (1961–63), he floated the notion of a "grand design" by which Europeans would, through the creation of an Atlantic free trade area and greater efforts at unification, reduce American costs of defending Europe so that the United States could focus on combating Soviet-sponsored "wars of national liberation" in the Third World.

Integral to the plan was British entry into the Common Market. But when this was vetoed by De Gaulle, and when the Cuban missile crisis (1962) dramatized that Europeans had no effective voice in U.S. nuclear strategy, the Grand Design faded away. A decade later it was revived in truncated form as a so-called Year of Europe. Its purpose, in the words of Kissinger, then Richard Nixon's foreign policy adviser, was to "strengthen the American moral commitment" that some Europeans questioned in the wake of a U.S.–Soviet détente. It also proposed to reinforce a "community of purpose" that had suffered considerably during the U.S. war in Vietnam.[5]

Europe's year came and went, however, leaving NATO basically unchanged. But the fall of the Berlin wall in 1989, and the collapse of communism in Eastern Europe and the Soviet Union, changed that equation. It raised in new form and intensity the question of what exactly NATO was containing. It dramatically diminished what had for decades been defined as the enemy. It redrew the borders of what had come to be called Europe. What exactly, many asked, was being contained, and what function did NATO serve in a Europe whose primary barriers to unification were internal?

The United States itself recognized that the problem in Europe was not primarily military and began withdrawing troops to ultimately one-third the Cold War level. Unintentionally, but inescapably, this opened for redefinition the fundamental question of America's role in Europe. The American guardianship, which had at times seemed so onerous, now became problematical. Europeans, who had come to take the American presence for granted, began to voice concern that the European pillar, such as it was, was in danger of standing alone.

The wars resulting from the breakup of Yugoslavia cast Europe's security dilemmas in a new light. Here was a conflict that had virtually nothing to do with the Cold War. In terms of a direct military threat it did not even concern the NATO members. Any intervention could be justified only on political grounds. Not only were the Americans not directly involved, they initially demonstrated that they did not want to be involved at all. Yet ultimately the Balkan wars became NATO's war as the European members of the alliance showed themselves incapable of either isolating or resolving it. Ruefully NATO's European leaders were driven to conclude that the American connection had not, after all, outlived its usefulness.

The acceptance of this reality was important to American officials, for whom NATO had never lost its relevance. Even as its security dimension shrinks, its political and economic dimensions make it of critical importance to America's global strategy. Even without the Cold War, the alliance continues to offer the United States leverage over virtually every aspect of European decision making, from diplomacy to military policy to trade relations.

NATO's military standardization ensures important markets for American weapons manufacturers, while Europe provides useful bases for the global projection of American power. Even within the European Union, questions such as the admission of additional states (strategically important Turkey, for example) or the role that American corporations may play in European markets fall under the shadow of Europe's dependent military relationship with the United States.

For strategists, NATO is seen as an effective instrument by which the United States can prevent a reversion to the anarchic state system that plunged Europe twice in the twentieth century into suicidal civil wars. It may indeed be no accident that Europe's current half century of peace coincides with its subordination to extra-European powers. With the Soviet Union gone and Russia cut down to the level of a middling power, only the United States, Washington believes, has the capacity to prevent any European power from seeking to aggrandize itself at the expense of the others. By this logic, Washington is the necessary guardian of Europe's peace and prosperity.

This is a view with which a number of European states, particularly the smaller and least influential ones, concur and which all accept. If they did not, the alliance could not have survived the disappearance of the Russian threat. Nor would it continue to prosper and even to expand as more European states press for admission into the club.

Because it values the maintenance of its leadership role in NATO as crucial, the United States was ultimately drawn into the Yugoslav civil wars. This was despite early efforts by the Clinton administration to stay out. The fighting in Bosnia and Kosovo may not have threatened European stability, but it did endanger the prestige of NATO and the position of the United States as the ultimate guarantor of European peace.

The often-voiced statement of American officials that the "United States is a European power" is not mere boilerplate. It means that the United States intends to maintain its position as Europe's protector and overseer.

By the same token, American strategists remain intent on maintaining a global military presence to prevent a breakdown of order in other areas of the world. Such a breakdown could lead to the disruption of supplies and markets that would imperil the global economic integration on which it is believed that American and European prosperity depends. This is why the demise of the Soviet Union did not mean the end of containment, let alone the "end of history," but merely a shift of concern to other areas.

In this regard the Gulf War of 1990–91 was not an aberration or even a sideshow but a necessary act of post–Cold War containment. The Iraqi attack on Kuwait and the danger to the oil fields of Saudi Arabia posed a potential threat to the energy sources on which both the Europeans and the Japanese were dependent. If the United States could not assure the stability, at a reasonable price, of this supply, then those nations harmed by a cutoff would have to acquire their own means of dealing with the problem. The structure of stability that had brought unprecedented prosperity to the industrialized nations would be imperiled. Under this rationale the United States response in the Gulf was not only logical but imperative.

The issue was addressed with instructive candor in a 1992 Pentagon internal document that became public when leaked to the press. Its authors argued that the United States "must discourage the advanced industrial nations from challenging our leadership or even aspiring to a larger regional or global role." To prevent this dispersal of power, the report continued, the United States must "retain the preeminent responsibility for addressing . . . those wrongs which threaten not only our interests, but those of allies or friends, or which could seriously unsettle international relations."[6]

The suffocation of disorder—or in the new terminology, the creation of a "stable international environment"—has now replaced the outdated containment doctrine as the national security formula for the post–Cold War world. In the maintenance of this stable environment, NATO plays a critical role for American strategists.

Guided by this logic—which is quite impeccable within its premises— we can expect a continuation of Cold War–level U.S. military budgets and periodic interventions like that in Iraq. Such budgets are quite manageable fiscally and, because they involve jobs as well as security, face little public hostility. The military interventions are also politically sustainable—at least so long as they rely on high technology, massive firepower, and low casualties.

The intervention in the Gulf, the "casualty-free" air war in Kosovo, and the antiterrorist war in Afghanistan exemplify a new strategy based on American political and military leadership. European participation will be allowed, or even sought, on an ad hoc basis, but only where it is not perceived as impeding Washington's freedom of action. As was made clear in the Afghanistan war of 2001, the United States will act alone when it believes a vital interest is at stake. Such independent action is something for which the European allies do not now have the capacity or, for the most part, even the will.

In NATO's vocabulary the notion of a strong European military "pillar" continues to enjoy a central place, at least rhetorically. To show that they are trying to implement this goal, the European members of the alliance have agreed to increase their military budgets and even to endow themselves with the capacity to conduct unspecified, but presumably low-level, peacekeeping operations within Europe.

In December 1999, a decision was made at the European Union summit meeting in Helsinki to create "an autonomous capacity to take decisions, and where NATO as a whole is not engaged, to launch and then conduct EU-led military operations in response to international crises."[7] By 2003 the ministers pledged to field a 60,000-person all-European force reinforced by warships and aircraft. This contingent is designed to enable Europeans to undertake peacekeeping missions that do not, or need not, involve NATO as a whole.

Pledging such an army is one thing; however, actually building it, or finding feasible tasks for it to perform, or achieving the consensus to use it in still-unforeseen situations may be something quite different. Lacking major logistical capacity, the projected force would be dependent on American support for even a Bosnia- or Kosovo-size operation. And of course an operation that large would likely be deemed to involve NATO as a whole in any case.

An effective interventionary force does not come cheap. For this, among other reasons, it should not be surprising that two years after the all-European army was announced with great fanfare, only eleven of NATO's nineteen members had increased their military spending.[8] As the European economy slows in the wake of a global recession, can Europeans be expected to do at considerable cost what the Americans have been willing to do for them? The freestanding pillar may not, to many, seem worth the price.

Britain's prime minister Tony Blair is fond of saying that Europe should be "a superpower, not a superstate." The formulation is in deference to the sensibilities of many British voters, who are resistant to seeing Britain as just another state in the European salad. But it could be argued that Blair has the formulation backward. What European officials are creating, what European publics have endorsed, is not a superpower, with its connotations of military might and geopolitical ambitions, but rather an economic entity (although something less than a state) of 375 million people. Some day there may be a European superpower with a unified will and the power to act unilaterally in the world. But that day seems no nearer than it was ten or even twenty years ago.

Europeans have never fully thought through what kind of Europe they want or what its relationship with the United States should be. Some dream of a union of equal superpowers, others of merely building an even more prosperous marketplace as they rest cozily under an American umbrella. Part of the problem rests on the fact than no single person or country can claim to speak for Europe. The European Union is itself a work in progress. Who can safely predict where it is going, or even what its ultimate membership will be?

The fact that a unified Europe is still in some sense a hypothesis does not prevent many from expressing an understandable dissatisfaction with America's dominant role in the alliance. This attitude was expressed with characteristic vigor by Foreign Minister Hubert Vedrine when in 1997 he told a group of French diplomats: "There is only one great power these days, the United States, but unless it is counterbalanced, that power brings with it the risks of monopoly domination." For this reason, he insisted, the EU "must gradually affirm itself as a center of power."[9]

But who will be at the controls of such a center of power? For other Europeans, particularly those from the weaker, poorer, and more geographically vulnerable states, part of the appeal of NATO is that the overwhelming power of the distant United States allows them to avoid being dominated by any of their own strong and ambitious neighbors. Not illogically, a good many European members of NATO consider themselves well served by the present situation.

Those who would like to create a European superpower may not have taken into account some of the real barriers to such an ambition. These barriers are not only the obvious military ones but the less obvious although no less pressing political, cultural, economic, and psychological ones. Where does Europe end? At the borders of the old Soviet Union, of the new Russia, of Asiatic Russia? Already, through the inclusion of Turkey, NATO Europe extends deep into the Middle East. What does it mean to speak of a Europe that borders on such distant states as Iran and Iraq?

Furthermore, with Cold War barricades now pulled down, the protected and privileged enclave of Western Europe is now wide open to the East (as well as to Africa and the Middle East) and to the flood of immigrants, both legal and illegal, who are transforming hitherto homogeneous societies. West Europeans, caught in a demographic dilemma, need more young workers to provide welfare and retirement benefits for an aging and shrinking population. But these immigrants bring with them traditions that clash with those of their newly adopted countries.

Europe is suddenly becoming multicultural, and it is having far more difficulty handling it than is the United States with its history of ethnic layering. The effect of this mass migration on European stability could be profound. For many years to come, Europe will be struggling with the problems of ethnic conflicts and maintaining its stability as a privileged enclave in a world churned by uncontrolled population growth, environmental degradation, and widening gaps between the fortunate and the desperate.

In addition to problems of identity and stability, what we call Europe lacks a fundamental quality that a state needs to be a major global actor. It lacks a will to power. Even the United States, which in terms of economic production was the dominant world state as early as 1900, did not seriously act like a global power until its entry into World War II in 1941. Europeans, unlike Americans, or Chinese, or Japanese, currently (and for understandable reasons) lack a sense of mission.

This lack is not necessarily a bad thing. They do not (at least since they lost their colonial empires) seek to create a "new world order" in their own image. They have no unified political will and are increasingly unlikely to develop one as the European Union extends eastward. They show little incentive to undertake the sacrifices necessary to project their power globally. They do not seem to be ready for, or perhaps they have had enough of, the imperial dreams that continue to seduce American elites. What the architects of a more ambitious European diplomacy seem to want is not sex but prestige—not the thrill of exercising power but the satisfaction of being admired.

If Europeans have not faced the implications of creating a political and military power roughly equal to that of the United States, neither have the Americans. What Washington envisages, for all its rhetoric about equality, is a somewhat stronger little brother who will help the United States in its self-assured role of stabilizing a free-enterprise but still politically anarchic world.

Yet a truly unified, or at least strongly confederated, Europe—if this is possible—poses greater potential problems for the United States than does a weak one. It would be both more assertive and more self-protective in the economic realm, blocking mergers of American corporations and challenging American dominance in key fields, as Airbus has already successfully challenged Boeing. It would be more accommodating to regimes such as Iran, Iraq, North Korea, and Cuba that the United States has labeled "rogue states." It would be less sentimental about Taiwan and forge closer ties with Russia, China, and Japan.

Such a Europe may never come into being. But an overly aggressive and unilateral American diplomacy could provide the spark to set in motion a self-assertive European diplomacy. A unified and self-confident Europe would have ambitions of its own that would not coincide with those of American policy makers. In such a case, Americans might conclude that they had created a kind of Frankenstein monster—a powerful creature that had escaped the control of its proud creator. This could set the stage for a conflict of wills and interests that would cause both pillars of the transatlantic house to crumble.

A more self-assertive Europe might also feed discontent in the United States over the cost of a military alliance and a political guardianship essentially unchanged since the end of the Cold War. A mismanaged and declining United States economy might lead American voters to conclude that the cost of being the guardian of a prosperous Europe rich enough to defend itself is a burden that need no longer be borne. Nations have been known, after all, to tire of imperial burdens.

As Americans now seemingly find it intolerable to accept military casualties in "peacekeeping" operations unrelated to U.S. security, they might well reject the optional duties prescribed for them by their leaders. This reaction becomes more likely now that the world has escaped the discipline imposed by the Soviet-American condominium and once-compliant client states become increasingly unruly and uncooperative.

The notion of a Fortress America retains a powerful appeal, as clearly evidenced by the unremitting search for a nuclear shield that will protect the United States from harm. Whether NATO Europe is invited to huddle behind such a shield (should it ever even be built) would almost certainly depend on the degree to which it was willing to remain subordinate to the United States in critical matters.

Forces are pulling at NATO from both sides of the Atlantic: from Europeans, who are trying to find some new form of identity in unification, and from Americans, who want a Europe that will be rich and tranquil but also can be taken for granted. Washington has shown that it can live with a divided Europe, a contentious Europe, a weak and dependent Europe, and a Europe that does not know who it is or what it wants.

But can it live with a strong, united Europe that will not automatically follow America's direction? Does it really want a twin pillar, a partner of equal power and weight? Indeed, is such a Europe possible? And more troubling for European architects, is it even desirable?

For the present time the dilemma seems more hypothetical than actual. In the absence of dramatic changes in the global political balance, it is virtually inconceivable that there will ever be twin pillars of equal power and importance holding up a common Atlantic bride. If the Europeans actually built a pillar roughly equal to the American one, they would gain the ability to pursue their interests independent of American wishes. In that case NATO would offer no advantages for the United States and would collapse into irrelevance.

Only by remaining weaker can the Europeans maintain the protective American connection. But only by pretending that they are making serious efforts to be strong can they dispel concerns that they are slackers content to ride freely on America's armored chariot. That is why the perpetual dream of a NATO composed of twin pillars is a fantasy. Everybody praises it, no one really wants it, and it will not happen because it is a logical impossibility.

NOTES

1. George Kennan, *Memoirs, 1925–1950* (Boston: Little, Brown, 1967), 399.
2. See, for example, James Chace, *Acheson: The Secretary of State Who Created the American World* (New York: Simon & Schuster, 1998), 202.
3. Melvin Leffler, "New Approaches, Old Interpretations, and Prospective Reconfiguration," *Diplomatic History* 19 (spring 1995): 189. Leffler's magisterial study, *A Preponderance of Power: National Security, the Truman Administration, and the Cold War* (Stanford: Stanford University Press, 1992), is a necessary starting point for all discussions of American policy in the early Cold War period.

4. Henry Kissinger, "What Kind of Atlantic Partnership?" *Atlantic Community Quarterly* 7 (summer 1973): 30.

5. Henry Kissinger, *Years of Upheaval* (Boston: Little, Brown, 1982), 706.

6. Patrick E. Tyler, "U.S. Strategy Plan Calls for Insuring No Rival Develop," *New York Times,* March 8, 1992.

7. EU Council, *Presidency Conclusions,* Helsinki, December 1999.

8. Michael Gordon, "Armies of Europe Failing to Meet Goals, Sapping NATO," *New York Times,* June 7, 2001.

9. Martin Walker, "What Europeans Think of America," *World Policy Journal* 17 (summer 2000): 26–38.

Utopia and Realism in Woodrow Wilson's Vision of the International Order

Massimo L. Salvadori

The Interpretative Dilemma

This chapter examines Woodrow Wilson and his foreign policy from three vantage points. First, it looks at evaluations by eminent post–World War I Europeans of Woodrow Wilson's controversial role in the peace process that put an end to World War I. Second, it examines a variety of assessments advanced by American historians and political scientists after World War II. Finally, it offers direct quotations from Woodrow Wilson to illustrate and clarify important aspects of his policy and ideology as a strategist of a "reconstructed international order." Through these perspectives, this chapter reinterprets Wilson's diplomatic achievements by answering the question of whether—and how—Wilson can be considered a utopian who ignored historical reality or a realist who was able to analyze the problems of his age by anticipating, at least partially, important future trends in international policy and diplomacy. The answer is that this ability made Wilson a more acute policy maker than most of his contemporaries. This chapter, then, reconsiders the role and the historical meaning of Wilsonianism between 1917 and 1920, and assesses its legacy.

Evaluations by Eminent Europeans after World War I

It is almost mandatory to begin this evaluation with John Maynard Keynes's well-known opinion of Wilson from his 1919 *Economic Con-*

sequences of the Peace. It was a sharply critical judgment, and at its core is the idea that the American president, whose virtues were essentially nonpolitical, played the role of the naive, noble spirit at the peace table, because he lacked that

dominating intellectual equipment which would have been necessary to cope with stable and dangerous spellbinders whom a tremendous clash of forces and personalities had brought to the top as triumphant masters in the swift game of give and take, face to face in council—a game of which he had no experience at all.[1]

In fact, although his book considered Wilson at length, Keynes undertook no analysis of Wilson's role or the historical meaning of the different policies the American president pursued, nor those pursued by Clemenceau and Lloyd George. Keynes was basically interested in stressing the inner limitations of the Treaty of Versailles and in emphasizing its complete failure. But Keynes was unfair to the American president when he accused both Wilson and Lloyd George of ignoring the fact that "the most serious of the problems which claimed their attention were not political or territorial but financial and economic."[2] Contrary to Keynes's judgment, one of the most important aspects of Wilson's policy was its insistence on a new international economic order as a prerequisite for a new political order.

It was Francesco Saverio Nitti—eminent economist and in 1919–20 prime minister of Italy—who, in his 1924 book *The Tragedy of Europe,* gave an insightful evaluation of what, in his opinion, was Wilson's fundamental mistake at the peace table. Nitti had a deep appreciation for Wilson's program of reconstruction, but he stressed that the American president was caught in the unbridgeable conflict between his program and that of the European powers that had won the war, and that eventually he made the mistake of accepting a treaty that fundamentally contradicted his own policy:

President Wilson managed to nullify all his programs, of which nothing remained except the deformed structure of the League of Nations, as he made a series of concessions whose relevance he was unable to understand. It was absurd to create a League of Nations to avoid conflicts among nations and, at the same time, to impose upon the losers conditions that were in blatant contradiction to all principles advanced during the war.[3]

As early as 1918, Luigi Einaudi—professor of economics and one of the most influential liberal thinkers in Italy at the time—advanced a radical criticism of the Wilsonian project of the League of Nations: Einaudi stressed that the league could not possibly function. It was contradictory to think that the principle of national sovereignty, resolutely defended by nation-states as their most important asset, could possibly be limited voluntarily. While Wilson supported limiting national sovereignty, he should have considered the example of the United States. In order to emerge as a nation, the United States had to move from an early confederate constitution to a second Constitution, which "did not talk of a 'union of sovereign states' anymore, and created instead a new, different, and superior State compared to the ancient states."[4] Einaudi thought that the league could not remain standing amid the conflicting interests of different sovereign states.

Wilsonianism was not seen, in Lenin's opinion, as a policy even potentially different from that of the European powers, because the Russian leader considered Wilson, Clemenceau, and Lloyd George the leaders of international capitalism in its final phase. He even wrote that "the idealized democratic republic of Woodrow Wilson has actually emerged de facto as one of the most unrestrained forms of imperialism, oppression and blatant strangling of small and weak peoples."[5]

There is a substantial parallel between the views of Lenin, the head of world revolution, and those of Benito Mussolini(albeit in different terms). The founder of Italian fascism thought that Wilson, Lloyd George, and Clemenceau were all participants in the "oligarchic plutocracy of Versailles," "the tyrants" who suffocated the just claims of Italy.[6]

It was Antonio Gramsci, the most brilliant Marxist intellectual and political leader of his generation in Italy, who in 1919 advanced an insightful, unconventional assessment of Wilson's strategy at the peace conference. He saw the United States and Great Britain as being opposed to the continental European states—because the latter embodied an old, nationalist capitalism, whereas the former provided examples of its internationalizing, modern version. "In Paris," Gramsci said, "two different notions of the armistice and the peace" and "two forces of the world bourgeoisie" are struggling: on the one hand, the supporters of free trade, universal competition, and the breakdown of national commercial monopolies; on the other, the backward-looking nationalist capitalism. As a consequence, Gramsci stressed, "the League of Nations is to be understood as the cosmopolitan city of capitalism, and the millionaires are its citizens." Wilson had framed his project of unifying the capitalist world as "a project entailing the *legal* [italics added] equality of all individuals, otherwise socially and economically divided between the bourgeoisie and the proletariat." This vision contrasted to the project of unification pursued by the communist proletarian International that posited instead—as one of its fundamental principles—the actual equality of individuals and classes.[7] Gramsci was obviously convinced that both brands of capitalism were bound to be defeated by the worldwide socialist revolution.

Karl Kautsky, another Marxist belonging to the social democratic school, approvingly compared, on the one hand, Wilson's plans with those of the European powers that had prevailed in World War I, and, on the other, American capitalism with its European counterparts. For years, Kautsky had been advancing the opinion that World War I had not been simply one necessary example of a series of intra-imperialist conflicts to which capitalism was doomed. It was, on the contrary, the result of a capitalist stage, which would be followed by what Kautsky called ultra-imperialism, that is, a stage characterized by the internationalization of capitalism, which would thereby overcome the constraints of imperialism. In his 1919 book *Die Wurzeln der Politik Wilsons* Kautsky stressed that the program inaugurated by Wilson and the League of Nations, together with the strength of the internationally oriented proletariat, could result in a kind of stable peace based not on violence but on an understanding among states and peoples. Wilson, who "had been elected as the enemy of imperialism and financial capital," was obviously a friend of capitalism, according to Kautsky, and as such could not help but recognize the fundamental role of financial capital, which represented "the highest form of capitalism." However, Wilson was special because he did not "bow" to the particular interests and aggressive superpower of financial capital.[8] In addition, Wilson's aim in the war had not been to annihilate Germany but to turn it into a democratic state. A peace of reason and understanding among peoples, said Kautsky, "is possible on the foundations proposed by Wilson," which stemmed from political methods and principles specific to America. Therefore, Kautsky concluded, it was to be expected that this brand of peace would inaugurate "an era of increasing socialization and, at the same time, Americanization of the world."[9] Eventually, such a peace would modernize international capitalism and thus create the prerequisite for the coming socialization of the means of production.

In different terms and with different conclusions, both Gramsci and Kautsky thought of Wilson as the strategist of the international modernization of capitalism, but Gaetano Salvemini, a prominent historian and political thinker, considered Wilson the father of international democracy, a new Mazzini, who, different from Clemenceau, Lloyd George, and Sonnino, had not "waged war on Germany on the basis of a German-style program."[10] Even these few, yet representative, contemporary European voices show that the discussion on Wilson's attitude at the peace table and its meaning received contrasting, irreducible interpretations.

Conflicting Images of Wilson after World War II

Post–World War II historians and political scientists interpreted Wilson's role showing contradictory points of view that parallel those conveyed by the few representative cases discussed above. Some significant examples of these conflicting interpretations follow.

The first approach can be termed apologetic; it portrays Wilson as the prophet of a better world, a Moses of peace-loving persons, whose ways, if adopted, would have saved humanity from World War II. Wilson's vision seemed utopian but, in light of what followed, turned out to be more realistic than those of the "realists" who had held center stage in 1918–20. Wilson seemed to be a statesman whose vision had laid the very real foundation for the dream of human peace that had been cherished by such figures as Erasmus of Rotterdam since the dawn of modernity. As early as 1919, William Archer wrote that the building of the League of Nations was an attempt at substituting "collective reason" for state violence in the conflicts among civilized peoples. It was the ideal—conceived by Erasmus, Grotius, the duke of Sully, Penn, and Kant—which, after existing for centuries only as a utopian dream, had then become "the most pressing and practical necessity of the future," to which Wilson had devoted his presidency.[11] In 1945, voices were immediately heard supporting the interpretation of a "realist" Wilson, whose realism had unfortunately been vindicated by disasters. Both the failure of the League of Nations after America turned it down and World War II shed light on Wilson's role as a pioneer of world democracy—which had failed once but should not fail again.

Scholars of high stature, such as William L. Langer and Arthur Link, have given dignity and strength to the apologetic interpretation; in their opinion, Wilson was a forerunner, and his success should therefore be analyzed through a timeframe in which 1917–20 is only the first step. Langer said openly that the post–World War II years and the creation of the United Nations "are eloquent proofs of the now general acceptance of Wilson's doctrine," to such an extent that "the main features of his foreign policy are no longer controversial. . . . Most of his principles and policies have, indeed, become integral parts of American thinking on world problems. . . . Wilson, like many great men, was patently in advance of his time."[12]

Wilson's most vigorous supporter has certainly been Arthur S. Link, his foremost biographer, whose interpretations fully summarize the apologetic opinion. In Link's view, Wilson was convinced that the American people "had a peculiar role to play, indeed a mission to execute, in history, because they were in so many ways unique among the peoples of the world," thanks to American institutions and history.[13] The reasons why Wilson failed to build a new world order are not to be found in his subjective shortcomings, as Keynes thought, but in the contemporary situation. The opinion that Wilson failed utterly, however, is unfounded, because any good that came out of Versailles was the result of his influence. If the international situation then degenerated, the reason was that the winners of the war did not have "the will to enforce what Wilson signed."[14] In the 1930s, the structure of collective security foundered not because of the defects of the League of Nations' machinery but because of insufficient will on the part of the peoples of the world, not only the American people, "to confront aggressors with the threat of war." The outcome was, as Wilson prophesied, the explosion of another world war, more terrible than the first, which finally managed to make the United States accept the international leadership that Wilson had called for. Wilson's role, therefore, was that of a prophet who has been fully vindicated by history.[15] Wilson's idealism was, according to Link, "a higher realism" than that of his European and American critics, who lacked historical vision. Wilson thought in terms of a real international order and was "a realist of a different sort" than were other managers of international relations, who measured national power in terms of material force. The latter were the unrealistic realists, whereas Wilson was the realistic idealist.

In particular, Link discussed why Wilson accepted and signed the Versailles treaty, which so contrasted with his purpose, and stressed that Wilson was persuaded the document contained whatever could be obtained, given "the circumstances of 1919." In the president's opinion, the United States would probably have been able to "rectify what he knew were the grievous mistakes" made at the peace conference if it had taken the leading role within the League of Nations. Therefore, Link's conclusion was that "President Wilson survives a more powerful force in history than when he lived because be gave us the supreme demonstration in the twentieth century of higher realism in statesmanship."[16]

To conclude this list of interpreters of the Wilsonian ideal as an anticipatory vision of the future, it should be recalled that in the mid-1990s, an observer who was pondering the end of the Soviet empire said that it was "as if Woodrow Wilson's great vision of a liberal international order, based on the shared values of the democratic societies, might come to pass."[17]

Walter Lippmann, Hans J. Morgenthau, George Kennan, and Robert E. Osgood are some of the most well-known American radical critics of Wilson's policy and opponents of the ideological myth of Wilsonianism. Lippmann's criticism of Wilson is particularly significant not only because it was later echoed in Kennan but also because—as Knock has stressed—"he had served as one of Wilson's bright young men." In 1943, Lippmann blamed Wilson for relying on "legalistic and moralist and idealistic reasons," because Wilson's concept of the League of Nations as a philanthropic enterprise ignored "the vital necessity of finding allies to support America's existing commitments in the Western Hemisphere and all the way across the Pacific to the China Coast."[18] In the early stage of the Cold War, Kennan revisited Lippmann's argument and talked of a "legalistic-moralistic approach," one that ignored the role of "the vital force for a large part of the world." Wilson was badly mistaken when he contributed decisively to destroying the former European balance. The consequence was that the peace of 1919 laid out the preconditions for "the tragedies of the future."[19]

Robert E. Osgood has offered a cohesive interpretation that clashes head-on with the notion of Wilson as a sort of Moses who managed to make of the United States the center of the United Nations and the leader of the anticommunist coalition. Osgood objected to this interpretation because it risked "falsifying Wilson's conception of economic security and—what is much more serious—misconceiving our own." Osgood made reference to Lippmann and Kennan, and supported their thesis that Wilson was unable to understand that "the decisive factor determining the effectiveness or ineffectiveness of collective security arrangements is not their legal and moral obligations but the accompanying configurations of power and interest."[20]

As a consequence, the roots of World War II were to be found in the inability of the United States to establish itself as the international leading power by checking fascist expansion, not in the unresolved dilemmas of the League of Nations. In much the same way, the "containment" of the Soviet Union by the United States was not related to how the United States behaved internationally "according to the United Nations Charter" but was an exercise of U.S. power and prestige in competition with the communist bloc.[21] It was America's international inexperience that made Wilson think that collective security could be based "upon the moral factor, as opposed to material power." The interpretation of America's role after 1945, in Wilsonian terms, showed an ideological desire and a noble end that could be considered "an ultimate aspiration," but—Osgood concluded—Americans should wisely "repay our debt to history with the candid acknowledgement that we live in a world he never envisioned."[22]

N. Gordon Levin has advanced a different interpretation in his 1968 book, *Woodrow Wilson and World Politics: America's Response to War and Revolution*. His interpretation turned upside down the idea that the post–World War II guidelines of American foreign policy were directly opposed to those of Wilson. In his opinion, Wilson was the architect of an international strategy that came of age after 1945: "The main outlines of recent American foreign policies were shaped decisively by the ideology and the international program developed by the Wilson Administration in response to world politics in the 1917–19 period."[23]

Wilson's approach was guided by two closely related aims. The first was to build "a stable world order of liberal-capitalist internationalism" able to face the threat of both imperialism from the right and revolution from the left; the second was to make the United States the backbone of this international strategy. Because he placed the United States at the center of his global arena, Wilson "could act simultaneously as the champion of American nationalism and as the spokesman for internationalism and anti-imperialism." It is a vision that showed "the crucial importance of Wilsonianism" and the origins of the policy of "later generations of American decision-makers" aiming "fully to realize Wilson's designs during World War II, [and] during the Cold War that followed."[24]

Wilson as an Interpreter of the Transition between Historical Ages

The previously discussed perspectives come either from Wilson's contemporaries or from scholars mostly active during the Cold War years. Today, in a context characterized by the international victory of liberal democracy and by economic globalization, how can we assess the American president and, in particular, the idealism-realism issue that characterized his policy?

Wilson certainly opened the way to the future, as Link holds, but—contrary to Link—this chapter argues that Wilson did not act as a modern King Arthur; he was instead the advocate of a need to restructure a world that was more advanced than that of his domestic and foreign opponents. In other words, Wilson by no means ignored the issues of power and strength; he did, however, interpret them differently than his contemporaries.

If success is the criterion for historical assessment, then Wilson's battle for a stable peace and an America that endorsed its international responsibilities to guarantee world order was anything but a complete failure—at either the peace table in Versailles or the U.S. Congress in Washington. To be sure, Keynes's opinion of Wilson's personal limits has merit. It is a fact that in 1919–20 Wilson was unable to lead his generation down the path he wished to go, which is why many critics have seen him as a utopian and unrealistic public figure. Yet it is inadequate to see Wilson as Link and others seem to—as a sort of Kantian philosophic statesman of the twentieth century, the prophet of justice, the holder of the right values, who has carved his place in history as the enemy of the old power politics, and as the world messenger of international justice and peace, freedom and democracy.

Among the several interpretations, Levin's, while not fully satisfactory, seems to contain a number of interesting insights. He has been able to escape the dilemma of whether Wilson's policy was coherent because of the president's ability to translate his values into reality amid the labyrinthine postwar international situation. Levin was able to understand how the American president expressed better than anyone else the awareness that World War I had opened an age of historical transition for both his country and the world. In addition, Levin stressed that Wilsonianism could be assessed only on the terrain—and this is the important point—of its objective role. Levin is persuasive when he states that Wilson was the spokesman for both a strong American nationalism and a liberal, capitalist internationalism, which was opposed to both right-wing imperialism and left-wing revolution, and that Wilson thought the United States should hold the leadership of a new political and economic international order. The limit of this interpretation is that it sees the Cold War as the peak of Wilsonianism, which actually had its climax in the liberal, capitalist internationalism of the post–Cold War years and in the role of an unrivaled superpower now vested in the

United States. Wilson held no strategy or ideology based on the competition between two centers of world power, heavily armed against each other and struggling in a world divided into spheres of influence. To the contrary, Wilson cherished the notion that these conflicts would be overcome by American primacy, basically conceived as a political and economic, rather than military, hegemony.

In assessing Wilson it is easy to be overwhelmed by the impression that he has been first and foremost a political preacher who, according to critics from Lippmann and Kennan to Osgood, saw wars and international conflicts with the eyes of a moralist and an idealist who ignored the laws of the balance of power. These critics, however, risk losing sight of an essential aspect of Wilson the politician: his missionary language and his emphasis on the great values of justice, ethics, and the law against pure force—whatever the good faith of the speaker—cannot be reduced to the individual temperament of the president. To be sure, Wilson's style followed his personal inclinations, but, more importantly, he was able to embody a style of politics and consensus building that, far from being archaic, was very modern. Such a style, first emerging during World War I and its immediate aftermath, was fully contemporary, as demonstrated by the great enthusiasm of the European masses for Wilson. His political and ideological role was, for Western democracies, what Lenin and Trotsky came to represent in revolutionary Europe, and Mussolini and Hitler in fascist Europe. Together with them, Wilson felt there was a need to address the common person beyond national frontiers and win consensus, and this awareness resulted in Wilson becoming a brilliant interpreter of the new needs arising from mass politics. In a world of utter crisis, Wilson emerged as a millennial liberal democratic preacher in the same way that Lenin was a millennial communist and Hitler a millennial Nazi. In addition, Wilson, Lenin, and Hitler were all internationalists: liberal-capitalist, anticapitalist, and racist, respectively. Each thought his country had been chosen by history as the foundation upon which to rebuild the international order. Wilson should be seen as the founder of the present-day Western democratic ideology that emerged during the Cold War and is peaking at the present time: it is permeated by appeals to human rights, democracy, popular self-determination, and political and economic freedom. Legitimacy is sought through placing, as Lippmann said, "legalistic, moralistic and idealistic reasons" at the forefront, while the reasons and interests of power politics are de-emphasized, even when they are actively pursued. The United States is the spokesman of this ideology that is held together by the glue of American supremacy. In this respect, Wilsonianism has conquered America.

Wilson definitely believed in his idealism, and this is why he appealed to it in an exaggerated fashion; his politics, however, cannot be limited to his moralism and idealism. In his policy, Wilson has in fact also shown many important traits of the old realist school, which stressed power relations and strength. The notion that his understanding of international relations and collective security did not conceive an order based on the balance of power is not persuasive. Wilson thought, on the contrary, that the old balance of power—the view of collective security based on the primacy of the European imperialistic powers and of individual states, which were free to act above any international consensus—had entered a historical decline and was to be substituted by a new principle based on four prerequisites: the democratic ideology and its institutions; the freedom of the market and trade; the founding of an international organization that would prevent and restrain wars created by an obsolete international system, using force if necessary; and a balance of power redefined by the United States's new position in the international order and its ideological, political, and economic supremacy.

It is true that Wilson failed in applying his strategy to the world that emerged out of World War I, because the residue of the old system, which he wrongly thought had been brought to an end by the war, remained. However, it is also true that the president was the correct interpreter of the historical crisis just beginning, the fundamental features of which he was effectively capable of discerning. He came to best embody the direction of the historic transition from one age to another, and was superior in this respect to Clemenceau and Lloyd George, who represented the old European centrality, to Lenin, who symbolized the reconstruction of communist internationalism, and to Hitler and Mussolini, who pursued the Nazi and fascist purpose of rebuilding the centrality of Europe. Wilson lost as a statesman but in the long run won as a political ideologist. Gramsci was right in thinking that Wilson was the spokesman of a capitalist internationalism that was in contrast to both the old capitalism of continental Europe and revolutionary internationalism, but he but was wrong in thinking that it was the historic destiny of Wilsonianism to be defeated by Lenin's plan.

During and after the war, Wilson conducted a vocal propaganda campaign on the character and purpose of American intervention in the war. The campaign has been frequently recalled in ways that make Wilson appear as the leader of virtue and justice. He said the war was the struggle between power and liberty, and that America was conducting an unselfish war aimed not at increasing power but at affirming the rule of law. He claimed it was time for a moral force to replace the armed forces as the fundamental historical motive. Yet, at the same time, he made it clear, again and again, that the security of the good cause rested in the hands of American power, a point of great relevance in assessing the realist/idealist divide.

At the beginning of 1919, Wilson said that American soldiers "came as crusaders, not merely to win a war, but to win a cause," that America was "the hope of the world."[25] In September, he said that "the isolation of the United States is at an end," not because the United States wanted to be engulfed by "the politics of the world" but because of the genius of its people and its increasing power, which had become "a determining factor in the history of mankind." The rhetoric of his ideological evangelism described the Founding Fathers as democratic Jesuses who "Said to the people of the world, 'Come to us: this is the home of liberty; this is the place where mankind can learn how to govern their own affairs and straighten out their own difficulties,'" and added, "and the world did come to us" (2:18–19).

There is, however, a different Wilson existing side by side with the framer of the new American democratic ideology that appealed to supreme principles and values, a Wilson whose realism consisted of a matter-of-fact vision of the various economic and political interests present in the international arena and in his calculation of mutual strengths, which stressed the primacy of the United States—a different Wilson who, when the situation required, indulged with no repentance in contradictory statements and stances, and in efforts to cover up their inconsistencies.

The same Wilson who had held that the war against Germany had not been a power game but a struggle for justice—a conflict between liberty and power—in the fall of 1919 outlined the nature of the Great War in terms that might have been uttered by Lenin. He said:

Let me say: is there any child here who does not know that the seed of war in the modern world is industrial and commercial rivalry? The real reason the war that we have just finished took place was that Germany was afraid her commercial rivals were going to get the better of her, and the reason why some nations went into war against Germany was that they thought Germany would get the commercial advantage of them. The seed of the jealousy, the seed of the deep-seated hatred was hot commercial and industrial rivalry. (1:637)

Together with the great economist Schumpeter, Wilson thought that the commercial and industrial rivalries among the imperialist, colonial European powers, whose international behavior generated the germs of war among states and classes, were the product of an age that was coming to a close. The need was to open the way to a new political and economic era characterized by democracy within states, cooperation among them, and American supremacy. While on the one hand Wilson tirelessly stressed his propaganda line that America "was not founded to make money" but "to lead the world on the way of liberty," on the other hand he never ceased insisting that what was needed was not only a new political order but also a new economic arena based on both the awareness that states were interdependent and the industrial and financial supremacy of the United States. Without peace "there is no foreign market that anybody can count on," and "if the rest of the world goes bankrupt, the business of the United States is in a way to be ruined" (2:92–93). It was only the leadership of the United States that could safeguard the world from falling into an era of "troubles," "age-long miseries," and "bloody revolution" (2:100). Wilson had no doubt that economic and political supremacy was to be America's. To his American listeners, he said quite openly:

Now, let us mix the selfish with the unselfish. If you do not want me to be too altruistic, let me be very practical. If we are partners, let me predict we will be the senior partner. The financial leadership will be ours. The industrial primacy will be ours. The commercial advantage will be ours. The other countries of the world are looking to us for leadership and direction. (1:640)

Americans were facing a historic alternative, and the choice was between being "provincials, little Americans, or big Americans, statesmen" (2:321).

Wilson the idealist bowed to the harshest laws of political realism and ideological make-believe to reach what he considered essential, that is, the ratifying of the Versailles treaty and the subsequent entry into the League of Nations. He extolled in bad faith the alleged virtues of the treaty, which in fact ensured a destructive peace and was openly at odds with his principles. He said the treaty was "unique in the history of mankind" (1:594), that everybody drew his fair share from it, that it protected the weak nations, that it had "no purpose of overwhelming the German people" (1:591), that it would prevent war, that it redressed "the age-long wrongs which characterized the history of Europe," and that it would extinguish the sparks of revolution because it respected the rights of all sides. Altogether, the treaty was a successful attempt "to right the history of Europe" (1:597–98). Wilson went so far as to say that, thanks to the treaty, "American principles" had not only touched the hearts of the great peoples of Europe but also those of its European framers, so that the treaty "in spirit and in essence is an American document" (2:1–2).

Wilson knew quite well that the treaty was a far cry from his plans, but "the utopian" coldly calculated means and ends. Whatever the treaty's deficiencies, he could not turn it down at Versailles. He pragmatically accepted it and tried to extol it as a success, in the hope that this act of realism would facilitate what he really considered essential—that the peace document would be ratified by Congress, and the United States would enter the League of Nations, which in his opinion was a development of worldwide import that, among other things, would allow the wrongs of the treaty to be righted at a later date. Herbert Hoover wrote that Wilson "was forced" to bow to the demands of European statesmen "dominated by the forces of hate and revenge," "in order to save the League, confident that it would in time right the wrongs that had been done."[26] When Wilson appealed to the country during the presidential campaign of October 1920, which had turned into a national referendum on the League of Nations, he said that the alternatives were relegating "the United States to a subordinate role in the affairs of the world" or accepting the "responsibilities" that history has reserved for America (2:504).

The historical irony is that the principles Wilson had boldly proclaimed to be in the hearts of the people of Europe and its leaders were turned down not only by the European powers but also by the majority of the American people as well as by those in the political class. Defeat made of Wilson's strategy a "utopia," but the future would vindicate it: first, in a negative sense by the new European and world tragedy, and then more positively by the expansion of a liberal, capitalist internationalism built on the economic and political leadership of the United States. Wilson's utopia is undistinguishable from his realism if only his effort and legacy are contextualized in the era of historic transition in which it took place.

NOTES

This article was translated from the Italian by Maurizio Vaudagna.

1. John Maynard Keynes, *The Economic Consequences of the Peace,* in *The Collected Writings of John Maynard Keynes* (London: Macmillan, 1971), 2:14–15.

2. Ibid., 92.

3. Francesco Saverio Nitti, *Scritti politici* (Bari, Italy: Laterza, 1959), 1:484.

4. Luigi Einaudi, *La guerra e l'unità europea* (Bologna: Mulino, 1986), 21.

5. Vladimir Il'ich Lenin, *Opere complete* (Rome: Editori Riuniti, 1967), 28:189.

6. Enzo Santarelli, ed., *Scritti politici di Benito Mussolini* (Milan: Feltrinelli, 1979), 195.

7. Antonio Gramsci, *L'ordine nuovo, 1919–1920* (Turin: Einaudi, 1955), 214–16.

8. Karl Kautsky, *Die Wurzeln der Politik Wilsons* (Berlin: Verlag Neues Vaterland, E. Berger, 1919), 26.

9. Ibid., 40.

10. Carlo Maranelli and G. Salvemini, *La questione dell'Adriatico* (Florence: Libreria della Voce, 1918), 217.

11. William Archer, *The Peace-President: A Brief Appreciation* (New York: Henry Holt, 1919), 109–10.

12. William L. Langer, "Woodrow Wilson: His Education in World Affairs," in *The Philosophy and Policies of Woodrow Wilson,* ed. Earl Latham (Chicago: University of Chicago Press, 1958), 166.

13. Arthur S. Link, *Wilson the Diplomatist: A Look at His Major Foreign Policies* (Baltimore: Johns Hopkins University Press, 1957), 15.

14. Ibid., 122–25.

15. Ibid., 155–56.

16. Arthur S. Link, "The Higher Realism of Woodrow Wilson," in *Wilson,* ed. John Braeman (Englewood Cliffs, N.J.: Prentice-Hall, 1972), 157–65.

17. J. A. Baker III, "Is History Repeating Itself in Europe?" in *Legacies of Woodrow Wilson,* ed. James M. Morris (Washington, D.C.: Woodrow Wilson Center Press, 1995), 62.

18. T. J. Knock, "Kennan versus Wilson," in *The Wilson Era: Essays in Honor of Arthur S. Link,* ed. John M. Cooper and Charles E. Neu (Arlington Heights, Ill.: Harlan Davidson, 1991), 305.

19. Ibid., 304–5.

20. Robert E. Osgood, "Woodrow Wilson, Collective Security, and the Lessons of History," in *Philosophy and Policies of Wilson,* ed. Latham, 188.

21. Ibid., 193.

22. Ibid., 196–98.

23. N. Gordon Levin, *Woodrow Wilson and World Politics: America's Response to War and Revolution* (New York: Oxford University Press, 1968), 1–2.

24. Ibid.

25. *The Public Papers of Woodrow Wilson: War and Peace; Presidential Messages, Addresses, and Public Papers (1917–1924),* ed. Ray Stannard Baker and William E. Dodd (New York: Kraus, 1970), 1:399, 437. Additional references to this volume are given in the text in parentheses.

26. Herbert Hoover, *The Ordeal of Woodrow Wilson* (New York: McGraw-Hill, 1958), 300–301.

The United States, Germany, and Europe in the Twentieth Century

DETLEF JUNKER

When we look at the twentieth century from an American perspective, we might venture to say that no country in the world has contributed so much to the ascension of the United States to superpower status and to the globalization of its interests as has Germany, Europe's central power.[1] It was primarily the triple challenge of the German problem in World War I, World War II, and the Cold War that established the United States as a military, economic, and societal power on the Eurasian continent, from which the United States had kept its distance in the nineteenth century, particularly in terms of military and alliance politics.

Germany was Public Enemy Number One in World War I, and the United States waged two wars against it: a military one in Europe and a cultural one against German Americans at home.[2] In World War II, for the American political and strategy elite, Nazi Germany remained the most urgent enemy to be defeated, even after the Japanese attack on Pearl Harbor. To be sure, after 1945 the American-Soviet conflict became the overriding structural principle of international relations and the German question was largely a dependent variable in the relationship between the two superpowers. However, Germany remained America's central problem in Europe. The power vacuum created in Europe by the unconditional surrender of the German Reich can be viewed as the most important cause of the emergence of Soviet-American antagonism after 1945. The establishment of NATO and the permanent stationing of American troops on German soil—both revolutions in

American foreign policy—were direct results of the fact that the major victors of World War II could not agree on a system of domestic order for Germany or on its proper place in Europe. The Berlin crises of 1948–49 and 1958–62 were among the greatest Cold War threats to world peace. Particularly the second crisis, closely related to the Cuban missile crisis, and the erection of the Berlin wall exposed the dilemma of the Americans, who wanted neither to die for Berlin and the Germans in an atomic war, nor to threaten their prestige and position as a European hegemonic power by withdrawing from West Berlin.[3]

Moreover, National Socialism pursued American foreign policy like a shadow after 1945, because, for this generation of American politicians, the overriding goal of containing the Soviet Union was combined with the major lesson learned from the failure of the Western democracies in the 1930s. Never again should a policy of appeasement be used toward dictatorships; there must be no second Munich, neither in Europe nor in Asia. This experience also gave rise to the domino theory, which was used in the United States during the Cold War as an all-purpose weapon for justifying alliances, military interventions, and economic aid in Europe, Asia, Africa, and Latin America, and which ultimately drew the Americans into the Vietnam War.[4]

From a geostrategic perspective, containing the power of the German nation-state in the center of Europe had been a leitmotif of American policy on Europe since the age of imperialism, when Kaiser Wilhelm II's Germany and an imperial America outgrew their status as regional powers to become competing world powers. Germany did not become a problem for the United States until it threatened to rise to the level of hegemonic power or oppressor of Europe. Unlike Germany's European neighbors, the distant United States never feared the German nation-state created in 1871 but always the rival world power.[5] That is why the United States not only fought the Germany of Wilhelm and the Germany of the Nazis in two world wars, but also sought to contain and stabilize the Weimar Republic through economic integration,[6] just as it attempted to do with the Federal Republic through economic, military, and diplomatic integration beginning in 1949.[7] European stability and German containment belong to the strategic objectives of American foreign policy in the twentieth century, from Woodrow Wilson to George Bush.

A telegram sent on May 11, 1949, by U.S. secretary of state Dean Acheson to the British secretary of state for foreign affairs Ernest Bevin and the French minister for foreign affairs Robert Schuman, clarified the basic American approach to the pending establishment of a West German Republic:

Our major premise is that our concern is with the future of Europe and not with Germany as a problem by itself. We are concerned with the integration of Germany into a free and democratic Europe. We have made and are making progress to this end with the part of Germany which we control and we shall not jeopardize this progress by seeking a unified Germany as in itself good. If we can integrate a greater part of Germany than we now control under conditions which help and do not retard what we are now doing, we favor that; but only if the circumstances are right.

Just as the unification of Germany is not an end in itself, so the division of Germany is not an end in itself. If, for instance, Russian troops were unilaterally withdrawn, we would not attempt—as an end in itself—by force to keep Eastern und Western Germany apart. Again the test is whether the unification can be achieved under conditions which help and do not retard the unification of a free Europe.[8]

Acheson's statement could just as well have been uttered by Woodrow Wilson in 1919, John F. Kennedy in 1961, or George Bush in 1990. One could argue that at Versailles, Wilson was forced to practice the very policy that he himself had pilloried as the greatest evil of the system of European powers and that he had intended to supersede by establishing the League of Nations. In other words, he had to act according to the principles that governed the balance of powers. In terms of power politics, Wilson's European policies already appeared to be those of triple containment. They aimed at containing the threat to Europe posed by Germany and the Soviet Union, coupled with the desire to meet French security concerns, while still not allowing France to become the hegemonic power in Europe. The most important means for containing a revisionist Germany was meant to be a postwar entangling alliance with Great Britain and France in which the United States promised the French nation to "come immediately to her assistance in the event of any unprovoked movement of aggression against her being made by Germany."[9] Of course, Wilson's grand design did not become reality. The Senate rejected Wilson's version of the League of Nations, did not even debate the Treaty of Guaranty for France, and the United States basically relied on economic means to reintegrate Germany into the world economy. Then the Great Depression deprived the United States even of this leverage. When Franklin D. Roosevelt was elected in 1932, he was an "unarmed prophet" as far as his policy toward Europe in general and toward National Socialism in particular was concerned.

U.S. policy toward Germany after World War II must be considered a direct consequence of the efforts undertaken by the Third Reich to force a racist regime of National Socialism upon a Europe extending from the Channel to the Urals. Even to the present day, this vision of the abyss of a Nazi-dominated Europe keeps alive the desire to contain Germany and integrate it into the West, so that it can never again pose a threat to the security and welfare of Europe, and thus the world—or, to borrow the wording of the title of the Morgenthau Plan, "to prevent Germany from starting a World War III."[10]

The August 1, 1945, Potsdam Agreements on the future of Germany were based on two prerequisites: first, the Allies were to act jointly at the European level to contain and control the further existence of a German state; second, decisions at the domestic level in Germany would be taken together. It is common knowledge, however, that between the summer of 1945 and the fall of 1947 it became sufficiently clear that the Allied powers were unable to agree on the domestic future of Germany or on its future role in Europe. The occupation zones began to develop in different directions. It proved impossible to define a common policy toward Germany, and the Allied Control Council was unsuccessful in developing a joint foreign trade policy.

The onset of the Cold War complicated the German problem. But the postwar generation of U.S. foreign policy makers—Truman, Acheson, Marshall, Kennan, and others—was up to the challenge.[11] From their point of view, the establishment of a West German state in 1949 constituted the beginning of the famous policy of double containment, that is, a policy aimed at simultaneously containing the Soviet and the German threat. West Germany became a bulwark against the communist threat, and its integration into the European and Atlantic organizations as well as its integration into the world economy were to guarantee that Germany would never again be a danger to the Western world. Political scientist Wolfram F. Hanrieder has written about the significance of this concept. Although he did not coin the term, he has contributed more astutely than anyone else to its diffusion:

Every major event in the postwar history of Europe follows from this: the rearmament and reconstruction of the Federal Republic within the restraints of international organizations, the development of NATO from a loosely organized mutual assistance pact into an integrated military alliance, American support for West European integration, and the solidification of the division of Germany and Europe. So long as the two components of America's double containment were mutually reinforcing, America's European diplomacy was on a sure footing. In later years, when tensions and contradictions developed between the two components, German-American relations became increasingly strained.[12]

One can even suggest that in 1948–49, American foreign policy again conducted a policy of triple containment, because the United States forced an economically weak France to agree to the creation of a West German state. The U.S. proposal to establish such a state not only triggered substantial concern about security issues among the French but also destroyed the dream of France as a world power that would exploit a defeated Germany and rise to become the leading European power with a modernized economy. The inherent promises of the Marshall Plan, coupled with the security guarantees of the envisaged NATO and the Ruhr and Occupation Statutes, convinced the French National Assembly to approve the plans for the establishment of a West German state by the slight majority of 300 to 286 votes. In a well-known quotation of Lord Ismay, to which the author takes the liberty of adding a few words, triple containment meant "keeping the Soviets out, the Americans in, the Germans down, [and the Europeans, especially the French, happy]."

The concept of dual containment has been criticized because the nature and scope, origin, and immediacy of the German and Soviet threats to the United States were fundamentally different. An analysis of the situation in Europe after 1945, purely in terms of power politics, would need to reject the idea that American policies toward Germany and the Soviet Union are even conceptually comparable, and therefore would also reject the concept of dual containment. But such a view of the Cold War geopolitical constellation ignores cultural and mental dispositions that arise during the collective interpretation of historical experiences. For example, the notion of a catastrophic German tradition from Luther to Hitler, popularized by William Shirer's bestseller in the 1960s, demonstrates that the Americans did not see their military victory over National Socialism as a definitive answer to the German problem.[13] German authoritarianism, Prussian militarism, and National Socialist fantasies of destruction could become virulent again—if not today, then tomorrow; if not in the same form, then a new form. Skepticism regarding the German national character linked the past and the future of

American policy, which actually sought to "contain" the latent danger of such excesses.

Herein lies the qualitative difference from the kind of hegemonic control that the United States sought to exert over France. The Western superpower never acknowledged France's *vocation mondiale et européenne*, its claim to the role of a major international power and a hegemonic position within Europe. For decades American politicians were bent on preventing France from using European integration to push the United States out of Europe and to free the Federal Republic from its dependence on the transatlantic colossus by making it France's junior partner in Europe. The United States wanted (and wants) to remain the decisive balancer and pacifier in Europe. Unlike the Federal Republic, France never accepted this claim.[14]

French President Charles de Gaulle, the self-appointed embodiment of "eternal" France, always envisioned a French-led Europe that would achieve parity with the two superpowers. The resistance of the Anglo-Saxons foiled de Gaulle's plans to be accepted into a nuclear directorate comprised of the United States, France, and Great Britain. In response, France took the liberty of denying Great Britain access to the European Economic Community (1963); it shocked the United States and NATO allies with its decision to withdraw French forces from NATO's integrated military structure (1966), called for the withdrawal of all American troops from French soil, undermined the American-dominated monetary system of Bretton Woods, and made a vain but daring attempt to forge a unilateral alliance with the Federal Republic in the Elysée Treaty.

Politicians in the Federal Republic dared not even dream of such latitude in dealing with the Western hegemonic power. That was due in part to the greater—indeed, existential—dependence of the Federal Republic on the United States in the area of security policy. It was also due to the fact that the legacy of National Socialism made an independent German claim to power untenable. The United States would not have tolerated it. American policy on containing Germany through integration was geared specifically toward withholding from the Federal Republic any military, political, or social basis for such a power play. German politicians understood this well and chose integration, self-containment, and multilateral routes for pursuing German interests.

Unlike Germany, France had not forfeited its right to conduct unilateral power politics. De Gaulle's hegemonic plans for Europe may have been inconvenient and annoying, but they could not shake a French-American trust, absent in the case of Germany, that was rooted in a two-hundred-year-old, shared tradition. The two nations perceived and continue to perceive themselves as standard-bearers of the universal mission of freedom, which began its victory march through the world with the American and French Revolutions. A veiled battle over the birthright of this mission is part of the tradition of French-American rivalry. Despite, or perhaps because of, this shared tradition, French national pride, born of the consciousness of French greatness and sovereignty, has chafed for several decades against American hegemonic policies in Europe, while the Federal Republic has viewed these policies primarily as protection and assistance toward the goal of integration. This wounded pride was the underlying reason for the series of French-American conflicts, all of which had repercussions for German-American and French-German relations, and forced the Germans into continual diplomatic gymnastics between the United States and France.[15]

Forty years later, during the revolutionary situation of 1989–90, the U.S. superpower again played the role of balancer and pacifier of Europe.[16] Again, the containment of Germany was the dominant goal, even the prerequisite for Germany's unification. Unified Germany was to remain a part of NATO and of a general European and Atlantic design; its neutralization or isolation was to be avoided at all costs. The rest of Europe had to be reassured in the face of newly rekindled fears about Germany, and America's influence in Europe had to be confirmed. The provisions of the Two-Plus-Four Treaty hinder a unified Germany from becoming a military threat to its neighbors. Within the terms of the treaty, Germany is incapable of either attacking others or defending itself on its own. The former Federal Republic had renounced the nuclear option in the nonproliferation treaty of 1968. And the repetition of this renunciation in the Two-Plus-Four Treaty, the diplomatic charter of the united Germany, was probably the single most important prerequisite for the international recognition of German unification. The renunciation of nuclear weapons and voluntary acceptance of a second-class military status was the raison d'être of the old Federal Republic, and these policies continue to play the same role for the united Germany—as long as the hegemonic power of the United States promises nuclear protection within the framework of NATO. After Secretary of State Baker met with Gorbachev and Shevardnaze on February 8–9, 1990, in Moscow, the American government was able to convince Gorbachev, step by step, that it would be better, even for the Soviet Union, to contain Germany according to the conditions set by the West than to leave it to its own resources.[17]

IN the first half of this century, the Germans not only served twice as the enemy but twice provided America with a powerful image of the enemy. The American civil religion certainly facilitated the propagandistic transformation of the German Empire of Kaiser Wilhelm II into the evil empire.[18] It was this Manichaean pattern of distinguishing between good and evil with religious fervor that permitted the Wilson administration to win the battle for the souls of the American people, who were none too eager to go to war.

Individuals or nations in the process of defining their own identities seem to have a hard time tolerating the idea of being merely equals of others. They attempt to arrogate to themselves some special significance that is supposed to render them different from, and superior to, other individuals or nations—indeed, to make them unique. In the process, they frequently invoke notions of exalted generality, such as God, History, Providence, Progress, or the Salvation of Mankind (all capitalized, of course). Like the citizens of so many other nations before them or since, Americans too have claimed to be a chosen people. The idea of America's special mission has been a self-evident aspect of its political culture since the founding of the nation. The Founding Fathers were shaped by the spirit of the Enlightenment. They integrated the Christian and Puritanical missionary ideas of New England's settlers—"the chosen people," "the Convenant people," "God's new Israel," and "God's last American Israel"—into the idea of a secular mission for America. It was this fusion of Christianity and Enlightenment that brought forth the civil religion so specific to America—that unmistakable admixture of Christian Republicanism and Democratic faith that created a nation with the soul of a church. The American nation has no ideologies; she herself is one.

The goals of America's mission have, of course, oscillated over time; they have combined with the dominant aspects of the Zeitgeist of different ages—such as, for example, racism in the age of imperialism—only to uncouple themselves again from such tendencies. They have transformed themselves, moving from the Puritanical mission of completing the work of the Reformation to the political mission of bringing freedom and democracy to the world—or in the words used by President Woodrow Wilson, a southern racist, in his declaration of war against Germany in 1917: "to make the world safe for democracy." Thus, the missionary goals of the United States changed from the passive notion of turning America into a new Jerusalem, whose example would be a beacon for the world, to the active missionary duty to elevate backward, less-civilized nations to the American level, to create a new world order, save the world, and bring about the millennium.

Every sense of mission grounded in a teleological view of history requires for its realization some concrete negation, its counterprinciple, an evil empire that has to be overcome by war in order to enable progress and fulfill the mission. Missionary zeal tends to cultivate a radical dualism; it has to divide the world and its governing principles into good and evil. This dualistic system of beliefs is known as Manichaeism, named after Mani, the Persian philosopher of late antiquity. A nation with the soul of a church can thus only justify entering an actual war on ideological grounds. It cannot fall back on material interests, reasons of state, or—*horribile dictu*—a violation of the balance of power. (By the way, it took Henry Kissinger almost a lifetime to come to terms with this American tradition.) At best, Manichaeism can refer to a violation of rights, because in this kind of reasoning, legality and morality are interchangeable. Thus, whoever gets involved in a conflict or war with the United States is automatically caught up in the Manichaean trap of America's sense of a special mission.[19]

The Indians were the first enemy caught in this trap. It was with them that the battle for territory was waged most ferociously, particularly after the greatest catastrophe of New England, in 1675–76. Under the leadership of Metacomet, chief of the Wamponoags, the Indians managed to almost destroy the New England settlers in a war that, in relation to the total number of inhabitants, was the bloodiest conflict in American history. Since those days, the Indians were perceived as savages who could not be civilized—indeed, as devils; the wilderness was equated with hell. The Indians had lost any right to stand in the way of the conquest of the West—a conquest that was pushed ahead during the nineteenth century by the massive employment of troops and capital. The Manichaean pattern of the ideology and mythology of the Indian Wars has determined the foreign policy of the United States throughout its history, up to and including the administration of Ronald Reagan.[20] Even after the secularization of America's sense of mission, this dualistic interpretation of the world played a key role in U.S. foreign policy. All the enemies of the United States were caught in the Manichaean trap: after the Indians were the French and the British—in America's first political best-seller, Thomas Paine's *Common Sense,* and in Thomas Jefferson's Declaration of Independence, it was King George III who embodied the principle; later it was the Spanish and Mexicans, and, in the twentieth century, primarily the Germans, Japanese, Russians, Chinese, North Koreans, Iraqis, and terrorists.

It was this transformation of the German Empire into the evil empire that enabled the American people in general, and President Wilson in particular, to put an end to the deeply ambivalent U.S. policy toward Europe of 1914–16, a policy that could not be maintained indefinitely. Wilson had, after all, won the election of 1916 because he had kept America out of the war. So the battle for the American soul, which was anything but ready for war, had to be won by revolutionizing the "threat perception" of the American people in order to be able to cross the Rubicon—that is, the Atlantic—and declare war on Germany. And, finally, after the United States entered the war, the propaganda machinery had to be set in motion, producing grotesque scenarios about the threat posed by German machinations in the Western Hemisphere to the domestic and external security of the United States.

The same pattern was repeated, more or less, between 1939 and 1941, with the exception of the witch-hunts against German Americans, whose ethnic identity had already been destroyed during World War I. Moreover—if I am here permitted to make a value judgment—while the situation in the Second World War was, of course, different (in that Germany actually was an evil empire), a comparison prior to 1914 of social and legal aspects, as well as of democratic theory, between Imperial Germany and the United States (including the South) would result in a highly complex and differentiated picture.

Wilson's deep ambivalence was based on the fact that although he did not like Europe, he was unable to leave the continent alone. He wanted to isolate the morally superior New World from the rotten Old World, while saving mankind and the international system from ancient evils.

From the German perspective, also, these two "battles for world power" represented the conflict between two opposing worldviews. Embodied by U.S. president Woodrow Wilson, America emerged in World War I Germany as the primary ideological opponent of the antiliberal, authoritarian camp in Germany. Behind the German debate over Siegfrieden and unlimited submarine warfare were differing views concerning not only strategy and war objectives but also the internal structure of the German Reich.[21] The enemy images established during World War I dominated the German image of America until well into World War II. Even in the years after 1939, two antagonistic ideologies confronted one another. The Americans saw National Socialism as the mortal enemy of democracy; Hitler saw democracy as the mortal enemy of National Socialism. Held together by anti-Semitism as its overall ideological framework, Nazi propaganda characterized "Americanism" as a scourge of humanity equal to, or even greater than, Bolshevism, not least because, as the war went on, the United States was becoming the most serious threat to the German domination of Europe. The Nazi-generated images of America built on traditional stereotypes, but beginning in 1938–39, they were increasingly dominated by the racist, anti-Semitic anti-Americanism of extreme right-wing Germans. Again, it was an American president who personified the ideological enmity toward America. According to Nazi propaganda, Franklin D. Roosevelt, the "main warmonger" and an agent of the world's Jews and the international Jewish-Bolshevist conspiracy, had driven the American people into war with the Third Reich.[22] Occasionally echoes of this radical, National Socialist criticism of America are still heard from right-wing anti-American elements in the Federal Republic.

THE Germans also played a central role in bringing about the positive flip side of this Manichaean pattern in American politics, the mission to bring freedom and democracy to the world. In this respect as well, the American Century is difficult to imagine without the Germans.[23] It was the German challenge that forced President Wilson to open up and globalize America's mission from the passive idea of turning America into a new Jerusalem, which would be a beacon for the world by virtue of its own example, to the active missionary responsibility of lifting those peoples who were less free and less civilized, who had been left behind, to the American level.[24] Wilson's call to make the world safe for democracy was the ideological climax of the declaration with which he justified his country's entry into the war against Germany in April 1917. Segments of the American political elite interpreted the failure of this mission in Germany during the period between the wars in part as a failure of their own country, which had withdrawn its military and alliance policy from Europe after the Treaty of Versailles, and had remained in Europe only in an economic and cultural role.

After 1945, therefore, the pacification and democratization of Germany—and Japan—were among the central goals of American foreign policy. Never before or after have the Americans expended so many resources to remake two foreign and occupied nations in their political, social, and cultural image. Under the influence of the Cold War, the United States incorporated the western part of Germany into an Atlantic community under American hegemony encompassing issues of security, values, production, consumption, information, leisure, travel, and entertainment.

The enormous influence of the United States on the security, politics, economics, culture, and society of the Federal Republic during the Cold War can essentially be attributed to seven factors, the first being the overwhelming political, military, economic, cultural, and technological status of the American superpower after 1945. Second, the foreign policy decision-making elite in the era of President Harry S. Truman from 1945 to 1952 possessed a determination and vision the likes of which the United States had not seen since the Founding Fathers. This elite drew its lessons from history and was determined to do everything in its power to prevent the Germans from ever again posing a threat to the peace of Europe or the world. The third factor was the dramatic transition from the wartime coalition with the Soviet Union to the Cold War and anti-Communism. Fourth, Americans' images of the enemy in Europe gradually shifted from a focus on the Germans to a focus on the Russians.[25] Closely related to this is the fifth factor, the shared German and American fear of Soviet aggression and expansion. Sixth, out of necessity, insight, enlightened self-interest, and a turning away from the past, the West Germans became willing to open themselves up to the West and see the United States, for the most part, as the guarantor of their own security and prosperity. The seventh and final factor was the increasing willingness of the West Germans, after the construction of the Berlin wall on August 13, 1961, to submit to the inevitabilities of détente by paying the price for the Western alliance—the de facto division of Germany. Over time, like the early Christians resigning themselves to the fact that the Second Coming was not imminent, Germans stopped waiting for reunification to materialize, and the issue became less and less of a burden on Germany's relations with the United States. Both Americans and Germans had given up the hope of achieving that goal in the foreseeable future.

Berlin, in particular, which had been the headquarters of evil from 1933 to 1945, became not only a symbol of the Cold War and a divided world, but also the outpost of freedom, the "city upon the hill," on which the eyes of the world were focused. For the Americans, nothing was a more obvious symbol of the victory of freedom over communism and dictatorship than the fall of the Berlin wall, to which they reacted almost more enthusiastically than many surprised and disconcerted West Germans.

As Berliners first danced on the wall and then began to tear it down, as freedom for the people of East Germany and the end of communism began to seem politically feasible, the majority of Americans warmly welcomed the unification of the Germans—despite old fears and a deep-seated mistrust of Germany, which were harbored especially among many intellectuals, in the academic world and in the Jewish community, and voiced chiefly in the *New York Times* and the *Washington Post*. Old images of the pathology of German history, from "Kaiser Bill" to Hitler and the Holocaust, overshadowed the experience of the last half of the century of a reliable German democracy that was the most important NATO partner in Europe. The World Jewish Congress stated on March 29, 1990: "The Jewish people, which harbors in its soul the nightmare of the most horrifying holocaust in the annals of mankind, cannot observe this process of unification indifferently but rather approaches it with immense feelings of fear and grave suspicion."[26] Old fears and anxieties of a united Germany were also expressed in Israel. In December 1989, Israeli prime minister Yitzhak Shamir and West German chancellor Helmut Kohl exchanged emotional letters. During his visit to the United States in late November 1989, Shamir declared that a united Germany could pose mortal danger to Jews; Kohl protested strongly against the equation of his country with Nazi Germany and stressed the democratic nature of West Germany. Nevertheless, polls from the spring of 1990 showed that 76 to 90 percent of Americans supported the creation of a free, unified Germany.[27]

When Chancellor Kohl received an honorary doctorate at Harvard, some people called out to him, "Mr. Chancellor, we are all Germans,"[28] meaning that they were all delighted that freedom had proven victorious. President George Bush had already stated in two interviews given before the fall of the Berlin wall that he could imagine a reunification of Germany as a free country. On September 18, 1989, he declared in his particular style: "I think there has been a dramatic change in post World War II Germany. And so, I don't fear it. . . . There is in some quarters a feeling—well, a reunified Germany would be detrimental to the peace of Europe or Western Europe, some way; and I don't accept that at all, simply don't."[29]

The early decision of the Bush administration to support German reunification was a powerful signal to the rest of the world, especially to

Gorbachev, Mitterrand, and Margaret Thatcher, who placed British interests in 1990 on equal footing with the glory of the victorious Allies
of 1945 and the partition of Germany. Kohl told Thatcher shortly after
visiting Churchill's grave that the difference between them was that he,
Kohl, lived in the post-Churchill era.[30]

Bush, Baker, and the small circle of advisors who demonstrated the
classic virtue of diplomacy with expertise, sound judgment, and finesse
knew that they actually had no other choice. Had the Bush administration stated publicly that the United States was continuing to uphold German partition despite the peaceful revolution in East Germany for
liberty, this declaration would have brought about a major catastrophe
in American policy toward Europe. Such a stance would have conflicted
with the "American creed," and with the nation's own image of itself as
an agent of Providence and progress, advancing the cause of freedom
and democracy. Such a statement would have rocked the perceptions of
Americans held by both themselves and the rest of the world, thrown
Germany and Europe into a severe political crisis with incalculable consequences, and led sooner or later to the breakup of NATO.

The Bush administration, however, acted precisely as Americans in
similar situations throughout history have always acted—as in 1848,
1871, and even in 1919 at the victors' conference at Versailles and 1945
in Potsdam. They always welcomed the prospect of a unified, democratic, peaceful, and midsized Germany. The initial American reaction to the
newly founded German nation-state in 1871 was typical. In an address
to Congress on February 7, 1871, only three weeks after the proclamation of the second German Empire at Versailles, President Ulysses S.
Grant stated that the unification of Germany under a form of government that, in many respects, mirrored the American system was received
with great sympathy by the American people. "The adoption in Europe," he declared, "of the American system of Union under the control
and the direction of a free people, educated to self-restraint, cannot fail
to extend a peaceful influence of American ideas."[31] Grant's address reflected America's hopes for the best of all possible Germanys: a distant
Old World country, freedom-loving, peaceful, Protestant, and with a
federal structure; a country of considerable size and weight, but one
without territorial ambitions in Europe, let alone any other part of the
world; a country without any serious conflict of interest with the United
States, and one called upon, as a freedom-loving European state, to emulate the historic mission of the United States by promoting the progress
of liberty and a market-oriented democracy throughout history. In 1871

and 1990, the United States chose to interpret German unity from this missionary perspective.

In 1919, at the Paris peace conference, of the three major powers, only the United States and President Wilson banked the American peace policy, without reserve, on the maintenance of a united German nation-state and a parliament that spoke in its name. In trying to define the role that Germany was to play in the world after the Allied victory in World War I, Wilson had already declared in his Fourteen Points address of January 8, 1918:

We have no jealousy of German greatness, and there is nothing in this program that impairs it. . . . We do not wish to fight her either with arms or with hostile arrangements of trade if she is willing to associate herself with us and the other peace-loving nations of the world in covenants of justice and fair dealing.[32]

Wilson could not deny self-determination to the defeated Germans; only a united Germany could preserve law and order, pay reparations, contain Bolshevism, and preserve a balance of power against a hegemonic France. As Wilson saw it, Germany deserved a chance—after an appropriate period of remorse, repentance, and reform—to return to the family of nations as a respected power and to prove itself as a liberal, capitalist democracy, as the "Little America" of Europe.

Even after World War II and the defeat of Nazi Germany, the United States initially favored a united Germany. Despite the well-known but unfounded myth that Stalin and Roosevelt had divided Europe and Germany, even the entire world, in a process of peaceful arbitration at Yalta, it is a fact that at the Potsdam Conference in July–August 1945, all plans for partitioning Germany had been abandoned, and the three Allies took it for granted that a German state would continue to exist. The Allied Control Council was to be responsible for Germany as a whole; agreed-upon plans had been set forth aiming to establish centralized administrative units, a future German government, and the possible conclusion of a peace treaty for all of Germany; and Germany was to be treated as a single economic area. The famous "four Ds"—that is, the political principles of denazification, demilitarization, democratization, and decartelization—were to be applied to Germany in its entirety. The foreign ministers were expected to draft a peace treaty for one Germany, and even the solution to the much-debated problem of reparations suggested that Germany was to be treated as a single economic unit.

It is, of course, common knowledge that between the summer of 1945 and the fall of 1947, it became abundantly clear that the Allied powers could agree on neither Germany's domestic structure nor the future role Germany should play in Europe. The conflict between the United States and the Soviet Union over the German problem was a major cause for the outbreak of the Cold War, and only the end of the Cold War made German unification possible. From the founding of the Federal Republic of Germany in 1948–49 until unification on October 3, 1990, the United States never wavered from officially and legally supporting the goal of German unification, although many Americans—much like the youthful Saint Augustine, who prayed "Grant me chastity, oh God, but not yet"— piously called for German unification, while assuming that this event would occur only sometime in a vaguely discernible future, if at all.

AT the outset of the new millennium, ten years after German reunification and the fall of the Soviet empire, it is fair to say that the containment and integration of a unified Germany into a wider Europe can be counted among the great achievements of U.S. foreign policies in the twentieth century.

For the first time in their history, Germans are enjoying the "unity and justice and liberty" extolled in their national anthem. Germany's political borders correspond with its cultural boundaries. For the first time, Germany no longer harbors revisionist ambitions; it has become a status quo power. There are four reasons for this, in my opinion.

First, seldom has a country learned so thoroughly from the mistakes of its history as has the German nation. Even today there is a strong rejection of militarism, nationalism, and unilateralism in matters of foreign policy. The Germans do not have a sense of mission; Germany has lost its rendezvous with destiny. Compared with the often vainglorious manifestations of nationalism, patriotism, and sense of mission ("the sole indispensable nation") found in the United States, Germany has become a civil society, a nation of producers, consumers, traders, and travelers—indeed, a "Greater Switzerland." To borrow a slogan from President Bill Clinton: "It is the economy, stupid," that matters for the Germans.

Second, ten years after reunification, it is becoming clear that the integration of the East German states into the Western fabric of economic and cultural life, to which there was no alternative, will greatly drain the resources of the Federal Republic for a long time to come. This transfer of resources, to the tune of $75 billion a year, already contributes significantly to the large national debt and the budget deficits of federal, state, and community governments. This greatly restricts the possibility for major changes in foreign policy. Even the financial basis of Germany's reduced armed forces is highly contested.

Third, the enormous pressure of transnational, even global problems—from immigration, environmental issues, terrorism, crime and drugs, to the challenges of the new global economy, unemployment, capital flight, and tax evasion—is forcing Germany, like all other countries, to cooperate on the international level, thereby diminishing the possibility for a unilateral foreign policy.

Fourth, Germany has experienced self-containment as the result of European integration. In this case we are also witnessing a historical process that was accelerated in 1990, the significance of which we can only understand from a long-term perspective. Throughout history, there has never been anything like a free ride. History, Bismarck once noted, is more accurate in all its revisions than the Prussian central audit office. In addition to the United States and the Soviet Union, Germany's most important neighbor in Western Europe, France, also demanded a price for German unification in 1990. During dramatic negotiations in March of that year, the Kohl administration promised the Mitterrand government that a unified Germany would allow itself to be absorbed into a unified Europe if the other European nation-states were also prepared to transfer major rights to a European union.[33] Ever since, the German government has never tired of repeating a quote from Thomas Mann: "We do not want a German Europe, but a European Germany." Many developments, such as the acceleration of the European integration process since 1990, the road to Maastricht I and Maastricht II, the struggle for a single European currency and a common European foreign policy, the debates on the widening and deepening of Europe, on a reform of many European institutions, and on a democratic legitimation of European policy, originate to a large degree from the desire harbored by Europeans to channel and restrict the influence of the major power among them. Despite the size of its population, its central location, and its economic resources, Germany is not allowed in the eyes of its neighbors to become the hegemonic power of Europe. What was prevented from occurring early in the twentieth century is also not permitted to occur in the twenty-first century.

Finally, Germany's containment and spiritual self-containment guarantee, as well, the future role of the United States as Europe's hegemon, balancer, and pacifier. The reason for that is simple, and Federico Romero, in his commentary on this chapter, expressed it clearly:

Germany . . . has renounced nuclear weapons: that is to say that the geopolitical core of the continent has been effectively disarmed and put under American protection. At the end of the day, the problem of European independence resides precisely in this conundrum, and no one can figure out how to solve it, unless you are prepared to gamble on a leap of faith into full-fledged federalism.

NOTES

1. On German-American relations in the twentieth century, see Hans W. Gatzke, *Germany and the United States: A "Special Relationship"?* (Cambridge: Harvard University Press, 1980); Manfred Jonas, *The United States and Germany: A Diplomatic History* (Ithaca: Cornell University Press, 1984); Frank Trommler and Joseph McVeigh, eds., *The Relationship in the Twentieth Century*, vol. 2 of *America and Germany: An Assessment of a Three-Hundred-Year History* (Philadelphia: University of Pennsylvania Press, 1985); Carl C. Hodge and Cathal J. Nolan, eds., *Shepherd of Democracy: America and Germany in the Twentieth Century* (Westport, Conn.: Greenwood Press, 1992); Klaus Larres and Torsten Oppelland, eds., *Deutschland und die USA im 20. Jahrhundert: Geschichte der politischen Beziehungen* (Darmstadt: Wissenschaftliche Buchgesellschaft, 1997).

2. On the American home front, see Frederick C. Luebke, *Bonds of Loyalty: German-Americans and World War I* (De Kalb: Northern Illinois University Press, 1974); Jörg Nagler, *Nationale Minoritäten im Krieg. "Feindliche Ausländer" und die amerikanische Heimatfront während des Ersten Weltkriegs* (Hamburg: Hamburger Edition, 2000).

3. John C. Ausland, *Kennedy, Krushchev, and the Berlin-Cuba Crisis, 1961–1964* (Oslo: Scandinavian University Press, 1996); Aleksandr Fursenko and Timothy Naftali, *One Hell of a Gamble: Krushchev, Castro, and Kennedy, 1958–1964* (London: John Murray, 1997); Ernest R. May and Philip D. Zelikow, eds., *The Kennedy Tapes: Inside the White House during the Cuban Missile Crisis* (Cambridge: Harvard University Press, 1997); Lawrence Freedman, *Kennedy's Wars: Berlin, Cuba, Laos, and Vietnam* (New York: Oxford University Press, 2000).

4. Frank Ninkovich, *Modernity and Power: A History of the Domino Theory in the Twentieth Century* (Chicago: University of Chicago Press, 1994).

5. Gottfried Niedhart, Detlef Junker, and Michael Richter, eds., *Deutschland in Europa: Nationale Interessen und internationale Ordnung im 20. Jahrhundert* (Mannheim: Palatium-Verlag, 1997).

6. On U.S.–German relations during the Weimar Republic, see Manfred Berg, *Gustav Stresemann und die Vereinigten Staaten von Amerika. Weltwirtschaftliche Verflechtung und Revisionspolitik 1907–29* (Baden-Baden: Nomos Verlagsgesellschaft, 1990); Frank Costigliola, *Awkward Dominion: American Political, Economic, and Cultural Relations with Europe, 1919–1933* (Ithaca: Cornell University Press, 1984); Melvyn P. Leffler, *The Elusive Quest: America's Pursuit of European Stability and French Security* (Chapel Hill: University of North Carolina Press, 1979); Charles S. Maier, *Recasting Bourgeois Europe: Stabilization in France, Germany and Italy in the Decade after World War I* (Princeton: Princeton University Press, 1975).

7. The vast research on U.S.–German relations after 1945 has now been summarized in Detlef Junker, ed., *Deutschland und die USA im Zeitalter des Kalten Krieges, 1945–1990*, 2 vols. (Stuttgart/Munich: Deutsche Verlagsanstalt, 2001). These volumes include 146 contributions by 132 authors from both sides of the Atlantic; an English translation will be published by Cambridge University Press in 2003.

8. *Foreign Relations of the United States* (FRUS), 1949, vol.3 (Washington, D.C.: U.S. Government Printing Office, 1974), 872–73.

9. *FRUS*, 1919, vol. 6 (Washington, D.C.: U.S. Government Printing Office, 1946), 736.

10. Wilfried Mausbach, *Zwischen Morgenthau und Marshall. Das wirtschaftspolitische Deutschlandkonzept der USA 1944–47* (Düsseldorf: Droste, 1996) Bernd Greiner, *Die Morgenthau-Legende. Zur Geschichte eines umstrittenen Planes* (Hamburg: Hamburger Edition, 1995); Warren F. Kimball, *Swords or Ploughshares? The Morgenthau Plan for Defeated Nazi Germany, 1943–46* (Philadelphia: Lippincott, 1976).

11. John L. Harper, *American Visions of Europe: Franklin D. Roosevelt, Georges F. Kennan, and Dean G. Acheson* (Cambridge: Cambridge University Press, 1994).

12. Wolfram F. Hanrieder, *Germany, America, Europe: Forty Years of German Foreign Policy* (New Haven: Yale University Press, 1989), 6.

13. Rohan H. Butler, *The Roots of National Socialism* (London: Faber & Faber, 1941); William Montgomery McGovern, *From Luther to Hitler: The History of Nazi-Fascist Philosophy* (Boston: Houghton Mifflin, 1941); William Shirer, *The Rise and Fall of the Third Reich: A History of Nazi-Germany* (New York: Simon & Schuster, 1960).

14. Frank Costigliola, *France and the United States: The Cold Alliance since World War II* (New York: Twayne, 1992); see also Klaus Schwabe, "Atlantic Partnership and European Integration: America's European Policies and the German Problem, 1947–1966," and Pierre Melandri, "The Troubled Friendship: France and the United States, 1965–1989," in *No End to Alliance: The United States and Western Europe: Past, Present and Future,* ed. Geir Lundestad (New York: Macmillan, 1998), 37–80, 112–33.

15. Georges-Henri Soutou, *L'alliance incertaine: Les rapports politico-stratégiques franco-allemands, 1954–1996* (Paris: Fayard, 1996), 131; Robert Paxton and Nicholas Wahl, eds., *De Gaulle and the United States: A Centennial Reappraisal* (Oxford: Berg, 1994).

16. On the United States and German unification, see especially Philip Zelikow and Condoleezza Rice, *Germany Unified and Europe Transformed: A Study in Statecraft* (Cambridge: Harvard University Press, 1995). In addition, see Elizabeth Pond, *Beyond the Wall: Germany's Road to Unification* (Washington, D.C.: Brookings Institution, 1993); Stephen F. Szabo, *The Diplomacy of German Unification* (New York: St. Martin's, 1992); Konrad Jarausch, *The Rush to German Unity* (New York and Oxford: Oxford University Press, 1994), 157–76. See also the following memoirs: James A. Baker III with Thomas M. Defrank, *The Politics of Diplomacy: Revolution, War and Peace, 1989–1992* (New York: Putnam, 1995); Hans-Dietrich Genscher, *Erinnerungen* (Berlin: Siedler Verlag, 1995) Horst Teltschik, *329 Tage. Innenansichten der Einigung* (n.p., 1991); Helmut Kohl, *Ich wollte Deutschlands Einheit, dargestellt von Kai Diekmann und Ralf Georg Reuth* (Berlin: Ullstein, 1996).

17. Baker, *Politics of Diplomacy,* 202–6; Zelikow and Rice, *Germany Unified,* 179–85.

18. Walter McDougall, *Promised Land, Crusader State: The American Encounter with the World since 1776* (Boston: Houghton Mifflin, 1997); Michael H. Hunt, *Ideology and United States Foreign Policy* (New Haven: Yale University Press, 1987).

19. Detlef Junker, "The Manichaean Trap: American Perceptions of the German Empire, 1871–1945," Occasional Paper 12 (Washington, D.C.: German Historical Institute, 1995).

20. Dieter Schulz, *Rothäute und Soldaten Gottes. Amerikanische Ideologie und Mythologie von der Kolonialzeit bis Ronald Reagan,* in *Kultur und Konflikt,* ed. Jan Assmann und Dietrich Harth (Frankfurt: Suhrkamp, 1990), 287–303.

21. Ernst Fraenkel, "Das deutsche Wilson-Bild," *Jahrbuch für Amerikastudien* 5 (1960):

66–120; Torsten Oppelland, *Reichstag und Aussenpolitik im Ersten Weltkrieg: Die deutschen Parteien und die Politik der USA 1914–18* (Düsseldorf: Droste, 1995).

22. See Philipp Gassert, *Amerika im Dritten Reich. Ideologie, Propaganda und Volksmeinung 1933–45* (Stuttgart: Steiner, 1997); Detlef Junker, "The Continuity of Ambivalence: German Views of America," in *Transatlantic Images and Perceptions: Germany and America since 1776,* ed. David E. Barkley and Elisabeth Glaser-Schmidt (Cambridge: Cambridge University Press, 1997), 243–63.

23. Tony Smith, *America's Mission: The United States and the Worldwide Struggle for Democracy in the Twentieth Century* (Princeton: Princeton University Press, 1994); Emily S. Rosenberg, *Spreading the American Dream: American Economic and Cultural Expansion, 1890–1945* (New York: Hill and Wang, 1982); Hunt, *Ideology and United States Foreign Policy.*

24. H. W. Brands, *What America Owes the World: The Struggle for the Soul of Foreign Policy* (New York: Cambridge University Press, 1998).

25. However, the American image of Germany after 1941 was not as bad as has long been assumed, nor was it as good as has been assumed prior to 1955. See Thomas Reuther, *Die ambivalente Normalisierung: Deutschlanddiskurs, und Deutschlandbilder in den USA 1941–1955* (Stuttgart: Steiner, 2000); see also Astrid Eckert, *Feindbilder im Wandel: Ein Vergleich des Deutschland- und des Japanbildes in den USA 1945 und 1946* (Münster: Lit Verlag 1999).

26. U.S. Holocaust Research Institute Archives, DrW / box 4, January 1–July 1, 1990.

27. *Süddeutsche Zeitung,* February 2, 1990; Kohl, *Deutschlands Einheit,* 241f.; Arthur M. Hanhardt Jr., *Die Deutsche Vereinigung im Spiegelbild der amerikanischen öffentlichen Meinung,* in *Die USA und die deutsche Frage 1945–1990,* ed. Wolfgang-Uwe Friedrichs (Frankfurt: Campus-Verlag, 1991), 407–16.

28. Teltschik, *329 Tage,* 264.

29. Zelikow and Rice, *Germany Unified,* 81. At this time, the more cautious Secretary of State Baker still preferred the words "reconciliation" and "normalization" to "unification" or "reunification"; see Baker, *Politics of Diplomacy,* 162f.

30. Zelikow and Rice, *Germany Unified,* 144f.; Kohl, *Deutschlands Einheit,* 196.

31. Quoted in Manfred Jonas, *The United States and Germany: A Diplomatic History* (Ithaca: Cornell University Press, 1984), 15.

32. Arthur S. Link et al., eds., *The Papers of Woodrow Wilson* (Princeton University Press, 1984), 45:538.

33. Zelikow and Rice, *Germany Unified,* 234f.; Kohl, *Deutschlands Einheit,* 230–38, 357f.; Teltschik, *329 Tage,* 175f., 178, 181.

PART TWO

CULTURAL RESPONSES

European Elitism, American Money, and Popular Culture

Volker R. Berghahn

In Europe the Cold War era began with a brief period of vacillation in 1945–46 when the Western Europeans, led by their intellectual and educated elites, resumed their search, begun during the interwar years, for a " third way" between American capitalism and Soviet communism. But many of them soon came to accept, albeit grudgingly, the leadership position of the United States in the emerging Western camp in power-political/military and economic/technological terms.

There was no total acceptance, however, in that those same elites continued to have great difficulties with concomitant American claims to cultural hegemony. However badly World War II had battered the Europeans' position industrially, commercially, and militarily, they continued to feel superior to the superpower across the Atlantic with respect to their intellectual and academic life that not even twelve years of Nazi barbarism had been able to dent. What Americans had produced in the way of culture was in their view at best derived from European high culture and at worst trashy, vulgar, and primitive. In fact, in the eyes of many on the right as well as the left of the political spectrum, what the Americans had achieved hardly deserved to be called culture.

Encountering these attitudes after 1945 among Western European intellectuals, academics, and the educated upper and middle classes more generally, American elites reacted with irritation to this criticism and developed an activist determination to change attitudes toward the United States. American economic and political hegemony in Western Europe,

117

they believed, would not be secure unless the Europeans also abandoned their cultural superiority complex and recognized as at least equal the achievements of the New World. Only if this acceptance was attained could the much-vaunted Atlantic community that was being built after World War II against the threat and challenge posed by the Soviet bloc become a reality not merely in material-economic and security terms but also in spirit and *Weltanschauung*.

The creation of an American-led Atlantic community seemed all the more urgent because the competition with the Soviets was not merely a struggle over military and economic leadership in Europe and other parts of the world but also presented an intellectual and philosophical challenge. In the tradition of the interwar period, the superpower in the East had begun to organize, soon after the end of the war, congresses of intellectuals and artists at which communists would meet with fellow travelers from the West to discuss and lay the cultural foundations of a Soviet-led world order. Now that this eastern model has collapsed, it is often forgotten that the Soviet bloc was perceived in the West to pose a comprehensive threat, not just a power-political and economic one. It is on this cultural challenge that the first part of this chapter concentrates. Subsequently, it moves on to discuss European fears of mass society before examining American popular culture and the role of "American money" in U.S. cultural policy-making.

One of the most notorious occasions of an East–West clash over the assumed superiority of their respective cultural systems was in Berlin in 1947 at the communist-sponsored international writers' congress at which, apart from a larger number of fellow travelers from Western Europe, a few anticommunist intellectuals turned up to debate Stalinist cultural policies and artistic production.[1] Feeling that the Western point should be put very firmly, a young American, Melvin Lasky, who worked for the American occupation authorities in Berlin at this time, intervened at one of the plenary sessions. His attack was so blunt and provocative that several communist intellectuals left the hall in protest.

After this there was a growing sense, especially among American writers and academics, that a countermovement had to be organized against the East. Consequently, with the encouragement and the financial support of the Office of Military Government U.S. (OMGUS) and leading West Berlin politicians, the first Congress for Cultural Freedom was organized in Berlin in 1950.[2] From this congress, which was a considerable success, there emerged a permanent association, the Congress for Cultural Freedom (CCF), with its headquarters in Paris and national chapters throughout Western Europe. There was also an American branch, some of whose members in fact took a lead in expanding the CCF network.

From the start, the new cultural association developed an activist program and organized several big congresses on major cultural themes of the Cold War era.[3] The first one following the successful Berlin meeting was held in Paris and was devoted to high culture and modern art. It was designed primarily to challenge communist art and the aesthetic theory of socialist realism and coincided, significantly enough, with an exhibition of Mexican art staged in the French capital with communist backing. At the CCF event, works by Alban Berg, Benjamin Britten, and Arnold Schoenberg were performed. Igor Stravinsky conducted *Oedipus Rex* for which Jean Cocteau had produced the stage set. There were literary debates and an exhibition of some 150 modern paintings, with due space given to French masterpieces but also to American ones. And in case anyone missed the ideological point, the organizers had works by Sergei Prokoviev and Dimitri Shostakovich performed (which had been banned in the Soviet Union) and arranged "church services for the victims of totalitarian oppression."

Next came a major CCF congress in the north German city of Hamburg under the heading Science and Freedom.[4] It was directed against Lysenkoism and the subjection of the sciences to state planning as well as the alleged needs of a socialist society. It was also supposed to counter "scientific Marxism" in the social sciences, and eminent philosophers and sociologists, such as Sidney Hook, Raymond Aron, Bruno Snell, Theodor Litt, and Edward Shils, were given ample opportunity to put their views on freedom of research and scientific opinion across to large audiences. Finally, in 1955, there was the Milan congress that focused on the theme "The Future of Freedom." Apart from academics and intellectuals, this congress attracted budding politicians from the "new" Social Democratic left in Western Europe and strong contingents from India, Japan, the Middle East, Latin America, and Africa.

Aside from organizing these congresses, the CCF became active in the field of highbrow journalism.[5] In 1953 it helped establish *Encounter,* which became a leading intellectual monthly in the English-speaking world. The CCF also took Lasky's *Der Monat* under its wing, which, founded in 1948, had provided the model for *Encounter. Der Monat* had been supported by OMGUS and later by the U.S. High Commission in West Germany, but in 1953 it lost this support and was therefore looking for a new patron. These and various other programs initiated by the

CCF swallowed up considerable amounts of money; the funds had come partly from the CIA and partly from the big American philanthropic foundations, the Ford Foundation in particular.

Although the Cold War confrontation and what has been said so far about the culture war against the Soviet bloc form the backdrop to the subsequent analysis, there is a puzzle to be solved that lies at the heart of this chapter: from the mid-1950s onward, a growing feeling was discernable in the CCF and among intellectuals and academics in the United States that the cultural Cold War against the Soviets was being won. The more information circulated both in the West and among intellectuals in Eastern Europe about Stalin's purges during the 1930s and the forms of Stalinization after World War II, the more intellectuals, academics, and artists who had once been attracted to communism began to dissociate themselves from their allegiances and fellow travelers. The Eastern cultural offensive against Western Europe that had looked so successful in the very early postwar years was manifestly failing ten years later. Socialist realism largely proved unappealing. Worse, there was a growing ferment among writers and academics in Poland, Hungary, and Czechoslovakia, who, especially after the death of Stalin in 1953, began to work ever so cautiously for a loosening of the ideological and artistic grip of Soviet communism.

For the CCF and its sponsors, the uprisings in Poland and Hungary in 1956 represented the clearest sign yet that, whatever Moscow's military might, the Soviet bloc was no longer a serious threat as a cultural competitor. Thenceforth they did their best to support the intellectual ferment in Eastern Europe through exchanges of students, scholars, and intellectuals, who were given fellowships to study or work in Europe or the United States for shorter or longer periods.[6] Although the impact of these programs as a way of promoting dialogue and debate between East and West should not be underestimated, and in fact must be seen in the larger context of the beginnings of détente, the sums of support involved remained relatively small—certainly in comparison with what the United States continued to spend on cultural projects in Western Europe. The reasons for this striking shift had little to do with the East–West conflict. Rather they must be sought in the larger framework of European attitudes toward America as a society and cultural system and the concerns that these European attitudes in turn generated in the United States.

Fundamental to European debates about American culture was not only the above-mentioned "superiority complex" but also a deep-seated fear among Europe's elites of the "masses." This fear was a response to their experience since the French Revolution, when the "people" had for the first time played a crucial role in radicalizing the revolt against the ancien régime. After July 1789 and even more so during the Terror, the floodgates seemed to have been opened to democratic politics. Although the revolutionaries were finally contained by Napoleon, his people's armies soon came to be seen by the rest of Europe as a *levée en masse* in a different guise. It therefore came as a great relief to the aristocratic elites of Europe, but also to the rising bourgeoisie, that the threat of the French Revolution could be contained at the Congress of Vienna and during the period of restoration that followed.[7]

The European revolutions of 1848–49 then shattered the belief that this restoration was permanent. The age of the masses had now definitely begun and could not be reversed. The most one could hope for was to channel the energies of those masses, as both Napoleon III and Bismarck tried to do when they introduced the universal manhood suffrage in hopes of playing the conservative peasants off against the "power-hungry" bourgeoisie and its claim to political leadership in the state.[8] Bismarck did not take the step into modern politics because he was a democrat who believed in the "rule of the people." Fittingly, he and his successors later bitterly regretted having promoted the plunge into mass politics. These masses were increasingly composed not of peasants but of industrial workers in the urban centers of Europe and represented by the socialists. By the turn of the century, it was thus no longer just monarchs and conservative aristocrats—the old elites of Europe—but also the new elites of the frightened educated and commercial middle classes who looked for ways of stopping the further advance of "democracy."

Worse from their point of view, there was not just the experience with the masses back home. With the shrinking of distances, improved communication, and the flow of information to Europe from immigrants to the New World, America appeared increasingly in the telescope of those Europeans who had stayed behind.[9] To understand elite responses, we must consider Alexis de Tocqueville's *Democracy in America,* which he wrote and published after visiting the United States for eighteen months in 1835.[10] For our purposes, it is not just what Tocqueville had to say about popular politics across the Atlantic that is important but also what he had to say about the egalitarian practices in the arts and artisanal production. Tocqueville wrote, thinking of Europe, that in aristocratic societies, the number of customers was strictly limited and the profit that artisans were able to make depended "principally on the perfection of their workmanship." In a society, by contrast, that was based on the "democratic principle," the artisan will be induced "to produce with great rapidity many imperfect commodities," and the consumer will have to "content himself with these commodities." In considering the lessons that Tocqueville was hoping to convey, Richard Pells is no doubt correct when he wrote that the French aristocrat "wanted primarily to warn his fellow Europeans about the perils of the democratic experiment which, he feared, would lead either to anarchy or mass conformity."[11]

It is no coincidence that after years of oblivion early on, *Democracy in America* received plenty of attention in Europe precisely at the turn of the century, when, as some feared, the experience of the United States pointed to a future that the Europeans likewise seemed headed for and yet desperately wanted to avoid. By the beginning of the twentieth century, cultural pessimists predicted an impending age of the masses and the attendant decline of elites and of received "civilized" values. Gustave Le Bon's famous book *The Crowd: A Study of the Popular Mind* chimed in well with this sense of impending doom.[12] There is no need to go into Le Bon's dire warning of an age of the masses and the barbarism it would bring, perpetrated on the ruins of the old hierarchical order. Nor is it necessary to discuss the counterstrategies that some intellectuals and politicians tried to develop in order to contain and channel this threat, for example, through "social imperialism."[13] The point is that the flood could no longer be stopped. If the fear of the masses had become deep-seated well before 1914, World War I with its mass mobilization and its revolutionary upheavals in Russia and elsewhere gave it a tremendous boost. And in 1917 in Russia, the radical Left and its followers were no longer just talking about revolution; they began to implement it, and they did so by attacking not merely the political and economic power structures but also society and culture.[14]

From the vantage point of Europe's conservative elites (and these now also included large sections of the once liberal middle classes), European societies found themselves on a downhill slope ever after. From the East, it was the threat of Bolshevism with its dictatorship of the proletariat; in Italy and, after 1933, in Germany, fascist mass movements had seized power, led by charismatic and demagogic upstarts, such as Hitler and Mussolini. As the Italian industrialist Gino Olivetti put it, the German and Italian elites, if not those in other European countries, had lost control of the masses; they had become an "ex-classe dirigente."[15] It is at this point that the European elites' horrific visions assume their full weight not only with respect to Bolshevism and fascism, but also with respect to the society that had unfolded across the Atlantic. As we have seen, the democratic politics and practices developed in the United States had caused elitist concern in Europe since the late nineteenth century, if not before. What was added in the 1920s was the specter of democratic participation of the masses in another field: the enjoyment of the material goods produced by an increasingly mechanized industrial economy.

It is important to emphasize that, unlike the Soviet model, the American model of rationalized production divided elite opinion in Europe even before 1914. There were those who were fascinated by Taylorism and the assembly-line production that Henry Ford had begun to develop at River Rouge. They wanted to transfer it to European industry.[16] But Fordist mass production with the aim of lowering prices and making cars and other consumer durables affordable to the masses also triggered worries and opposition to its consequences. As Daimler Benz, the makers of fine motor cars, pointed out before World War I and with some relief: "Over here we are still a long way from the American situation where every Mr. Jones owns a car. With us the automobile is for the most part a vehicle for the better-off classes."[17]

It is worth pondering this quotation in conjunction with the European reception of Tocqueville's *Democracy in America*. In the eyes of Europe's elites, the masses were not only volatile and irrational in the rising age of mass politics but also "greedy" as producers and consumers of cheap, mass-produced industrial goods. To the growing concern over what this ominous brew of mass production/consumption along with the political mass market and universal suffrage might do to existing patterns of privilege and elite status was finally added the worry about mass culture. Europe's elites had traditionally defined culture narrowly as "high culture," which comprised only the "great" works of literature, painting, theater, music, and ballet, and they were to be enjoyed exclusively in the performing arts centers of the cities at prices beyond the means of the "uneducated masses." There was, of course, something like "low culture," but it was deemed vulgar and primitive, an *Unkultur.*

The trouble was that mass culture, next to mass politics, mass production, and mass consumption, was not only proliferating in the United States but—by the 1920s, if not before—was also "swamping" Europe. By 1925, America, its political isolationism notwithstanding, had reappeared in Europe not only as an industrial and commercial power but also as a purveyor of mass culture. Millions of "ordinary Europeans" would go to the movies every week to watch primarily Hollywood products.[18] With film came American popular music, Josephine Baker, and the Tilly Sisters. From the point of view of Europe's elites and their conceptions of social stratification, culture, and politics, the "age of the masses" had begun, and American popular cultural imports were viewed by them not only with disdain but also as a threat to their notions of social order.[19] Next to their anti-Bolshevism, an anti-Americanism, that is, a rejection of what the United States seemingly represented as a society, a culture, and a democratic political system, took deep root. It harmonized well with the widespread cultural pessimism of the interwar period. For Europe's educated elites, the world was out of joint. Their feelings were neatly summarized in a best-seller titled *The Revolt of the Masses,* which the Spanish philosopher José Ortega y Gasset published in 1932.[20]

The outcome of World War II did not fundamentally alter the pessimistic attitudes of right-wing intellectuals and Europe's conservative elites. They remained staunchly anti-Bolshevik, but they also continued to harbor strong reservations about the United States. Meanwhile, left-wing intellectuals, as we have seen, had developed sympathies for the Soviet experiment, which implied that they not only fought fascism, but also capitalism, not least in its American guise. Worse, in their eyes, there existed a direct link between this American model of capitalist production and the commercialized mass culture it espoused.[21] The scathing criticism of the United States as an economy and a culture that this attitude produced was not abandoned when, by the 1950s, the Soviet model was gradually losing its luster among these fellow travelers. Nor did the European cultural pessimists on the Right change their mind about America after 1945. In short, old attitudes toward America as a society and cultural system persisted, even as the Cold War against the Soviet bloc was being won in intellectual terms.

We have thus reached the point where we can take the final analytical step and move to relating European elitist attitudes toward American popular culture (rooted in the first half of the twentieth century) to the role of "American money" and in particular to that of the big philanthropic foundations.[22] The policies of the largest among them, the Ford Foundation, provide a good case in point. In the 1950s and 1960s, this foundation came to play a very influential role within the triangle of American big business, Washington politicians, and intellectuals and academics based mainly in New York or at Ivy League universities along the East Coast.

These men (and a few women), while still taking the Cold War against the Soviet Union seriously in military and economic terms, had, like the CCF leadership with which they cooperated, come to the conclusion that communism no longer posed a major intellectual and cultural threat. At the same time they were keenly aware of the persistent cultural anti-Americanism among Western Europe's elites. Many of them had experienced it firsthand when they went to Europe during the interwar years and listened to European criticism of America as an *Unkultur.* Traveling in Europe after 1945 or working for extended periods for American reconstruction agencies in occupied Germany or elsewhere, they knew about their country's economic and military superiority, but they also learned that Europe's elites refused to accept America'a claims to cultural leadership. Indeed, they were dismayed and irritated by what they heard being said about the culture of the United States. It was—as they had been told before 1945 and were now told again—vulgar, trashy, and incomparably inferior to anything the Europeans had produced. Convinced not only that this criticism was unfair but also that American leadership in the emergent Atlantic community would remain precarious unless European elitist perceptions were changed, they set out to achieve just that. The CCF with its congresses and intellectual journals became a key instrument in this effort.[23]

The determination of the East Coast internationalist elites to win this second Cold War of culture of the 1950s and 1960s suffered from one serious handicap. In the early postwar years, Washington and the U.S. Congress had footed the bill. In occupied western Germany, the military government and, after 1949, the U.S. High Commission had spent millions not only on intellectual journals like *Der Monat* but also on America Houses and in subsidies to a still fragile democratic press.[24] In other countries of Western Europe, pro-American attitudes had been promoted through the Marshall Plan and other programs. But after the end of the Korean War, the new Republican Congress began to cut public expenditures, and the efforts of the State Department and the U.S. Information Agency were reduced. In the eyes of those who knew about European criticism of the United States and about the undiminished strength of cultural anti-Americanism and who wanted to build an American-led Atlantic community, this policy was shortsighted, and it was one they decided to try to counteract. One of these supporters was Allen Dulles, chief of the CIA, who had at his disposal covert funds not subject to the public scrutiny of isolationist and parsimonious politicians in Washington. Accordingly, he decided to commit secretly funds to the

CCF as a major promoter of the idea that America did have a "high" culture to be shown with pride to skeptical Western Europeans.[25]

Dulles's funds were not unlimited, however, and the cultural ventures of the CCF were expensive. Fortunately for him and for the internationalist foreign policy establishment in the East, there were like-minded people who similarly knew Europe from the interwar period or from assignments after 1945. Some of these individuals had meanwhile risen to influential positions in large philanthropic foundations, where they were in charge of millions of dollars to be given to deserving applicants.

One of these men was Dr. Shepard Stone, a protégé of John J. McCloy, who became the key person to develop the international program of the Ford Foundation. After years of pushing within the organization, Stone persuaded the foundation hierarchy to commit itself. Although it is not possible to give a full presentation of the rich material relating to its cultural efforts in Europe, it should suffice to quote a few pertinent passages from the archives and to mention a few initiatives that the Ford Foundation launched in the 1950s, when the second culture war against Western European anti-Americanism had begun.

Discussing the potentialities of the CCF after one of his trips to Europe in 1954, Stone called the Congress "the most effective organization in Europe among the political, intellectual and cultural leaders" there that deserved the Ford Foundation's support.[26] He added with reference to the shift of emphasis in America's cultural Cold War that "in the past the Congress had concentrated on combating Communist efforts among the intellectuals of Europe and Asia." But now, he added, it "intends to emphasize the positive aspects of freedom and a free society." The new confidence toward the Soviet bloc and the focus on Western Europe are clearly reflected in Stone's subsequent recommendation that the foundation "consider the allocation of funds for sending American plays, art, orchestras to Europe." The main problem, he continued, "is not to convince the Europeans that we have a culture. As a matter of fact, Europeans are becoming bored with our insistence that we are a cultured people. Informed Europeans know it. But they want to see it for themselves. They read our books and periodicals, and they now want to see our art, our theater, and to hear our music." One U.S. ambassador, he added, "has made a strong plea for sending 'Porgy and Bess.' . . . He believes that the political and psychological results of such a visit would be astonishing." Meanwhile, "Ambassador Dillon in Paris" had, according to Stone, "strongly" urged "us to support the American Art Festival which will take place in the spring in theaters, museums, and halls being put at the disposal of the American people by the Government of France and by the City of Paris." Cultural efforts of this kind, Stone concluded, "can have important effects politically."[27]

However, it is important to realize that Stone and the men of learning, business, and politics involved with his sprawling European program had a broader definition of "high culture than the traditional European one that focused on the arts and philosophy. For them it included the institutions of higher learning, and not just those in the humanities but in the social and natural sciences as well. Indeed, their cultural system was comprehensive, although—like that of the Europeans—centered on high culture. Accordingly, the Ford Foundation's international program began to support the expansion of Oxbridge colleges. It helped to establish the Maison des Sciences de l'Homme in Paris and the Institute of European Sociology that Raymond Aron headed in the 1960s.[28] It gave money to the Free University in West Berlin for the construction of the Ford-Bau, a big lecture hall in the modern style, and for the building of an American Studies program. It funded the institute of Niels Bohr, the famous Danish physicist, who also acted as a bridge to colleagues in Eastern Europe.

The strategy behind these projects, of which only a few have been listed here, was just as political as Stone's aid to the CCF's cultural and artistic enterprises had been: to combat European cultural anti-Americanism and to promote institutions, intellectuals, and politicians who were known not to share the negative images of America as a culture. This was not easy, because these efforts coincided with the massive return of American mass culture to Western Europe during the 1950s. As in the 1920s, this return was spearheaded by Hollywood films and jazz. But it was soon followed by something that many European intellectuals and educated middle-class people found even more objectionable— Elvis Presley and Bill Haley.[29] At first the experts and family politicians thought that Western Europe's youth would be immune to the rhythms and gyrations of American rock musicians. But when the first youth riots occurred in cities in the wake of their concerts, the alarm bells began to ring loudly again. Was this the beginning of a cultural rebellion of the lower classes against prevailing elite perceptions of culture? And what if these outbursts of irrationalism became politicized? Would Europe not lapse back into the mass hysteria of the totalitarian 1930s?

At this point we turn to the final aspect that is relevant to our topic: the appearance on the foundation- and CCF-funded lecturing circuit in Europe of a number of highly influential social scientists who interpreted to their audiences of educated people, full of anxiety about American mass culture and its impact on their societies, what this mass culture was really about. These scholars had cut their teeth in debates about the same topic and about the direction of American "mass society" that had taken place in the early 1950s in the Ivy Leagues and among New York intellectuals in particular. These protagonists had responded to criticisms of the United States and its future that were strikingly similar to the arguments European intellectuals had advanced since the interwar period. For example, in the United States the writings of Dwight Macdonald had upset many people when he attacked the depressing standards of American "Midcult" and "Masscult."[30] The response came from a number of sociologists who had a different take on popular culture. One of the most widely read was Daniel Bell, whose famous study *The End of Ideology* has often been seen as an exposition of Deweyan pragmatism and reformist management of modern industrial societies after an era of ideological dogmatism during the interwar and early postwar years.[31] On closer inspection, Bell's book is also a defense of the pluralism and richness of American popular culture. To him, society was everything but standardized and gray, vulgar and barbaric; it was diverse and colorful and manifested itself at the grass roots of society in a myriad of cultural groups and their activities.

It is safe to say that Bell's arguments did not convince many European intellectuals when they were first published in the early 1960s. But attitudes have changed since then. Thanks to the activities of the CFF and American philanthropic organizations, these elite groups had become more appreciative of American high culture by the end of the twentieth century, whether in the narrow sense of the arts or in the broader sense of the country's educational and scientific achievements. Meanwhile the traditional disdain for American mass culture also mellowed. At first the slow pace of this process led to frustrations. They are reflected in a report that a Ford Foundation official sent to Stone after attending a CCF-run conference of European intellectuals at Lourmarin in 1959.[32] Businessmen and politicians, Waldemar Nielsen wrote, had begun to change their mind about America as the leading cultural power of the West. The problem, according to him, was that the intellectual and academic elites were "lagging behind" in the "healthy development going on in other groups." He had been upset by the "sickness" of many of the participants, "particularly the French." To be sure, most of them had given up the early postwar fellow-traveling and admiration for communism. But their cultural anti-Americanism had not diminished. Accordingly, they had "spent a lot of time worrying and stewing and griping about the United States, about American domination, about the inferiority of our values and so on."

Yet it is safe to say that forty years later, at the beginning of the twenty-first century, there has been a tangible change in European intellectuals' attitudes toward American mass culture. It may still be criticized for its trashiness, but in their weaker moments, even those critics have come to enjoy it. In this respect Richard Peterson is probably correct when he asserts that most European intellectuals have, culturally speaking, become "omnivores."[33] The old elitism and rejection of popular culture have noticeably declined. As to "American money" and the official and private support of American culture in Europe, very much less is spent today on its promotion. This may in part be because America's "high" cultural achievements are now much more widely recognized and its mass-cultural products much more widely consumed than they were in the 1950s and 1960s. But it is also due to the withdrawal of the foundations from the initiatives of that earlier period. This retreat had no doubt much to do with the crisis that resulted from the revelation of covert CIA funding in the rebellious 1960s, the generational shift that occurred in those years, and the new concentration of the philanthropies on helping to solve the social and economic problems of the developing world.[34] Compared with the magnitude of those problems, perceptions of American popular culture by Europe's intellectual elites had become marginal. And after the end of the Cold War against the Soviet bloc, the small dose of European cultural anti-Americanism that is still around is much less worrisome than it had been in those tense 1950s and 1960s.

NOTES

1. See Peter Coleman, *The Liberal Conspiracy* (New York: Free Press, 1989), 4; Frances S. Saunders, *The Cultural Cold War* (New York: New Press, 1999), 17ff.

2. See Coleman, *Liberal Conspiracy*, 46ff.; Pierre Grémion, *Intelligence de l'anticommunisme* (Paris: Fayard, 1995), 22.

3. See Coleman, *Liberal Conspiracy*, 56; Richard Kuisel, *Seducing the French: The Dilemma of Americanization* (Berkeley: University of California Press, 1993), 28.

4. See Coleman, *Liberal Conspiracy*, 104ff.; Grémion, *Intelligence de l'anticommunisme*, 125ff.

5. See Coleman, *Liberal Conspiracy*, 93f.; Saunders, *Cultural Cold War*, 27ff.

6. See Volker R. Berghahn, *America and the Intellectual Cold Wars in Europe* (Princeton: Princeton University Press, 2001), 187ff.

7. See, e.g., R. J. W. Evans and Hartmut Pogge von Strandmann, eds., *The Revolutions in Europe* (Oxford: Oxford University Press, 2000).

8. See, e.g., T. S. Hamerow, "The Origins of Mass Politics in Germany," in *Deutschland in der Weltpolitik des 19. und 20. Jahrhunderts,* ed. Imanuel Geiss and Bernd Jürgen Wendt (Düsseldorf: Bertelsmann, 1973), 105–20.

9. See, e.g., Volker R. Berghahn, *The Americanization of West German Industry, 1945–1973* (New York: Cambridge University Press, 1986), 26ff.

10. Alexis de Tocqueville, *Democracy in America,* 2 vols. (New York: Vintage, 1945), 2:48ff.

11. Richard Pells, *Not Like Us* (New York: Basic Books, 1997), 97.

12. Gustave Le Bon, *The Crowd: A Study of the Popular Mind* (London: T. F. Unwin, 1910); originally published in French as *La psychologie des foules* (Paris, 1899).

13. See, e.g., Edward R. Tannenbaum, *1900: The Generation before the Great War* (Garden City, N.J.: Anchor Books, 1976), 348f.

14. See, e.g., Charles S. Maier, *Recasting Bourgeois Europe* (Princeton: Princeton University Press, 1975), 19ff.

15. Quoted in E. Nolte, "Die 'herrschenden Klassen' und der Faschismus in Italien," in *Faschismus als soziale Bewegung,* ed. Wolfgang Schieder (Hamburg: Hoffmann & Campe, 1976), 192.

16. Mary Nolan, *Visions of Modernity: American Business and the Modernization of Germany* (New York: Oxford University Press, 1994).

17. A. Kugler, "Von der Werkstatt zum Fliessband," *Geschichte und Gesellschaft* 13 (1987): 316.

18. Thomas Saunders, *Hollywood in Berlin* (Berkeley: University of California Press, 1996).

19. See, e.g., Frank Costigliola, *Awkward Dominion: American Political, Economic, and Cultural Relations with Europe, 1919–1933* (Ithaca: Cornell University Press, 1984); Philipp Gassert, *Amerika im Dritten Reich* (Stuttgart: DVA, 1997).

20. José Ortega y Gasset, *The Revolt of the Masses* (London: Unwin, 1969).

21. See, e.g., Theodor W. Adorno and Max Horkheimer, *Die Dialektik der Aufklärung* (New York: Social Studies Association, 1944); Jerry Z. Muller, *The Other God That Failed* (Princeton: Princeton University Press, 1987).

22. See Giuliana Gemelli, ed., *The Ford Foundation in Europe (1950's–1970's)* (Brussels: European Interuniversity Press, 1998).

23. Berghahn, *America and the Intellectual Cold Wars,* 108ff., 178ff.

24. See O. Schmidt, "Protecting the Civil Empire" (Ph.D. diss., Harvard University, 1999).

25. Saunders, *Cultural Cold War,* 82ff.

26. Quoted in Berghahn, *America and the Intellectual Cold Wars,* 176.

27. Ibid., 201ff.

28. See J. Krige, "The Ford Foundation, European Physics and the Cold War," *Historical Studies in the Physical and Biological Sciences* 29:333–61.

29. See, e.g., Heide Fehrenbach and Uta Poiger, eds., *Transactions, Transgressions, Transformations. American Culture in Western Europe and Japan* (New York: Berghahn Books, 2000).

30. Michael Wreszin, *A Rebel in Defense of Tradition* (New York: Basic Books, 1994).

31. Daniel Bell, *The End of Ideology* (Glencoe, Ill.: Free Press, 1960).

32. Quoted in Berghahn, *America and the Intellectual Cold Wars,* xi.

33. Quoted in Herbert Gans, *Popular Culture and High Culture* (New York: Basic Books, 1999), 9.

34. Berghahn, *America and the Intellectual Cold Wars,* 250ff.

American Myth, American Model, and the Quest for a British Modernity

David W. Ellwood

The Meaning of a Choice

Within the next five years, the United Kingdom will almost certainly be obliged to decide whether to abandon its age-old currency, the pound sterling, and embrace the euro, the common money of the European Union. The closer this milestone approaches, the more intense becomes the debate on the meaning of Britain's experience in the twentieth century, which is still thought to be the factor more likely than any other (e.g., globalization) to decide Britain's fate in the century now opening. Like all the nations of Europe, Britain faces this decision during a prolonged spasm of national self-interrogation triggered by the end of the Cold War. Germany gradually is coming to terms with the double trauma of the end of the East–West confrontation *and* re-unification; France is trying to redefine its position in the Atlantic community and the European community; Italy disputes whether fascism, communism, or Catholicism should take the most blame for its unsatisfactory sense of nationhood. The British worry most about "Europe": specifically the past, present, and future; the costs and the benefits of their membership in the institutions of the European Union.

All these national debates share a tendency to condense a great many issues—some old, some new, some borrowed, some imposed—into one overriding, never-ending argument. But of all the uncertainties, none is deeper than that concerning the link between modernity and sovereignty, or modernization and self-preservation: that is, how to build and defend a distinctively Italian or French or German path to the future, one a people can recognize as its own, balancing the most attractive of the new and the best of the old. What distinguishes the French, the German, and the British varieties of this debate, and differentiates them from the others, is the importance of the role of America in their discussions; not American policy or personalities, of course, but a real or imagined United States, one that includes all the forms American power has taken on in these national scenes over the years.

The pages that follow focus on how the American inspiration has functioned in Britain's key identity debates, stretching from the start of the last century, through the post–World War I version of the 1920s, the post-imperial phase of the 1960s, the era of renewal under Mrs. Thatcher, and so on down to the present. The central question concerns the role of the American myth and model in the United Kingdom's search for a satisfactory, stable modernity of its own: one that enjoys consensus, legitimacy, and—above all—*success*.

At this point, though, an obvious distinction needs to be made. Many German and French commentators on these questions seem to speak from a feeling that their nations have been to some extent forced to come to terms with the presence of America in their midst, often relating it to circumstances that were disagreeable, or at best unsought. British sentiment springs from quite different impulses. At the turn of the new millennium, the evidence began to mount that the nation most concerned about the role of America as culture, society, or power in the definition of its options was no longer the Federal Republic of Germany or the France of the stereotypes but the "cool Britannia" of Tony Blair and New Labour. In contrast, though, with Continental debates on American power in all its forms, which often complained of an excessive supply of models, products, languages, symbols, and so forth, conflict in Britain revolved round the demand side of the equation: after years of effort to bring the country up to the prevailing standards of modernity and progress, just how much like the United States did the country want to be?

Writing in the *Financial Times* in 2001, the commentator Michael Prowse argued repeatedly that the British government of the time was in danger of becoming "obsessed" with a cure-all it believed it had found for all the country's ills: turning everything it could touch, even education, into a "business" experience that would bring the magic of private enterprise to the rescue of all things public. Citizens would be turned into consumers and the disciplines of the market place applied to the supply of schools and prisons, hospitals, roads, and all the rest. "This compulsion to emulate the U.S. is nothing short of pathological," concluded Prowse. "In the case of education it is also irrational."[1]

The former editor of the center-left daily *The Guardian,* Peter Preston, described the then-leader of the opposition Conservative Party William Hague as "pathetically desperate to worship at the Washington court" and denounced the unquestioning reverence of British politicians for the American way.[2] A leading political philosopher, John Gray, had already gone further, attacking directly Labour's commitment to "the United States as the paradigmatic modern country, which Britain should take as a model." With no credible alternative visible in Europe, the government was urged to stop looking abroad for ready-made notions of the sort of country Britain should be.[3] The Oxford historian Timothy Garton Ash asked simply "Is Britain European?" And once again, it was the American question that presented itself as the one unavoidable point of reference. If law and governance were by now oriented formally to Europe, the content of policy owed most to America: "This is something that both the Thatcher and Blair governments have had in common: a fascination with U.S. policy and U.S. solutions."[4]

But positions such as Garton Ash's were only the latest contributions to a weighty and enduring debate on the national identity question in the United Kingdom. Continuing a line established in the 1980s by books such as Martin Weiner's influential *English Culture and the Decline of the Industrial Spirit, 1850–1980,* on through texts such as *On Living in an Old Country,* to the pronouncements of popular culture discoverer Richard Hoggart in *The Way We Live Now,* and New Labour–leaning economist and social commentator Will Hutton in *The State We're In,*[5] the fundamental question seemed always the one originally identified in 1968 by Eric Hobsbawm:

the vested interest in the past has been unusually strong, more complacent, because more protected; and perhaps also more unwilling to try new paths for its economy, because no new paths seem to lead to half so inviting a prospect as the old ones. These may be now impassable, but other roads do not appear very passable either.[6]

In such a context, America seemed to represent the last, best hope—not of mankind, but of a leading element of Britain's political class and its mass media, the only route left for them to try after so many disappointments in spheres such as the Commonwealth and the Common

Market. Commenting on the incompatibility of British and European visions of the future, the BBC World Service economics correspondent concluded that "in Britain it is so incorrect to see anything good in Europe that the U.S. is constantly evoked as an ideal model and partner."[7] Jonathan Freedland, a *Guardian* journalist, wrote an entire volume dedicated to teaching Britons how they could "live the American dream." The solution in his view was a fundamental constitutional reform, first to eliminate the monarchy and its trappings, followed by the installation of a republic based on the U.S. Constitution. That document after all had been written by English-nurtured rebels in those thirteen colonies and was rooted in English radicalism. Now was the time to "Bring Home the American Revolution!"[8]

The Origins of an Attitude

Contemporary attention to the meaning of America's development for Britain has its roots in what Gladstone at the end of the nineteenth century called "the paramount question of the American future" in his nation's life. The first grand pronouncement anywhere in Europe on the dangers of not taking the Americans seriously appeared under the pen of the London journalist W. T. Stead, in his *Review of Reviews* of 1902, titled: "The Americanisation of the World or the Trend of the Twentieth Century." Although Stead was eager to document and denounce the ever-increasing presence of American products, methods, and people in British society, the key question he posed in the article was strategic: How could the British keep their world status and continue to compete on a basis of equality?

Stead had been one of those most excited by the Spanish-American War of 1898, an event that much British opinion defined as America finally facing up to the challenge of imperial rivalries. But the rejoicing in London at this spectacle was based on the conviction that the new American power in the world would immediately be available for the benefit of the Mother Country. The war fever was greatly stimulated, of course, by contemporary notions of the workings of Darwinist principles in international life, and schemes flourished on all sides for friendship clubs, alliances, and unions.[9] Two consequences of the episode would be of lasting significance. One was the birth in continental Europe of the daunting prospect of a common Anglo-Saxon front, one whose potential for adding power to British purposes seemed unlimited. The other lay in the new, made-in-England vision of a "union of the Anglo-Saxon peoples." Only partly discouraged by the events of World War I and Versailles—which included Woodrow Wilson's outspoken rejection of any such link[10]—this impulse would reappear in World War II under Winston Churchill's powerful patronage and eventually attain a permanent status in the British myths that came out of the Atlantic Charter of 1941.

As part of the British illusion on her place in the world after 1945, and the nation's capacity to rebuild her Great Power status, the fantasy lived on. One wartime humiliation after another at American hands did not prevent Churchill's celebrated Iron Curtain speech of March 1946 from including an eloquent call for "a fraternal association of the English-speaking peoples." The vision of "a special relationship" between the United States and the British Commonwealth was evoked by the great hero. This would rebuild the combined war machine of the glory days and might even point the way to a form of common citizenship.[11] Whenever Churchill's hallowed name was brought before American audiences by Mrs. Thatcher at the height of her powers, the old notion was given another spin. It was hinted at even after the Iron Lady left office, in her calls for a North Atlantic free trade area to be set up under Anglo-American auspices. And without any warning it was to return from the grave as the new millennium opened.[12]

America and Britain's First Identity Crisis

The decade that followed the First World War changed Britain in ways the country was neither prepared to face nor much cared for when they happened, and tensions with America were among its most characteristic and unwelcome features. These were for the most part grim years in which the heart of the Empire sought to find some sort of headway after the great catastrophe, uncertain whether to try simply to rebuild the old world as it was imagined to have been—the main thrust of economic policy—or recast the nation's standing on some new basis. Brought up sharp at the great postwar crossroads where mass democracy, mass production, and mass communications met, Britain's finance- and commerce-based capitalism struggled to adapt. The challenge, say the specialists Cain and Hopkins, was not simply to organize the exchange of "tradition" for "modernity" but to manage "a selective amalgamation of elements inherited from the past with introductions from the continuously evolving present."[13] The unspoken question concerned how much sovereignty Britain now really commanded to control the ever more complicated processes of selection and amalgamation.

At the time, the introductions that most severely challenged governments and their officials were economic in nature and came from across the Atlantic. At the end of the decade, a U.S. journalist published a dramatic account of all the conflicts in course or looming between the two sides, and predicted the outcome: American business would soon comprehensively defeat that of the old Mother Country. Ludwell Denny's "record of economic war" was in fact a compendium of the American nation's economic and commercial triumphs, leading to a warning that the British Empire would never be able to withstand the ever-rising competition from the United States as well as from Europe. "Britain," he diagnosed, "is approaching the time when she must decide on a working agreement with the European cartel alliance or with the United States. As yet there is much confusion in the British mind between these alternatives."[14]

Of all the strategies proposed at the time to cope with this situation, there was only one destined to endure. The new world challenger must be beaten at its own game: British industries should take over America's methods and thoroughly modernize themselves with Fordist techniques and attitudes. The 1920s were a time when many enduring patterns of transatlantic action and reaction were created, and this was one of them. A limited and *controlled* adjustment to American patterns was to be attempted, one of the few effective responses possible to the rising challenge of U.S. economic power across an ever-increasing number of sectors and markets.

But these political and economic developments took place in a very special cultural context. The Americans were now applying their technology and their commercial methods to create new kinds of industry, in communications and entertainment. Their products were achieving overwhelming mass appeal and were starting to arrive on an ever-increasing scale in Britain and Europe. Movies, music, dances, advertising, and all the systems of promotion that come with them began to represent a quite new kind of American challenge. Traditional cultural authorities did not like what they saw. As Frank Costigliola remarked, they "interpreted every manifestation of American culture, whether it was music, films or automobiles, as the product of a society dominated by technology and the machine."[15]

The outcome was a prolonged battle in Britain between the "commercial" and the "cultivated" spirits for the definition of a satisfactory national identity in the new era. As intensely as the masses embraced the new amusements the United States sent over, so the cultivated elites denounced them and rushed to set up bulwarks against them. The 1920s saw the first explicit use of the term *anti-Americanism,* and the culture of the crowd, of popular democracy and commercial modernity, was the force that provoked it.[16] Hostility to whatever idea or practice stood for the United States had never been absent among European elites. But the arrival of Hollywood and its stars, jazz, advertising, streamlining, chain stores, chorus girls, and all the making-getting-spending philosophies that stood behind them was profoundly upsetting to cultural authorities anxiously engaged in trying to re-establish their positions in society in the wake of the great catastrophe.[17]

Cinema was seen as the key battleground, not only because of the size of the audience—roughly 20 million spectators per week in 1927—but also because America's market share was so overwhelming: 95 percent on average at this time. The answer was cultural protectionism. As in most countries in Europe at the time, a system of quotas was installed, the hope being to restore the balance of cultural power and domesticate the beast, as was happening in the burgeoning worlds of recorded sound, jazz, and dancing. In this way, tradition might re-assert itself and Americanization become "something recognizably British."[18]

On Losing an Empire and Searching for a Role

By the time former Secretary of State Dean Acheson made his famous remarks in December 1962 about Britain's loss of empire and inability to find a new way forward in the world, the British intellectual and media debate was already counting the costs of the nation's difficulties in adapting to the new postwar universe of decolonization, seemingly perpetual Cold War, and ever-increasing economic competition. The financial and industrial contest with the United States had of course long been lost, with Britain facing bankruptcy after 1945 and barely surviving on austerity and American loans. Atlanticism and the doctrine of the "Special Relationship" were the supreme means for coping with all this, ever since the Labour government had formally recognized in 1949 that the Anglo-American connection must be the keystone of Britain's foreign policy.[19] After the Suez crisis of 1956, and the bitter end of the postwar illusions that the country might rebuild its great power status by reconstructing and modernizing its empire, British dependence on American political and strategic strength was generally no longer hidden.

These moments were still recalled forty years later in debates on national identity and the "decline" theme in the story. Acheson's phrase, it was recalled, had been explicitly and forcefully rejected by Mrs. Thatcher in 1983: "I want the 1980's to be the decade when we get back on course."[20] But Stuart Hall, a leading expert on the evolution of contemporary popular culture, evoked it again in 1999 when commenting on the parallel decline of the formal British Empire and the rise of the informal American equivalent to take its place. "Locked into a subordinate position" as a result of the Second World War, the United Kingdom now "resentfully learned the [Fordist] game" from the United States, while the rest of the world came to Britain to "learn how to be traditional!"[21]

No matter how tightly the hard realities of geopolitics bound Britain to NATO and Washington, learning the Fordist game and modernizing along American lines were in fact far from the most obvious priorities for domestic policy or society at large in the first postwar years. The "occupation" of Britain by almost three million U.S. soldiers, sailors, and airmen during World War II had changed the nation in a hundred subtle ways and gave solid grounds to preexisting images of the affluence, self-assurance, and optimism of the average American citizen. But it did not lead to any traceable Americanization of Britain.[22] Likewise, the Marshall Plan in its U.K. incarnation failed to inspire any revolution in British ways of production and consumption, in spite of very explicit efforts in this direction.[23]

But along with the rest of Western Europe, Britain began to regain its confidence in the future as it gradually began to feel the buoyancy effects of the new, unexpected tide of 1950s affluence. While governments concentrated on building the welfare state and making the "mixed economy" work, a new kind of prosperity started to assert itself from below: consumerist, private, and dynamic. Characterized later as "an ever-expanding prosperity for an ever-expanding majority," at the time it was simply called "growth."[24] There was little doubt of its origins. In 1967 the Cambridge economist Michael Postan explained:

Both openly and discreetly the wish to catch up with the USA became the ambition of governments and the public. . . . American affluence and American levels of consumption—motor cars, domestic gadgets, and all—were held up as rewards to come. In short, America's very presence provided an impulse to European growth and a measure of its achievements.[25]

The changes in market relationships involved in the Americanized era of "high mass consumption" touched every social class and brought new groups forward to enjoy its benefits: most of the working class, women, and youth.[26] American myth and American model merged in the Hollywood cinema, never again as influential as in the years 1945–54. While productivity stood as the key to the supply side, a force like Hollywood's worked on the demand side of the economic and social transformation, speeding and channeling the changes in mentality and behavior. So by pointing out the most credible, alluring path forward in a hundred different ways—films, personalities, products, magazines, advertising, television, fashions, "lifestyles"—America's experience was exported and turned into a new kind of British "Americanisation."[27]

Although the cultivated elite had lost a good deal of its force in the era of the welfare state, conservative critics were not slow to express their dismay. In a 1951 collection of essays edited by Bertrand Russell on the impact of American culture in Europe, the Anglo-American historian J. E. Morpurgo accused Hollywood of having reinvented and amplified the most decadent aspects of traditional European culture, Americanizing hedonism and self-indulgence in order to retransmit them as the new mass satisfactions, easy to acquire, easy to enjoy.[28] In 1955 the writer and broadcaster J. B. Priestley, long a skeptic, would publish his grand denunciation of the mass-production-for-mass-consumption society, termed by him "Admass," and inspired more or less directly by the American experience.[29]

But figures such as Morpurgo and Priestley were not simply armchair regurgitaters of the starchy Victorian denunciations of mass society. Names such as these were invariably among those consulted when film censorship bureaucracies had to be set up and run or television regulation invented. As Valeria Camporesi has demonstrated, during the British debate on the introduction of privately run commercial television in 1954—the first nation in Europe to make this choice—the influence of such figures was crucial in ensuring that the American model in this field would *not* be emulated, just as in the early 1920s they had rejected the American model of commercial radio at the time of the BBC's founding.[30]

Yet the 1959 election under Harold Macmillan's premiership was carried on under a slogan *The Economist* had invented in 1954: "You've never had it so good." The leader of the Labour Party opposition, Gaitskell, was forced on the defensive. "Compared with prewar, most people are a good deal better off," he agreed. The consequences were worrying for a left-wing politician: "There are signs of the breaking up of traditional political loyalties." Specifically, wrote the British commentators Bogdanov and Skidelsky, "polarisation between worker and management was dissolving into the subtler hierarchies of a world based upon 'status symbols,' as measured by consumer goods—badges of the new affluence." Labour accused the Tories of substituting these symbols for issues, of selling Macmillan like a detergent, and of introducing "the worst sort of Americanisation."[31]

Whether the American cultural hegemony of the postwar years was stronger in Britain than in the other major Western European countries remains controversial. There was certainly no strong reaction against it as there had been in interwar Germany or postwar France.[32] For certain, British people lived through their own "revolution of rising expectations" in the 1950s and 1960s, and went on to demonstrate that out of it they could successfully produce their own new forms of mass culture—in television, music, fashion, advertising, and lifestyles. This spontaneous and youthful effort often involved building ingenious mechanisms for "appropriating" whatever was new and successful in the United States and transforming it, more or less consciously, more or less ironically, into a form of expression that was different and yet unmistakably British.[33]

The irony was that when the reaction to all this eventually found political expression in Britain, at the end of the 1970s, it was to another imaginary America that the new saviors of society looked for their ideals, their inspiration, and their vision of the good life.

The Thatcherite Crusade for Renewal

Thatcher admired America. Whenever she returned from a visit to the States, she was buzzing. This too was different from most of her predecessors. Old-line Tory thinking had customarily looked at America as a volatile, overgrown juvenile that would be much improved if it could just learn to be a bit more British. Thatcher reversed this by saying that Britain was a fine old place but should learn to be a little more like America.[34]

This was Raymond Seitz speaking, a career diplomat who had uniquely risen to the post of ambassador to the Court of Saint James and, equally exceptionally, wrote a memoir of his experiences, set in the era of the Major government between 1991 and 1994. By now it was legitimate to pass judgments on the results of the Thatcher years, and Seitz was not backward in coming forward with his own. The transformation, compared with the England he had first known in the 1970s, was, he said, "little short of miraculous." The "harrowing sense of British free-fall

[had] finally come to an end," because the economic agenda of the nation had been rewritten and the old stereotypes broken up. The place was "more flexible, adaptable, educated and competitive."[35]

Assuming all this to be true (and ignoring the costs and the contradictions), how had the American connection Mrs. Thatcher made so much of contributed to the result? Ever since World War II, the British had been looking for some new source of power to replace those that history had forced them to discard. Mrs. Thatcher believed that in her own person, by the force of her example, her convictions, and her results, the country might once more make its impress on the world. Among those convictions was the centrality of the "special relationship" to Britain's strength and sense of purpose in the world.

Historians have made much of the political consequences of all this, emphasizing the record number of Anglo-American summits held in these years, the closeness of the military and intelligence connections, the Falklands experience, and the collaboration generally on the renewal of the British nuclear deterrent, the Libya bombing of 1986, the Strategic Defense Initiative, cruise missiles, and Cold War strategy.[36]

Yet by the time Ambassador Seitz arrived in London, only months after Mrs. Thatcher's downfall in November 1990, he had vowed to himself never to use the phrase "special relationship": "Like a brass plate on a church floor, the words seemed a little worn from years of hard rubbing." But Seitz realized just how much it still meant to English ears. For some it was automatic and unquestionable, for others "a bromide should Europe prove ultimately indigestible." For the majority, though, it endured as a deep source of comfort and reassurance, especially during a Cold War crisis. Seitz, however, made clear that the last moment of glory for this postwar version had come and gone in the Gulf War collaboration of 1991. With the Cold War ended and no totalitarian enemy to face in Europe, America would look elsewhere for its priorities and its problems to solve, most likely starting at home.[37]

Meanwhile, Mrs. Thatcher's internal reforms had set the scene for a different kind of intertwining between the two nations. As the prime minister told a joint session of Congress on one of her most triumphal visits to Washington: "We are having to recover the spirit of enterprise which you never lost. Many of the policies you are following are the ones we are following." Citing the monetarist approach to inflation control, the elimination of bureaucracy and regulation, liberalization, privatization and popular capitalism, Mrs. Thatcher extolled the success of her new post-industrial version of the British economy. It was confirmed by the embrace of entrepreneurs and financiers across the Atlantic Ocean:

"America is by far the largest direct investor in Britain and I am delighted to say that Britain is the largest direct investor in the United States."[38]

From the beginning, political styles were thoroughly Americanized as the Conservative Party embraced without reserve all the latest techniques of political marketing in its election campaigns and party conferences.[39] As for the substance of policy, certain public sectors, in particular the school and university systems, were reformed again and again in the hope of hooking them up to the motor of economic growth in the way their equivalents were supposed to function in the United States.[40] Employment policy was explicitly modeled on Reaganite ideology and experience, as David Dolowitz has shown in a detailed, operational study of the transfer process. As well as specific policy structures, even the wording of legislation was directly copied.[41] The highly regulated broadcasting duopoly of the BBC and the Independent Television network was attacked frontally with the aim of producing a market-led commercial system, and the "enterprise culture" was imposed throughout the institutional world of the arts. Even inner-city renewal was promoted using models and connections from the United States.[42]

But the enduring legacy of all the policies and all the years of reforming zeal was much more mixed than these images would suggest. By the end of the 1980s, says Arthur Marwick, a leading social historian, social attitude surveys confirmed the persistence of "uniquely British characteristics, few of them conforming to Thatcherite ideas." In particular, attitudes to wealth creation, job security, and social services all continued little changed from previous eras of the welfare state. It was Marwick's conviction that "despite a Government openly admiring of American ways of doing things, and the spread in Britain, as never before, of a universalized American style and gimmickry, the Britishness of British life was still abundantly in evidence."[43] In the intense debate that followed her fall in 1990 on the meaning of the Thatcher years for the nation's past, present, and future, America and Americanization were barely mentioned.[44]

Now the Cold War Is Over—The British in the Age of Globalization

The world needs us to be different. I feel sufficiently confident in British capability to believe we have something important to offer. To be the bridge between the US and the EU would alone justify the argument I am making. But our influence can and should go far beyond that.[45]

This was what Tony Blair, in a major foreign policy speech of November 2000, called "enlightened patriotism," the Labour government's answer to the search for Britain's role in the post–Cold War world of the European Union and globalization. "There is a new world order whether we like it or not, and we need to decide our place in it," the prime minister declared.

Blair knew he could count on a sympathetic audience in Brussels for his ever-more arduous task of fighting British standoffishness to the European project and preparing public opinion for the great decision of whether to abandon the pound sterling. He also knew that, as ever, official attitudes in Washington would support a British government as long as it persevered in this direction. But Blair was clearly determined to turn his back on all the efforts made to discourage him and his predecessors from any other flight of fancy. In his 1998 memoir, Ambassador Seitz repeated the message he had been trying to get across throughout his sojourn, that harping on the "special relationship" was worse than useless—it was irrelevant: "For decades, America's transatlantic policy has been European in scope—one continent to another—not a series of compartmentalized, bilateral policies."[46]

Yet a senior American journalist in conversation with Tony Blair in April 2000 found that the bridge metaphor was not just a rhetorical device but reflected "a deep belief" about Britain's position in world affairs. Blair put himself forward as aiming to "help Europe understand where America is coming from, and to explain European concerns to America" on such issues as trade, missile defense, and the European intervention force. A year later, in a speech titled "Celebrating Britishness," his foreign secretary, Robin Cook, restated the point, as did the chancellor of the exchequer in July 2001 when promoting new multilateral trade talks.[47]

The problem Blair and his government seemed unable to grasp was that at the same time the Americans were explicitly setting aside his notion of Britain's bridging function, the Europeans were simply ignoring it. They had become used to addressing their concerns directly to the American president, and by the late 1990s they were beginning to express one particular preoccupation, which the British official mind did not appear to comprehend, let alone share. This was that the most powerful form of the rising force of globalization was in many respects just a new and more virulent variety of the old Americanization challenge. As such, opinion leaders in continental Europe were beginning to see in it a renewed threat to their various forms of national sovereignty, especially where the latest expressions of technological and commercial modernity were thought to impinge most, at the level of collective identity. On the occasion of the meeting of the Third Way leaders in Florence in November 1999, Chancellor Schroeder of Germany, President Chirac of France, and the host Italians through their culture minister, Giovanna Melandri, separately and together made points on this issue. Of British intervention in this area there was no discernible trace.[48]

The open pleas by European leaders on this occasion for the United States to respect all the forms of "cultural diversity" on display in the Old World reflected a growing sensitivity to the fact that traditional divisions between political, economic, and strategic power, on the one hand, and the force of America's mass culture on the other, were breaking down. Some years earlier, the Harvard political scientist Joseph Nye had identified and categorized these elements as "hard" power and "soft" power, with soft power being the ability—as he put it—to make others like what America liked. Now, it seemed, they could no longer be so easily separated: "hard" questions were getting softer, and "soft" questions harder. In the contemporary international or globalized system of production and consumption, mass culture was now recognized for what it had in fact always been since the 1920s: a form or currency of power.[49]

Although hardly ever debated as such in the United Kingdom, the British version of a common European experience was not difficult to trace. In April 1998, reported *The Economist,* "of the current top ten movies in Britain's cinemas nine are American, in France's seven, in Spain's ten, in Germany's nine and in Italy's nine." At the end of 1999, out of the ten most-visited Internet sites in the United Kingdom, eight were American owned.[50] During that decade the country had witnessed the arrival of discount shopping malls, twenty-four-hour hypermarkets, Wal-Mart, Borders, and Starbucks. By the year 2000, the total number of McDonald's "outlets" was 884, putting the number of hamburger franchises in Britain second in Europe behind Germany. Meanwhile the Perfect Pizza company's research indicated that "if, as expected, we follow the American trend in eating and lifestyle, the British will soon be eating three times as many pizzas as they do now."[51]

Yet opinion makers in politics, the media, and the leading national institutions dwelt less on the workings of American power in their midst than on their own renewed sense of rootlessness and loss of self-confidence. The consequences of the end of the Cold War and the prospect of a European monetary union were realities that could not be avoided, but they felt so much more difficult to face up to as new internal fractures opened up with the repeated crises of the House of Windsor, the rise and fall of hopes in Ireland, and the ever more vociferous demands for decentralization coming from Scotland and Wales. Although the economy was eventually stabilized after a phase of panic in 1992–93, and Tony Blair would go on to claim it was the fourth largest in the world, a high-tech model for the rest, few outside the country were convinced.[52] Above all, the long-term effects of the Thatcher revolution were becoming increasingly obvious, dividing more sharply than ever the winners from the losers.

The authoritative cultural historian Robert Hewison blamed the impact of Thatcherite values for what he perceived as a new crisis of national identity. Dominated as these values were entirely by the priorities of the marketplace, the Thatcherite legacy could not possibly transmute into "fresh symbols of national significance." Once there had been enduring ideas binding people to the national destiny—"community, cohesion, discipline, endurance, a shared sense of history"; now "these themes have been re-arranged as the muzak of theme-park Britain," courtesy of the Department of National Heritage.[53] The veteran social commentator Paul Barker announced a new quest for the meaning of Englishness, one that was more "urgent" and "fraught" than ever. The English were feeling squeezed, he reported, caught between Scotland, the European Union, and the United States. The London media were reduced to judging cultural output only in terms of its success across the Atlantic: "How un-self-confident can a nation get?"[54]

Again, the old shibboleth of Americanization was called on to bear some of the strain of the argument. A *Guardian* writer talked of a land where "almost every provincial town has a greenfield development complete with multiplex cinema, tenpin bowling, a fast-food joint and acres of parking space."[55] Bishops, arts critics, and prison reformers alike denounced the "slavish" dedication of the Conservative governments to the American example in the preceding seventeen years. So surprise and dismay accompanied the discovery that the bright new Labour government of Tony Blair was even more enthralled by the U.S. model than were its unloved Tory predecessors. Its supporters in the think tanks urged the prime minister and his colleagues to look specifically to California for their most relevant model, while friends in the Goldman Sachs Foundation promised to finance a new government program aimed at promoting "a new U.S.–style culture of entrepreneurship" among young people. In a rather maladroit effort to satirize all this, former *Guardian* editor Peter Preston wrote a fantasy novel, *51st State,* in which a grotesque series of political misadventures transform the United Kingdom, by way of NAFTA, into one of the United States, eventually propelling its bewildered ex–prime minister into the White House.[56]

This Gale-Swept Chip

In 1964 the distinguished Harvard political scientist Stanley Hoffmann was already able to discern how "The more European societies become alike in their social structures and economic makeup, the more each national society seems to heighten its idiosyncrasies."[57] In contrast with much continental experience, British political and media culture seemed to seek as comfortable an accommodation with whatever the United States offered as could profitably be arranged. "Labour is pragmatic, and will cherry-pick ideas from anywhere provided they work," said a *Guardian* commentator soon after the 1997 election. "As far as Labour is concerned, the U.S. works when it comes to job creation, and Europe doesn't."[58]

Britain was once characterized by a Welsh political scientist, at the end of a long study on the subject, as a "much governed nation." Ever since the beginning of the century-long debate on national decline and how to reverse it, the assumption was that, in any event, control, governance, and order would be maintained and that no matter how hard the blows of fate, whatever became of British society was exclusively the responsibility of the nation's people and its rulers. No one else could be blamed if things went wrong and disappointments piled up.[59] So as a fresh wave of setbacks crashed over the islands from the mid-1990s onward, the process of self-analysis was once more set in motion.

The intractability of the nation's problems was demonstrated by the fate of the National Health Service. Opinion polls repeatedly expressed comprehensive support for the service—"the institution that always comes out on top . . . as the one that represents the best about being British," said Labour's leading expert on national identity.[60] And yet years of effort to reform, refinance, and re-launch the system were clearly failing. As in so many other areas of public provision, the disasters multiplied, public discontent soared, and no amount of extra funding from a government that had identified its very destiny with this keystone of the welfare state seemed able to guarantee its effectiveness. In the end, said a large-scale *Wall Street Journal* survey, one question stood out above all others:

Britain hasn't decided whether it wants to be a Continental European-style welfare state, with the government ensuring high-quality social services for all, or a U.S.–style bastion of capitalism, with lower taxes and services left largely to local authorities or private enterprise.

Lower taxes guaranteed poor-quality schools and hospitals, said the survey, yet eighteen years of the Thatcherite supply-side revolution had failed to revolutionize either the public or the private sectors in the way the United States had done. A prominent German businessman with long experience in the country was quoted as saying that the country was "falling between the two models," gaining few of the advantages of either of them, "but many of the disadvantages that the U.S. suffers from."[61]

As the day of the great currency choice approached, British ministers insisted their economy was structurally "in synch" with America's rather than Europe's, even though its performance was but a pale shadow of what had happened on the other side of the Atlantic in the 1990s. In the end, the Tory Party had torn itself apart over the dilemma of the two models and its inability to link them with the best of Britain's heritage to create something distinctively national and unmistakably successful. As the rest of the nation's experts, politicians, opinion makers, and voters contemplated the symbolic nature of the decision awaiting them, it looked as though a similar fate was hanging over them all.

Notes

1. *Financial Times,* February 24–25, 2001.

2. *The Guardian,* March 12, 2001.

3. *The Guardian,* January 5, 2001.

4. *Prospect,* February, 2001, 28.

5. Martin Weiner, *English Culture and the Decline of the Industrial Spirit, 1850–1980* (Cambridge: Cambridge University Press, 1981); Patrick Wright, *On Living in an Old Country: The National Past in Contemporary Britain* (London: Verso, 1985); R. Hoggart, *The Way We Live Now* (London: Chatto and Windus, 1995); Will Hutton, *The State We're In* (London: Jonathan Cape, 1995).

6. E. J. Hobsbawm, *Industry and Empire: An Economic History of Britain since 1750* (London: History Book Club, 1968), 7.

7. James Morgan, *Financial Times,* August 31–September 1, 1996.

8. Jonathan Freedland, *Bring Home the Revolution: How Britain Can Live the American Dream* (London: Fourth Estate, 1998), esp. chap. 10.

9. Cf. Norman Rose, *The Cliveden Set: Portrait of an Exclusive Fraternity* (London: Jonathan Cape, 2000), 2–3, 45, 214–15.

10. Conversation between Wilson and King George V, quoted in David Dimbleby and

148   *David W. Ellwood*

David Reynolds, *An Ocean Apart: The Relationship between Britain and America in the Twentieth Century* (London: Hodder and Stoughton, 1988), 64.

11. D. Reynolds, "Roosevelt, Churchill, and the Wartime Anglo-American Alliance, 1929–45: Towards a New Synthesis," in *The Special Relationship": Anglo-American Relations Since 1945*, ed. William R. Louis and H. Bull (Oxford: Clarendon Press, 1985), 17–41, quotation on 17.

12. In 2000, a new pressure group, the Anglosphere, emerged to unite prestigious conservative believers in the Anglo-American connection; see O. Harries, ed., "The Anglosphere Illusion," *National Interest*, spring 2001.

13. P. J. Cain and A. G. Hopkins, *British Imperialism: Crisis and Deconstruction, 1914–1990* (London: Longman, 1993), 298.

14. Ludwell Denny, *America Conquers Britain: A Record of Economic War* (New York: Knopf, 1930), 123.

15. Frank Costigliola, *Awkward Dominion: American Political, Economic and Cultural Relations with Europe, 1919–1933* (Ithaca: Cornell University Press, 1984), 19.

16. D. L. LeMahieu, *A Culture for Democracy: Mass Culture and the Cultivated Mind in Britain between the Wars* (Oxford: Clarendon Press, 1988), chap. 3.

17. George Harmon Knoles, *The Jazz Age Revisited: British Criticism of American Civilization during the 1920s* (Stanford: Stanford University Press), chap. 2.

18. Andrew Higson, *Waving the Flag: Constructing a National Cinema in Britain* (Oxford: Clarendon Press, 1995), 9–13; LeMahieu, *Culture for Democracy*, 82, 88–98.

19. R. Ovendale, "The End Of Empire," in *Rethinking Britain's Decline*, ed. Richard English and Michael Kenny (London: Macmillan Press, 2000), 261–62.

20. Quoted in Robert Eccleshall, "Party Ideology and National Decline," in *Rethinking Britain's Decline*, ed. English and Kenny, 175.

21. S. Hall, interview, ibid., 110–11.

22. David Reynolds, *Rich Relations: The American Occupation of Britain, 1942–1945* (London: HarperCollins, 1995), chap. 24.

23. J. Tomlinson and N. Tiratsoo, "Americanisation beyond the Mass Production Paradigm: The Case of British Industry," in *The Americanisation of European Business: The Marshall Plan and the Transfer of U.S. Management Models*, ed. Matthias Kipping and Ove Bjarnar (London: Routledge, 1998).

24. Definition supplied by E. Luttwak, *Times Literary Supplement*, June 10, 1994.

25. M. M. Postan, *An Economic History of Western Europe, 1945–1967* (London: Methuen, 1967), 49.

26. Dick Hebdige, *Hiding the Light: On Images and Things* (London: Routledge, 1988), chap. 3.

27. Ibid., 52–58; Christopher Booker, *The Neophiliacs* (London: Fontana, 1970), 32–33.

28. J. E. Morpurgo, "Hollywood: America's Voice," in *The Impact of America on European Culture*, ed. Bertrand Russell (Boston: Little, Brown, 1951); Hebdige, *Hiding the Light*, 56–58.

29. J. B. Priestley and J. Hawkes, *Journey down the Rainbow* (London: Collins, 1955), 43–45.

30. Valeria Camporesi, *Mass Culture and National Traditions: The BBC and American Broadcasting, 1922–1954* (Florence: European Press Academic Publishing, 2000), 43–48.

31. Quotation in David Ellwood, *Rebuilding Europe: Western Europe, America, and Postwar Reconstruction, 1945–1995* (London: Longmans, 1992), 229.

32. J. Black, *Modern British History since 1900* (London: Macmillan, 2000), 326, 330–31.

33. Cf. ibid., 283–84; Booker, *Neophiliacs*, 228–29; Hebdige, *Hiding the Light*, 73–74.

34. Raymond Seitz, *Over Here* (London: Phoenix, 1998), 318–19.

35. Ibid., 221–24.

36. Alan P. Dobson, *Anglo-American Relations in the Twentieth Century* (London: Routledge, 1995), 150–62.

37. Seitz, *Over Here*, 325–27.

38. Speech of February 20, 1985, reprinted in M. Thatcher, *In Defence of Freedom: Speeches on Britain's Relations with the World, 1976–1986* (London: Aurum Press, 1986), quotations on 112–13.

39. Eric J. Evans, *Thatcher and Thatcherism* (London: Routledge, 1997), 48.

40. See P. R. G. Tomlinson, "The Schools," and Peter Scott, "Higher Education," in *The Thatcher Effect: A Decade of Change*, eds. Dennis Kavanagh and Antony Seldon (Oxford: Oxford University Press, 1991), 183–97 and 198–212, respectively.

41. David P. Dolowitz, *Learning from America: Policy Transfer and the Development of the British Workfare State* (Brighton: Sussex Academic Press, 1998), 26–27, 108, 143; quotation at 175.

42. Robert Hewison, *Culture and Consensus: England, Art and Politics since 1940* (London: Methuen, 1995), chaps. 7 and 8.

43. Arthur Marwick, *British Society since 1945*, 3d ed. (London: Penguin, 1996), 371–72.

44. Hugo Young, *One of Us: A Biography of Margaret Thatcher* (London: Pan Books, 1990); Ivor Crewe, "Values: The Crusade That Failed," in *Thatcher Effect*, eds. Kavanagh and Seldon, 239–50. F. Bédarida, *A Social History of Britain, 1851–1990*, 2d ed. (London: Methuen, 1991), postscript.

45. Tony Blair, speech of November 13, 2000 (www.fco.gov.uk).

46. Seitz, *Over Here*, 308–9, 334.

47. Jim Hoagland, *International Herald Tribune*, April 17, 2000; cf. former secretary of state for Northern Ireland, Peter Mandelson, *The World Today*, November 2000; Cook's speech at www.fco.gov.uk; Brown's at www.hm-treasury.gov.uk.

48. On Jospin, *Le Monde*, November 23, 1999; Schroeder interview, *Le Monde*, November 20, 1999; Melandri, *L'Unità*, November 13, 1999.

49. Joseph S. Nye, *Bound to Lead: The Changing Nature of American Power* (New York: Basic Books, 1990), 31–35.

50. *The Economist*, April 11, 1998; Internet figures quoted in *Financial Times*, January 8, 2000.

51. Figures on McDonald's from the annual report, January 2000; on pizzas, *The Guardian*, August 30, 2000.

52. A large-scale survey of images of the United Kingdom among young people worldwide by the British Council, the official cultural and educational organization, reported: "They are critical of our social relationships and do not regard us as especially creative or innovative. In general [they] respect us more than they like us—and they find America more attractive" (www.britishcouncil.org/work/survey).

53. Hewison, *Culture and Consensus*, 307.

54. *The Guardian*, December 22, 1997.

55. *The Guardian*, April 30, 1996.

56. C. Leadbetter, *Britain: The California of Europe?* (London: Demos, 1997); on Goldman Sachs Foundation, *Financial Times*, June 1, 2001; Peter Preston, *51st State* (London: Viking, 1998).

57. The title refers to literary critic Cyril Connolly's ironic contribution to the influential collection *Suicide of a Nation?* (London: Hutchinson, 1963). The quotation is from

Stanley Hoffmann, "Europe's Identity Crisis: Between the Past and America" (1964), in Hoffmann, *The European Sisyphus: Essays on Europe 1964–1994* (Boulder, Colo.: West-view Press, 1995), 18.

58. *The Guardian,* December 22, 1997.
59. W. H. Greenleaf, *The British Political Tradition,* vol. 3 (London: Methuen, 1987).
60. Interview with Michael Wills, *New Statesman,* March 26, 2001.
61. *Wall Street Journal,* March 9–10, 2001.

American Religion as Cultural Imperialism

R. LAURENCE MOORE

A passage in Salman Rushdie's *The Ground Beneath Her Feet* neatly characterized the propellant force of American cultural imperialism as "greenbacks, set to music." He meant rock music and jazz, not Charles Ives. Rushdie's phrase invites endless expansion. Hollywood obviously. Casual fashion, soft drinks, fast food, Michael Jordan. America's marketplace of commercial culture is vast and has over the past century extended itself around the globe. This chapter is an effort to view Protestant evangelical religion, in its many American styles, as one important item in that marketplace. As a beginning point, it takes seriously the politically heated charge made by Alfredo Silletta, an Argentine, that American sectarian religions are the not-so-spiritual counterparts of American multinational corporations. They have acted as *multinacionales de la fe* and in that role have promoted American interests abroad. Bill Gates may be important, but Billy Graham prefigured him.[1]

Silletta worries primarily about what he calls American cults, a loaded term that signifies to him a motley range of rapidly growing non-Catholic groups that are funded from the United States. The Jehovah's Witnesses, the Hare Krishnas, Moonies, and the Children of God are more than nuisances. Stilletta regards their aggressive adherents as carriers of ideological and cultural assumptions that threaten to disrupt progressive elements in Latin America and perpetuate regimes friendly to Yankee corporate interests. Silletta's general point of view has been bruited almost everywhere in Latin America. American *evangelistas,* and

151

one can throw into the mix all Protestant missionaries, are agents of the CIA. Roman Catholic officials have not discouraged this opinion; it operates, however, in a political context that is recognizably Marxist. Protestant proselytizing, so the charge goes, is enlisted to dampen revolutionary activity against authoritarian regimes. Encouraged by Washington, Protestant sects accepted a covert mission to prepare Latin America to welcome the particular brand of capitalism exported from America.

The American government has done plenty to make these views plausible, even if it has not been an important sponsor of American religious groups in South America or anywhere else. Unquestionably, aggressive religious proselytizing, privately sponsored, has acted in concert with more obvious forms of state-sponsored intervention. American missionaries have wittingly and unwittingly promoted abroad various versions of the American model for organizing religious communities. Along with a host of elected and appointed officials in the United States, they have sanctimoniously charged other countries with the repression of religious freedom. These actions, whether or not they may be justified, are interventions that have convinced many people that Americans, whenever they talk about religion elsewhere, are selling a whole gamut of American political and economic values.

After the Great War, when American power took a great leap forward, officials in the Middle East, in Asia, and in Africa often viewed American efforts to Christianize the world as equivalent to efforts to establish American interests abroad. One can track in the *New York Times* of the 1920s regular reports about the alleged political meddling of American missionaries in other nations' affairs. This chapter focuses on Europe. The issues here are somewhat different than in other parts of the globe. The United States, after all, is largely Christian because Europeans were largely Christian before they crossed the Atlantic, and American missionaries in the nineteenth century learned their craft from the Europeans who preceded them to outposts in Asia and Africa. In the twentieth century, therefore, American Protestant missionaries had to profess to aims in Europe that were other than its "Christianization." Even so, although the goal was not conversion, although much of the work in Europe was relief work, American religious workers hoped to change the forms of Christianity they found in Europe. To do that, they exported a particular style of religion that many Europeans, especially on the Continent, viewed as an effort to imprint the American Way firmly upon European cultures.

American Religion on the World Stage: The Origins

In 1900, when grievances against European imperialism had already stirred significant political opposition, the United States had only begun to operate on a world stage. In 1900 the target of most indigenous complaints made in Asia and Africa was European missionaries, not American ones. Nonetheless, in religious matters the United States moved quickly to the forefront. Arguably it became the major missionary power of the world faster than it achieved clear dominance in any other area. Good reasons quickly developed to link the twentieth-century work of Protestant missionary groups with general programs to Americanize the world.

American religious triumphalism had long been in the making. It burst into spectacular view during the World's Parliament of Religions, an extravagant event that was held in conjunction with Chicago's Columbian Exposition in 1893. That affair, made famous by a press corps awed by the pomp and color exhibited by religious dignitaries from non-Christian parts of the globe, just preceded America's most ambitious initiatives in expansion beyond its continental borders. The timing was coincidental, but what happened at the parliament set the tone for America's spiritual self-confidence when loosed upon the world.

The World's Parliament of Religions was an invention of American liberal Protestantism. Judged against many dogmatic Christian spokesmen who wanted no part of the parliament, the Presbyterian John Henry Barrows, who chaired the sessions, was a tolerant man who was genuinely interested in learning about the other great religions of the world. He and other organizers were in their own way thrilled to welcome in Chicago leading religious teachers from Asia, including most famously Swami Vivekananda from India. Yet although the event deserves recognition for encouraging the study of comparative religion, it was also part and parcel of a heady and aggressive movement within American Protestantism to "evangelize the world in this generation."[2]

Several years after John Barrows had banged the final gavel closing the Parliament of Religions and had assumed the presidency of Oberlin College, he articulated the popular opinion that the United States bore the responsibility for world redemption. For almost the first half of the twentieth century, America's most famous missionary voice belonged to the remarkable John R. Mott. Mott was a Cornell graduate who turned the intercollegiate YMCA movement into a potent religious force on American campuses and spent his life working for the Y in its foreign missions. The Student Volunteer Movement for Foreign Missions that he founded in 1888 became the World's Student Christian Federation. These agencies along with the missionary societies of individual denominations and the Foreign Missions Conference of North America provided a significant portion of the money and personnel of American Protestant missionary work in the world. Mott's prominence owed something to his political connections, which in turn gave Mott a reputation for conflating Christian expansion with American expansion. He was a friend of Woodrow Wilson and accepted diplomatic missions both in Mexico and Russia. He also was close to Herbert Hoover, who was one of those who nominated Mott for the Nobel Peace Prize that he finally won in 1946.

Mott was cosmopolitan by the standards of the time, an indefatigable and curious world traveler. His unabashed goal, however, was to participate in an American transformation of international affairs through Protestant evangelical work. At the turn of the century, American money was making a difference in the World Missionary Conference, an organization centered in Great Britain but with Continental and growing American participation. Missionary societies in Great Britain had total resources of more than $9 million in 1900, followed by an American total of just under $6 million. The gap was closing. Mott, who reflected the American obsession with growth in numbers, celebrated the leadership of the American YMCA for gaining statistical superiority over England's YMCA. England had invented the YMCA, but Americans made it powerful: "We have the men, we have the money, we have the methods. . . . It is estimated that at least five-sixths of the employed officers and five-sixths of the property of the Associations of the world are on this side of the two oceans."[3]

The financial and other advantages of the United States increased dramatically after the outbreak of war in Europe in 1914. During the course of the war, the American YMCA raised more than $150 million in relief funds and served more than twenty million soldiers.[4] It worked in prisoner of war camps, both before the United States entered the Great War and during the period of American involvement. It set up recreation areas for allied soldiers, trying hard to maintain a distance from America's war policy or for that matter from its own brand of Protestant Christianity. Wherever it had authority to do so, it established religious services for all creeds and denominations.

Even so, American YMCA workers acted in ways that left little doubt about their national provenance. To host countries, American religious workers looked much the same as American Red Cross workers or the Americans that Herbert Hoover mobilized for relief work at the end of the hostilities. They sold themselves as agents of American goodwill that European prisoners of war would remember "as they set their faces toward home." According to training instructions given to American Y workers, disinterested but highly visible work in Greece, Rumania, Russia, Poland, and Czechoslovakia would "prove in the end of the greatest advantage to the interests of America." "It showed that what the other nations call our 'passion for uplift' is not so dangerous as they are inclined to believe, that service does not necessarily mean patronage or coddling. It exhibited the conception of a Christianity of practical effort, dissipating many fears generated by oppressive religious systems of the Old World." American ideals, exemplified in this way, held great promise for the future.[5]

The war decimated the resources of European missionary societies. In contrast, the financial gifts to American Christian agencies for relief work and missionary enterprises both in Europe and elsewhere continued to swell into the early 1920s. One reason for the increase was a sensed opportunity to expand American influence. Clear lines between economic influence and religious/moral influence did not exist. American missionaries adopted an unyielding opposition to the newly formed Soviet Union, both because of its godlessness and its opposition to capitalism. Mott, who remained a world ambassador for American Christianity, declared to a group of Chicago businessmen in 1925 his "unqualifiedly uncompromising warfare" against the Bolsheviks. Both their economic theories of class warfare and their attempt to build a nation without religion threatened Christianity. Mott urged his audience to donate generously to American missionary enterprises as a sound investment in pressing American economic advantage in the world.[6] Speaking in Egypt in 1926, he joined the work of the YMCA with that of the World's Bankers Association, the World's Chamber of Commerce, and the World's Advertiser Clubs: "The world expansion of commerce, industry, and finance constitutes another great force which should tell more and more for the stabilization, unification, and upbuilding of the world."[7]

In this context, Europeans began to voice their first concerns about the threat of American hegemony. After the Great War, other American missionary leaders traveled regularly to Europe to participate in congresses dedicated to the joint American/European project of enlightening the rest of the world. The weight of American influence became a subject of explicit criticism, especially from the defeated and economically devastated Germany. Some prominent German theologians charged that the American evangelicals were up to no good in Europe. The German Heinrich Frick wondered suspiciously why so many American missionaries in the 1920s were working in Europe. Why were they seeking to convert people who were already Christian? Or was there another agenda beyond conversion? Europeans needed to understand that Mott was "first of all an American and then a Christian."[8]

Frick had special reasons to complain. The Treaty of Versailles had in effect placed Germany's missionary property under American and British control. However, other European religious leaders emphasized the difference between an American style of religion and what most of them valued. Continental critics of American Protestant Christianity warned against its activist and result orientation. It was, they said, too much focused on numbers—the number of missionaries in the field, the amount of money raised, the number of missions opened, the body count of alleged conversions. Quick results were all that mattered, especially after the American missionary establishment took as its own the slogan "Evangelization of the world in this generation." In this discussion clustered all of the clichés about American practicality and materialism.

American Protestants did not shrink from the accusation of practicality. It was in fact a trait they embraced along with the need for Madison Avenue–style advertising. To them, the favorable consequences of practicality were obvious. American churches were growing. Attendance at European churches was declining. Slowly, however, American missionary leaders in the 1920s began to worry about the perception that their Christian activism was merely another manifestation of American boosterism. They told themselves that their relief work was an absolutely necessary and much appreciated act of charity and that their work to establish various Protestant churches in Europe was politically neutral. However, they also knew that they never meant to leave things in Europe quite as they found them.

American Baptists and Methodists had not even tried to disguise that fact when they first set up missions in Catholic Italy. A celebratory book written in 1929, *Southern Baptists in Sunny Italy,* was part of a long history of conflict between Italian authorities and American Protestant missionaries. It had started as early as 1869 when the Foreign Missions Board of the Southern Baptist Convention first thought of giving attention to Europe. To justify an effort there, the board wrote: "It is a mournful fact that the wide prevalence of anti-Christian doctrines and forms of worship has rendered many portions of that continent as truly in need of Christian sympathy and missionary enterprise as any portion of the heathen world."[9] American Methodists, no less than Baptists, courted unpopularity in Italy in the late nineteenth and early twentieth century. One Methodist leader after another attacked Italian Catholicism as pagan, intellectually sterile, bacchanalian, and downright evil. They made it their mission to show the Italian people that Roman Catholicism is not Christianity.

In the early 1920s American Methodists proceeded with plans to build a boys' collegio on Monte Mario, a site about a mile from the Vatican with a view overlooking the Vatican gardens and Saint Peter's. The American side termed it an effort to emancipate Italian youth from a church hostile to free thought: "The only imperialism in it [the collegio] is the imperialism of a pure Gospel." But for the rest of the decade this educational institution became, from the viewpoint of Italian journalists and public officials, a symptom of American "empire" building. It was an assault on national integrity: "These Methodist institutions, no matter how carefully they seek to disguise themselves in the flags of the various nations among whom they spread their propaganda, are effective organs of Anglo-Saxon propaganda and penetration. It is a movement which must be closely watched, because it is against out interests and against the peoples, the civilization and the traditions of the Latin world."[10] The Methodist school was an insult not just to Catholicism but to the Italian nation and its culture.

The battle over the Methodist school on Monte Mario resulted mostly in an Italian victory. Italian culture survived the American Methodist onslaught. However, the process made explicit how close to the surface was American Protestant disapproval of European religious practice. During the 1920s, American Protestants had fewer nasty things to say about European Protestants than about European Catholics. The European Protestant state church was nonetheless a mistake. Every church that Americans funded in northern Europe represented an effort to spread the American gospel of church disestablishment. Bishop Daniel Goodsell of the American Methodist mission called the ministers of German Lutheranism "state-hired, time-serving functionaries." Germany's national church," he continued, "is associated with a social system favorable to the few and rich and resting as a burden on the heavily taxed, landless, and exploited poor."[11] The resident Methodist bishop assigned to Copenhagen, the Reverend Anton Bast, was equally blunt about the Lutheran state churches in Scandinavia: "There are now—thank God for the Methodist Episcopal Church of America—Methodist Churches distributed over the whole territory of Scandinavia and Finland." Even if the state churches did not die out, they would be forced to become more democratic.[12]

Underlying the suspicion of American utilitarian Christianity and its espousal of church/state separation was fear of the formidable American money machine. By 1925, the United States accounted for two-thirds of the total amount of Protestant missionary funds raised in Europe and America. That ratio encouraged Americans to speak openly of European decline. At the end of 1922, Cornelius H. Patton enthusiastically surveyed the opportunities awaiting Americans around the world:

We can no longer count upon continental Europe to assume any considerable part in the evangelization of the world. The great Powers of the continent are bankrupt and broken. Europe has become a liability instead of an asset. . . . To prosperous and powerful America comes the call to assume the heavy end of the load. Can there be any question that God is calling upon us to lead off in this mighty undertaking?[13]

Mott, as usual, lumped American diplomatic undertakings together with religious initiatives. In 1925, at a conference of the Foreign Missionary Convention of the United States and Canada, addressed by President Calvin Coolidge and attended by Secretary of State Charles Evans Hughes, Mott followed other speakers in urging closer cooperation between churches and American diplomacy. "The moment has come," Mott said, "when we must emphasize as never before the drawing together of Christian forces. The nearly 30,000 missionaries whom we represent should be regarded not only as ambassadors, but in reality, as they are, interpreters and mediators between peoples and civilizations."[14] Mott's enthusiasms managed to link American Christianity with the American railroad system. American railroads were by far the best in the world because "we had liberty. We didn't have impossible restrictions, we had a long enough period to work out our very best ideas singly and cooperatively before we had anything that would put limitations upon us." So it was with American religion, which prospered everywhere because of the lack of restriction and the freedom for private individuals to work out strategies unmolested by government.[15] The American ideals that built railroads and churches would shape the next generation of leaders in Europe.

One positive side of Mott's spirit was its opposition to any form of American isolationism. Along with Mott, most Protestant missionary journals strongly endorsed American diplomatic efforts during the 1920s on behalf of world peace. They cautioned national leaders against any temptation to retreat into internal matters or to break intellectual and political links with Europe. American Protestant churches deserve some credit for their awareness that Europe was headed for another disaster. The downside of Mott's approach was that it fully endorsed American unilateral action. It was willing to use aggressive means to export American standards to unwilling markets. They did not always work. Nothing better illustrated this fact than the efforts made by American Protestant during the 1920s to sell American Prohibition to the nations of Europe. Reports that the French and the Italians were about to give up wine, and the Germans and English, beer, were unaccountably glowing and led to disappointment. There was other evidence of failure as well. American-funded churches in Europe remained marginal operations. By the middle of the 1920s, American contributions to missionary societies were sinking and Protestant societies cut back their programs in Europe.

Some Protestant groups welcomed the retreat and raised questions about the appropriateness of what they had been doing. They took notice of their European critics. For example, J. H. Oldham, the editor of the *International Review of Missions* published in Edinburgh, had warned shortly after Versailles against the danger of missionary work "dominated by the financial objective." The campaign for war bonds, with all the attendant advertising, should not be the model for raising funds for missionary work: "The Church of Christ has fundamentally different aims from war loans and even from the Red Cross Society; and certain vital aspects of the Church may be obscured in the public mind if it comes to be thought of primarily as a body engaged in raising large sums of money." The very ability of American agencies to raise money led to fears about Americanization. "The world is not willing to be americanized any more than it is willing to be anglicized or germanized."[16]

Oldham did not use the word *imperialism,* but others did. The American retreat from Europe was hastened in the 1930s by events in Germany, Italy, and Spain, and the missionary work of America's largest and oldest Protestant denominations went through a period of redefinition. One lay group of liberals, representing seven Protestant denominations, issued in 1932 an important report on American missions in China, Japan, Burma, and India. The study, titled *Re-Thinking Missions: A Lay-*

man's Inquiry after One Hundred Years, sharply criticized Western arrogance toward other world religions. The strong report suggested that trying to implant the Christian church as a superior religion ignored the richness of other cultures. Perhaps conversion should no longer be the central aim of missionary activities. Although "conversion" had never been the announced intention of Protestant missionary work in Europe, the aim had gone well beyond relief work. American Protestant missionaries wanted to change the church habits of Europeans. Thus, many of the strictures raised by this study were as relevant to American missionary work in Europe as to work in Asia.

Despite the cautions and the actual reduction of activities, the leadership of American Protestant missionary societies and of the YMCA movement did not entirely give up their vision of bringing the world under a single order sponsored by Christianity. It was Americans who drove the move to found the World's Council of Churches in 1948. Among the prominent people participating in that organization was the future American secretary of state John Foster Dulles, who in the early 1940s warned of the danger of secular faiths, by which he meant communism. It was incumbent on the United States, he said, to lead a worldwide crusade for a religion to unite all countries. He had Christianity in mind. Dulles had moved only slightly beyond the perspective of the American Protestants who had organized the World's Parliament of Religions. The Second World War gave that perspective a new lease on life. The American Century recommenced, with the dangers of secular faiths that Dulles had warned of now crystallized in the Soviet Union.

The Cold War

The devastation of Europe's civilian populations during World War II surpassed by far what had happened to them between 1914 and 1918. American relief societies, which included religious groups, again had the opportunity to work in Europe. The more important fact, however, was the onset of the Cold War, which effectively turned American religious denominations into partisan supporters of Washington's efforts to defeat the "godless" Soviet Union. The American Protestant denominations that had been most active in Europe in the early twentieth century were now less evident in Europe. They were replaced by a whole new set of religions that included independent Baptists, none more important than Billy Graham, the Pentecostals, Jehovah's Witnesses, and Mormons. As we shall see, the new groups became emblems of freedom in the Cold War ideological struggles. Even so, the older Protestant groups in the United States first defined what was at stake and gave a political tone to all American evangelical activity.

In 1947 delegates to the fifty-third annual meeting of the Foreign Missions Conference of North America urged an effort to push back the "steadily increasing adherence to the materialistic faith of Marxian philosophy, fostered by the expanding influence of the Soviet Union." Its resolution pinpointed the danger of Stalin's "military conquests, political coercion and able propaganda" as forcefully as any statement issued by the U.S. State Department.[17] A year later, at a World Mission Assembly sponsored by the Foreign Missions Conference of North America, Dr. Ralph Diffendorfer, the secretary of the Missions and Church Extension of the Methodist Church, warned again of "Communist ideology." It spoke "to the hungry and the landless, the debt-ridden and the oppressed. . . . They [the communists] can be pushed back only by the forceful offensive of an idea and program that stops them in their tracks. Christians must either serve the needs of all God's men better than the Communists do or else prepare to yield ground to them. The issue is that clear." Diffendorfer's doctrine of Christian containment tracked closely the more famous document penned by George Kennan.[18]

The tone of urgency swelled yearly at the meetings of the North American Foreign Missions Conference. By 1949, Soviet ideology had become the church's "number one rival." "Not since the spread of Islam from Arabia in the seventh and eighth century," a detailed conference document declared, "has the church met such a combination of fanatical zeal and political expansionism." Such statements made it easy for communist and leftist leaders in Africa, Asia, and Latin America to equate American Protestant activity with American foreign policy. American missionaries were variously branded as apostles of colonialism, imperialism, and white supremacy. In India, a government investigation into missionary activities in the state of Madhya Pradesh concluded that "evangelization in India appears to be part of the uniform world policy to revive Christendom for re-establishing Western supremacy and is not prompted by spiritual motives."[19]

Although the United States government in fact moved slowly to inject human rights, including religious freedom, into the rhetoric of the Cold War (it had too many allies around the world that cared little about human rights, and it had its own domestic problems with racial injustice), religion became a useful issue in the early Cold War—for both the Soviet Union and the United States. The United States linked efforts to restrict religious expression in Communist countries to their Marxist godlessness. For its part, the Soviet Union happily cast religion, especially sectarian groups founded in the United States, as enemies of the state. Both sides played their roles predictably for at least twenty years with little variation in the script.

Americans scripted a drama with religious groups playing roles that accentuated the differences between countries on opposite sides of the Iron Curtain. In the early 1950s, Jehovah's Witnesses were in constant trouble in Eastern Europe. Already in 1947, a trial in Zagreb sentenced three Witnesses to death for working against the interests of the state and sentenced eleven others to prison terms ranging from five to fifteen years. The Polish government in 1951 put seven Jehovah's Witnesses on trial for conducting espionage on behalf of the United States. All seven were convicted and sentenced to prison terms. In 1955 Poland jailed five more Witnesses who, according to the prosecution, had close contact with the United States and worked against the interests of the government. In the Soviet Union, Witnesses faced the longest series of trials. *Pravda* in 1957 accused "American imperialists" of organizing them to undermine work programs in Kazakhstan. The Soviet Union repeatedly identified the Witnesses as an "American-sponsored" religion that took orders from its Brooklyn headquarters. The charge perfectly mirrored the long-held American assertion that the Communist Party of America slavishly followed directions from Moscow.

American missionary activity was outlawed in Warsaw Pact countries. This gave Czechoslovakia a reason in 1951 to oust all American Mormons as spies. However, by the beginning of the Cold War, some churches that had been founded in the United States already had a Russian or Polish or Czech membership. They bore the brunt of future repressive measures in the East, which ensured for a few Seventh-day Adventist groups, a few Pentecostal churches, and a few clusters of Jehovah's Witnesses extensive press coverage in the West. During the 1980s, and Ronald Reagan's final showdown with the Evil Empire, Pentecostals took center stage when a number of them sought refuge in the United States embassy. Several spent nearly five years in the embassy before they were allowed to emigrate. That was more than sufficient time for Congress and the White House to use their plight to condemn Soviet violations of human rights.

There was a problem with this strategy, however. The hope of the United States that the governments of Western Europe would react with dismay to examples of religious persecution in Eastern Europe was often disappointed. In fact the Warsaw bloc nations were not the only countries to take legal action against the Jehovah's Witnesses. In 1952, the French government banned the *Watchtower,* the group's magazine, from France and all French territories. Italy ousted a Jehovah's Witness preacher in 1955. In 1963 Greece banned all public meetings of Witnesses and sentenced one of them to death for refusing military service. Spain arrested fifty-five members of the "sect" in 1969 for holding an "unauthorized assembly." None of these incidents was used by the United States to illustrate religious intolerance.[20] Publicizing differences of opinion among the Western allies did not serve American interests.

In one case that started in Italy in 1953, the United States government made an exception. To American Protestants, it was an old story of Catholics behaving badly. Italian officials in Livorno and Rome sought to restrict the activities of a Texas-supported church affiliated with the Church of Christ. In Livorno the police broke up a religious meeting of the group, and in Rome officials tore down the sign in front of its headquarters. The new U.S. ambassador to Italy, Clare Boothe Luce, lodged a protest with the Italian government and spoke, less than truthfully, about the "unfavorable reaction that results in the United States from any illiberal action" in the matter of religious freedom. Luce, a Catholic convert, may have harbored doubts about the moral position of the United States in complaining about Italian intolerance, given that anti-Catholicism remained a potent political force in America. In this case, however, the American government persisted. The matter dragged on for several years until Italy's high court upheld the right of all religious communities to open and operate houses of worship without police authorization.[21]

The United States was less interested in Franco's Spain, where it had no leverage. In 1954 Spain closed a church belonging to the Southern Baptist Convention for illegal proselytizing (Spanish law forbade the dissemination of non-Catholic propaganda). Southern Baptists then urged a worldwide prayer campaign to end restrictions on religious liberty in Spain, a campaign that failed to elicit much support in Europe or from the American government. The episodes in Spain and Italy did introduce an important change in the rhetoric of American Protestant groups. Attempts to restrict Protestant activities in Catholic parts of Europe were no longer blamed on the pope but on communist and fascist influences.

The Cold War colored the European crusades of America's most famous evangelistic preacher, Billy Graham. Graham owed at least part of his early success to Henry Luce and the publicity he received in *Time* and

Life. Luce—born in China, the son of Presbyterian ministers—in a fitting way carried forward his parents' work when he heralded the "American Century" early in 1941. Graham emerged as the poster boy of a campaign to identify the United States with moral goodness. Already in the mid-1950s he "challenged the leaders of the Soviet Union to allow him to preach the Gospel throughout the country without restriction." His petition went unheeded for many years. Ironically when he was finally allowed to carry his crusade to Moscow in 1982, he traveled against the strong urgings of the Reagan administration. America's hardened Cold Warriors of the 1980s no longer deemed Graham a reliable spokesman of anticommunism. Nonetheless, Graham had had a good run as a sponsor of Western religious freedom. His efforts during the 1950s and 1960s to work in Soviet-controlled countries were calculated to demarcate the differences between East and West. When Graham preached to large crowds in Berlin in 1960, he set up his tent and loudspeakers so that his voice carried into East Berlin. This was before the Berlin wall was constructed, and Graham's campaign boasted about the thousands of East Berliners who crossed into West Berlin to hear the American. Graham's first visit to a communist country was to Yugoslavia in 1967, followed ten years later by visits to Hungary and Poland. American officials who had little use for Graham at home took pleasure in the crowds he attracted.[22]

In fact, the East–West demarcation was far from absolute. Although Graham faced no legal obstacles in organizing religious crusades in Western Europe, his reception in NATO countries suggested that many European religious leaders still resented the intrusion of what they labeled American-style religion. That his European crusades during the 1960s drew big crowds made the problem worse. When he went to London in 1966 to conduct revival meetings at Earl's Court, some British scoffers attacked the campaign for its emphasis on the size of the crowds, the number of people converted, and the amount of money collected. The criticisms precisely recalled those made by European religious leaders in the decade after World War I.

Graham's visit to Scandinavia in 1978 met organized opposition. Newspapers in Sweden and Norway complained about the emphasis on money, about foreign "methodology" in religious matters, and about Graham's friendship with Richard Nixon. The Lutheran bishop of Oslo rejected the example of America-style religion exemplified by Graham because the excitement of one week of heated meetings erased the importance of what happened daily in Norwegian churches over many years. Quieter was better, certainly in spiritual matters. One writer accused Graham of "spiritual rape" and urged that children be protected from his appeal. Back in England in 1980 to hold meetings in Oxford, Graham found his official reception chilly, with some church leaders complaining of "too assertive a form of Christianity." When Graham went to France in 1986, he received, more predictably, discouraging advice from Henri Tincq, the religion editor of *Le Monde:* "Go back to America and forget about your plans for France." No self-respecting French person would turn up to hear an evangelist "parachuted" from the United States who presented a "made-in-USA religion extravaganza," which ignored "our special French mentality."[23]

What the Cold War tried to obscure was the fact that Americans and Western Europeans did not always agree about the terms of religious tolerance. Americans often regard European reactions toward American religious imports as a case of ridiculously overstated anti-Americanism. However, those reactions are grounded in serious disputes. Europeans do not consider American-style religious proselytizing, especially when it involves fund-raising and strongly separatist communities, as a religious practice that automatically merits legal protection and privilege.

Scientology and the American Way

We come then to the strange case of the American government's support for Scientology in Europe. Washington, in reviewing critically Germany's concerted efforts during the 1990s to make life difficult for Scientologists, framed the dispute with charges of religious intolerance. Germans, for obvious reasons, have special problems in dealing with all charges that touch on human rights, and the willingness of the Clinton administration to raise this issue outraged the German government. It also struck many Europeans as an example of American hypocrisy. When L. Ron Hubbard had published *Dianetics* in 1950, he made no claims that this venture into the market for psychological self-healing had religious significance. But within four years, the Church of Scientology was lining up members by boasting the therapeutic value of a device that Hubbard called an E-meter. For the next forty years the Church of Scientology waged a series of mostly losing battles to maintain tax-exempt status in the United States. In the late 1970s, members of the church, including Hubbard's wife, were jailed for stealing government documents from the Justice Department and bugging a conference room in the Internal Revenue Service offices. This did not deter the church from harassing public officials and journalists who criticized its practices. Only in 1993 did the United States government consent to grant tax exemption to the Church of Scientology and 150 of its related corporations, which were collecting about $300 million in annual fees. Even then the deal between the IRS and the Church of Scientology had the odor of sleazy business. Under a secret agreement, the IRS granted tax-exempt status in return for a payment of $12.5 million and a pledge by the church to drop more than two thousand lawsuits against the agency and its past and present officials.[24]

The United States, which stretches its laws to protect almost any claim of religious practice, treated the Church of Scientology for many years as a public enemy, rather like it had treated the Church of Latter-day Saints in the nineteenth century. Given this record, and given the church's own dubious commercial ventures and disregard for the civil rights of its critics, it is hard to imagine why the United States should have objected when other countries judged Scientology a less than welcome import and refused to recognize it as a religion. In fact, during those years when the United States was pursuing its own quarrels with Hubbard, the United States raised not a peep about prejudicial treatment accorded to American Scientologists abroad. In 1968 England had refused visas to Americans who arrived at Heathrow with the intention of enrolling at a Scientology Study Center in Sussex. A year later the British High Court ruled that Scientology was not a religion. The U.S. State Department said nothing. Nor had it mattered to the United States that France and Italy also applied restrictive measures to Scientology. In 1996 France set up a thirty-member government policy committee to track sects, most of which were blamed on the influence of the United States.[25]

To be sure, measures taken in Germany have been severe. In 1994, leading members of the German government and opposition denounced the "American-based Scientology" as a danger to democracy and proposed an absolute ban on its existence. Scientologists in Germany immediately responded that they were victims of right-wing terrorist campaigns similar to those that had been unleashed against Germany's Jews in the 1930s. Its charges appeared as paid advertisements in the *New York Times* and *Washington Post*. Charges and countercharges escalated. Scientologists were barred from membership in Germany's major political parties. Germans urged boycotts of the film *Mission Impossible* because Tom Cruise, the movie's star and producer, was a Scientologist; for the same reason they advocated boycotting the American jazz pianist Chick Corea. The German state of Bavaria required all state employees to fill out forms detailing any connection they might have with Scientology and effectively barred Scientologists from public service jobs. In 1997 Germany placed the church under nationwide surveillance for one year.[26]

In response the Clinton administration labeled Germany's actions a "campaign of harassment and intimidation against the church." It suggested that German actions against the Scientologists were not much different from the ethnic cleansing occurring in Kosovo. Germany understandably bitterly resented the implication that its treatment of Scientology smacked of Nazi tactics rooted in the German character—the precise charge of a $56,000 full-page advertisement placed in the *International Herald Tribune* in January 1997 and signed by thirty-four show business personalities, including Goldie Hawn, Dustin Hoffman, and Oliver Stone. As Frank Rich pointed out in the *New York Times,* more than half of the signatories had professional ties, worth a great deal of money, to Tom Cruise and John Travolta.[27]

What could seem more predictable? The stars of America's premier engine of cultural imperialism, Hollywood, rose to the defense of another powerful engine for spreading the American way: aggressive, proselytizing, money-collecting religion. This merger of interests makes the notion that Scientology is a "multinational corporation of faith" entirely plausible. It is doubtless unfair to equate those American religions that worked in Europe over the course of the twentieth century with Scientology. Even to its worst critics, the religiously sponsored relief work that put Americans in Europe during and after the two world wars cannot look much like the Scientologist invasion of Europe. Nonetheless, an American effort to erode the legitimacy of European state churches has run through the whole story of American religious work in Europe. American religious leaders have sought to pass America's singular system of religious arrangements to the rest of the world. That system prohibits the state from contributing one cent to promote a religious enterprise but gives legal protection to almost anything claiming to be a religion. It regards proselytizing in airports, in residential areas, and on the streets as a private matter. Gathering people into a closely contained, armed commune is also a private matter, not subject to the same rules that apply to nursing homes and day-care centers.

Elsewhere in the world, state authorities and ordinary people often view proselytizing as aggressive efforts to turn people against legitimate rules that regulate public life. Therefore, they demand public scrutiny and sometimes restrictive regulation. Russia's post–Cold War definition of religious freedom has not welcomed the "marketing of salvation." It permits restrictive religious laws that disadvantage religious groups newly arrived from abroad. When Nikolai Volkov, a provincial bureaucrat who was trying to dislodge Lutherans from an area in Siberia, was asked where the "nontraditional" religions that threatened Russia had come from, his instinctive answer was "America—a sewage ditch—when it was created all sorts of rabble thronged there."[28]

What Americans need to consider is that a pledge to support their program of free trade in religious ideas is not an adequate measure of a country's commitment to religious tolerance. American religion, whatever else it is, is an export commodity in today's highly competitive world market. America's style of religion was shaped from the early nineteenth century by the convergence of a constitutional system of church voluntarism, an emergent market economy, and an aggressive evangelical style.

Americans will not stop exporting their views. That much the American Century has made clear. But Europeans will continue to resist. They have their own historically conditioned reasons to view some of what is being offered for emulation as the cultural equivalent of genetically engineered food. It may have variety, but it threatens traditional ways of doing things. It is possibly bad for your health. And it can be tasteless.

NOTES

1. Alfredo Siletta, *Multinacionales de la fe: Religión, sectas, e iglesia electrónica* (Buenos Aires: Contrapunto, 1988), 154.

2. John R. Mott, *The Evangelization of the World in This Generation* (New York: Student Volunteer Movement for Foreign Missions, 1904); Clifford Johnson, "Changing Attitudes in the Student Volunteer Movement of Great Britain and North America, 1886–1928," in *Missionary Ideologies in the Imperialist Era, 1880–1920*, ed. Torben Christensen and William R. Hutchison (Arhus, Denmark: Aros, 1982), 131; Richard Seager, *World's Parliament of Religions* (Bloomington: Indiana University Press, 1995), 13, 274; John Henry Barrows, ed., *The World's Parliament of Religions*, 2 vols.(Chicago: Parliament, 1893), 2:1577–78.

3. *Addresses and Papers of John R. Mott: The Young Man's Christian Associations* (New York: Association Press, 1947), 3:214.

4. Kenneth Scott Latourette, *A History of the Expansion of Christianity* (New York: Harper's, 1945), 11:69.

5. *Fighting Men: An Account of the Work of the American Young Men's Christian Associations in the World War*, 2 vols. (New York, 1922), 2:237, 252, 334, 479, 486.

6. *Addresses and Papers of John R. Mott*, 3:336.

7. Ibid., 343.

8. William R. Hutchison, *Errand to the World: American Protestant Thought and Foreign Missions* (Chicago: University of Chicago Press, 1987, 136–38; Hutchison, "Innocence Abroad: The 'American Religion' in Europe," *Church History 5* (March 1982): 71–84; C. Howard Hopkins, *John R. Mott, 1865–1955* (Grand Rapids, Mich.: Eerdmans, 1979), 630.

9. Baker J. Cauthen, *Advance: A History of Southern Baptist Foreign Missions* (Nashville: Broadman Press, 1970), 187.

10. "The School on Monte Mario," *Christian Advocate* 96 (July 7, 1921): 876.

11. J. Tremayne Copplestone, *History of Methodist Missions: Twentieth-Century Perspectives* (New York: Board of Global Missions, 1973), 317.

12. Reverend Anton Bast, "Why Do We Need a Methodism in Scandinavia?" *Christian Advocate* 97 (November 2, l922): 1372.

13. Cornelius H. Patton, "The World at the Turn of the Year," *Christian Advocate* 97 (December 28, 1922): 1630.

14. H. E. Woolever, "Foreign Mission and the United States Congress: Relationship of Church and State," *Christian Advocate* 100 (February 12, 1925): 208.

15. *Addresses and Papers of John R. Mott*, 3:647.

16. *International Review of Missions*, April 1920.

17. "Protestants Hit Marxism Growth," *New York Times*, January 17, 1947, 6.

18. "Bids Missions Rise to Times or Perish," *New York Times*, October 8, 1948.

19. "Communist Gains Put Up to Churches," *New York Times*, January 7, 1949, 18; "Indian State Asks Missionary Cuts," *New York Times*, July 19, 1956, 14.

20. "France Bars Watchtower," *New York Times*, December 28, 1952, 4; "Italy Ousts Jehovah's Witness," *New York Times*, October 27, 1955; "Greeks Bar Witnesses Rally," *New York Times*, July 26, 1963; "Greece to Review Army's Verdict of Death for Jehovah's Witness," *New York Times*, August 17, 1966; "Spain Announces Arrests," *New York Times*, September 14, 1969. For reports of recent conflicts, see Jane Lampman, "Europe Spars over Faith," *Christian Science Monitor*, March 25, 1999.

21. "Italy Again Bans U.S. Sect," *New York Times*, April 15, 1953, 9; "Mrs. Luce Pledges Aid on Missionaries," *New York Times*, April 17, 1953, 8; "Leghorn Police Arrest Minister in Raid on Protestant Church," *New York Times*, February 13, 1954, 1; "Protestant Liberty Upheld in Italy," *New York Times*, November 12, 1954, 1; "U.S. Embassy Acts in Rome Sect Feud," *New York Times*, March 3, 1955, 2.

22. "Graham Proposes Russian Crusade," *New York Times*, June 10, 1957; "Graham Defies Reds," *New York Times*, September 29, 1960; "Graham Preaches in Zagreb Church," *New York Times*, July 9, 1967; "Billy Graham, Defying Critics, Journeys to Soviet," *New York Times*, May 8, 1982.

23. Edward Plowman, "The Scandinavians: No Neutrality on Graham," *Christianity Today*, October 20, 1978; "Reaction to Graham in Britain's University Towns Hardly Detached," *Christianity Today*, March 21, 1980; "Media Opposition and Bombings Fail to Damage Graham's Paris Crusade," *Christianity Today*, November 7, 1986.

24. "Scientologists Granted Tax Exemption by U.S.," *New York Times*, October 14, 1993, 1; "Agency Hints at Inquiry on Leak on Scientologists," *New York Times*, January 1, 1998.

25. Anthony Lewis, "Britain Curbs Activities of Cult of Scientologists," *New York Times*, August 1, 1968; Gail Chaddock, "With New Zeal: France Screens Religious Sects," *Christian Science Monitor*, November 18, 1996.

26. Alan Cowell, "Germany Says It Will Press On with Scientology Investigation," *New York Times*, February 1, 1997, 1; Alan Cowell, "Germany Will Place Scientology under Nationwide Surveillance," *New York Times*, June 7, 1997, 1.

27. Frank Rich, "Show Me the Money," *New York Times*, January 25, 1997, 23.

28. Adrei Zolotov, "Why Russia Restricts Religions," *Christian Science Monitor,* October 28, 1997, 18; Lawrence Uzzell, "Repressive Religion Law Has Russian Faithful on Edge," *Christian Science Monitor,* April 22, 1998, 19. For pressure on the State Department to make religious freedom central to foreign policy, see Robert Marquand, "Cry Is Heard to Fight for Freedom of Faith," *Christian Science Monitor,* December 24, 1996.

Western Alliance and Scientific Diplomacy in the Early 1960s: The Rise and Failure of the Project to Create a European M.I.T.

Giuliana Gemelli

This chapter discusses three arguments related to the emergence of large-scale scientific cooperation in the Western world. The first concerns the role of cross-disciplinary strategies in strengthening scientific cooperation; the second analyses the effects of institutional competition in shaping large-scale scientific cooperation during the Cold War; and the last concerns the resistance of European institutions and institutional actors to the dissemination of American educational patterns in the framework of international scientific cooperation. These arguments and the ways they interrelate are developed by looking at the attempt, in the late 1950s and early 1960s, to create a European equivalent of the Massachusetts Institute of Technology (M.I.T.).

The Cold War and Its Stereotypes: Human and Social Sciences at M.I.T.

The prevalent image of M.I.T. during the Cold War was that it was an institution that provided a strictly technological educational environment with little or even no room for the humanities. The 1953 novel *Fahrenheit 451* helped crystallize this stereotype by presenting a world in which the humanities, social sciences, and philosophy had been banned from the most prestigious scientific and engineering schools.

In fact, the strengthening of social and human studies at M.I.T. occurred precisely during the warmest phase of the Cold War, particularly

171

in 1951 with the creation of the Center for International Studies under the direction of Walter Rostow. In 1954 the center received a $2 million grant from the Ford Foundation and was considered the core of an institutional experiment especially well suited to "an understanding of the world of the second half of this century."[1]

The Center for International Studies was to be an interdepartmental institution that allowed interdisciplinary ties and included representatives of the department of humanities as well as of the School of Industrial Management and the department of political science. A report of the center stressed the fact that "the cross-departmental walls are not often so low as they are at M.I.T. Students in this political science option are encouraged to take electives in subjects of economics and industrial relations, which deal with governmental policy concerning business, labor, money and banking."[2] Considering the effects of the warmest phase of the Cold War, which were characterized by increasing development of Soviet manpower and production of well-trained engineers, it was also significant that one of the center's main goals was to develop the study of "the quality of Soviet higher education in science and technology and the social, economic, political and military measures necessary to counter Communist attempts at subversion, in less developed countries."[3]

In September 1957, a committee on the social sciences was created, supported by M.I.T.'s chancellor Julius Stratton and president James Killian, as well as by such outstanding scholars as economic historian Alfred D. Chandler, social psychologist Erik Erikson, political scientist Kenneth Arrow, and economist Howard Raiffa.[4] The committee was at the core of a transformation that made cross-disciplinary work in particular areas a long-term institutional goal. This change, combined with the shock of the Soviet Union's technological prowess in launching the Sputniks, played an important role in transforming an institutional "bricolage" into a focused, large-scale strategy. M.I.T.'s leading personalities did not reply to the Soviet challenge simply by intensifying their offerings in space science and technology. Rather they hoped to redesign engineering education by not only strengthening scientific training but by developing general education and cross-disciplinary approaches.

There is an important distinction to be made between scientific and technical education and scientific and technical training, Max F. Millikan, director of The Center for International Studies, wrote:

From narrow immediate purpose, educational programs emphasizing the training of specialists to perform certain high priority technical assignments may produce a more rapid rate of progress in the short run than a broader emphasis on fundamental education in both the social and natural sciences. There is some evidence that part of the explanation of the apparently rapid rate of Soviet industrial growth lies in their concentration of attention on the rather narrow training of a large number of engineering specialists. In the long run, however, it is probable that a broader concept of education, with a somewhat less limiting focus on the immediate priority tasks, may produce a more substantial and rewarding kind of economic progress, even though its immediate fruits may be somewhat less visible.[5]

This educational orientation was strongly supported after the shock of Sputnik, particularly at the level of the President's Science Advisory Committee (PSAC), which was placed under the leadership of the president of the M.I.T. Corporation, James Killian. He was firmly convinced that support for basic research and the strengthening of American science were two sides of the same coin.

Strengthening International Scientific Policies in the Sputnik Era: M.I.T., NATO, and the Ford Foundation

Why and how, between the late 1950s and early 1960s, did this focus on interdisciplinary education at the postsecondary level become a compelling influence in shaping strategies of international cooperation? This shift in focus was related to several factors set into motion by the Soviet challenge: (1) the necessity of strengthening the Western Alliance by enhancing the role of Europe as an equal partner not only in political diplomacy but also in technology and science; (2) the strong support of the Ford Foundation for accelerating innovative engineering education; (3) the prominent role played by M.I.T. president James Killian, as the first presidential science advisor; and (4) the decision taken in 1959 by the NATO Science Committee, in existence since December 1957, to study the needs of Western science as well as its institutional development and cooperation. In the immediate post-Sputnik era, this study indicated a shift in interest among member governments of the Atlantic community, from concerns based exclusively on defense strategies and toward recognition of "the growing quantity and quality of scientists and engineers in the Soviet Union, which threatened to outstrip the supply of manpower in the United States and Western Europe. One of the main tasks of the NATO Science Committee was to redress this educational imbalance."[6]

How did these factors' mutual influence enhance the role of educational policies as a strategic concern in Atlantic community policies?

John Krige has rightly stated that the NATO Science Committee's preferred means of achieving its objectives was international collaboration. An international program could not simply be imposed on NATO members, because it had to respect the national sovereignty of member countries in matters of science and technology policy. Rather, the circulation of scientists, along with their ideas and skills, was seen as a fruitful way of building a scientific community that could dominate the frontiers of research in a number of strategic fields.[7]

Another important framework for developing international cooperation was created as a result of the relationship between M.I.T. and the Ford Foundation. One of the leading personalities at M.I.T., Julius Stratton, was a trustee of the foundation. Another link was created as a result of the foundation's increasing interest in developing an international affairs program, an interest that enhanced the appeal of M.I.T.'s Center for International Studies for the foundation's programs. These links also favored the development of large-scale educational programs, such as the revamping of engineering education. Killian sent his recommendations to the president of the Ford Foundation, Henry Heald, in December 1957, and also defined the project's international goals. "Engineering education," Killian wrote,

has today an unprecedented responsibility and opportunity to bring about this much-needed advance in the professional excellence and constructive influence of engineers. . . . We believe too that this enlarged concept of engineering education involves the development of an even deeper interpenetrating between engineering and science and the identification of a new area of symbiotic association between engineering and the humanities and the social sciences. We believe that . . . engineering methods of thought . . . can contribute importantly to a liberal education, especially apt and meaningful for the conditions of modern life.[8]

The proposal was accepted by the foundation's trustees, and in 1959 the program "for Engineering curriculum development and experiments" was granted $7.85 million. This chapter's central argument is that Killian, as the president's scientific advisor, was able to enter the system of decision making and create, within the institutional framework of M.I.T., an emerging and growing "epistemic community"—that is, a "network of professionals with recognized expertise and competence in a particular domain and an authoritative claim to policy-relevant knowledge."[9]

More than half of M.I.T.'s Ford Foundation grant went to help develop Killian's institutional blueprint, which had at its core strengthening the areas of information theory and applied systems analysis, as well as improving cross-disciplinary approaches that were relevant to these research fields.

Killian was firmly convinced of the necessity of developing human sciences as a crucial foundation for working in the fields of information theory and computer science, and he criticized the educational patterns of technical schools in Europe, especially in Germany: they were too specialized and discipline-bounded. And he endorsed the opinion of a M.I.T. visiting professor in Germany, who said that

German[s] are quite competent but their training is severely limited to the application of computer techniques to problems arising out of numerical analysis of models of physical systems. . . . Their tunnel vision is, in my opinion, caused by their teachers' distrust of any interdisciplinary activity . . . the German professor seems to feel that contact with another domain is by definition dilettantism, hence unprofessional. He considers it his responsibility not only to avoid potentially contaminating interdisciplinary contacts, but also to build positive safeguards against possible incursions into its own activities.[10]

Killian also emphasized the role foundations could play in developing strategies for international cooperation.[11] In his role as a consultant, Killian supported the Ford Foundation's policy of strengthening European scientific cooperation as well as the idea of developing a science policy not entirely dependent on security goals and military research contracts. Under Killian's influence, the Center for International Studies at M.I.T. changed its agenda so that its concerns became broader than merely evaluating Soviet manpower and technological development. It should be stressed that Killian was skeptical that Soviet science was surpassing American science in quality, and he was also skeptical about the worth of quantitative comparisons. He was, however, strongly convinced that the Western Alliance in general was not training enough scientists and engineers. He felt that what was needed was a larger concept of educational and professional training focused on "global interdependence, with special attention to the consequences of technological change, social control of the effects of technology . . . and problems of policy-making in this changing international environment."[12]

In 1959, within this framework, Killian met and supported the decision of the Ford Foundation to grant $75,000 to a study group concerned with the "means of increasing the effectiveness of Western science," on the condition that the grant was not related exclusively to a military organization, such as NATO. Killian's argument, and the Ford Foundation's concern, was that NATO recognize it was faced with a new challenge that was largely nonmilitary in character. Although maintaining strict cooperation with NATO (which also granted the study group $75,000), the study group was based at an independent institution, the Belgian Foundation Universitaire, whose president, Jean Willems, had been one of the founding fathers of CERN, the European Organization for Nuclear Research, and its treasurer. Willems also had good personal relations with Paul Henri Spaak, who "appointed the Working group while secretary general of NATO."[13] The strong concern of NATO's Science Committee with fostering international cooperation favored agreement among the institutional partners of the study group.

The uneasiness over the Soviet Union's technological challenge was the most visible but not the only concern among American scientific-industrial-military networks. After 1957, in fact, they became increasingly uneasy about the extension of the contractual system to European countries—through the signing of research contracts with industrial or military firms—and the fact that this process could create a disadvantage for American technological development, "because," as Killian observed, "they can hire scientists at about half the cost that they could hire them over here."[14]

In this shift in educational policy between the end of the 1950s and the beginning of the 1960s, the interest in European scientific and institutional development was based on a Janus-like pattern. On the one hand, there was continuity with mainstream Cold War policies, that is, helping technologically backward Europeans, in order to strengthen the "free world" of sciences, by developing cooperation in the Atlantic community. On the other hand there was a growing concern about "who leads in scientific research" based on increasing competitive cooperation between the United States and Europe, with the Americans looking for a beachhead inside the superior European scientific tradition. In the early 1960s, Killian found in the Ford Foundation policy in Europe both a channel and a support to explore and to shape this framework.

The Armand Study Group and Western Science

Interestingly, the activities of the Study Group on Western Sciences reveal this complex dynamic, which involved some antinomies of the period, such as the national state versus supernationalism, and American supremacy versus European autonomy. These antinomies produced contrasting effects of cooperation in supporting and imitating American programs in the framework of European institutions, as well as academic resistance vis-à-vis the attempts to create an American institutional beachhead in Europe. In some cases, these two kinds of behavior could be found within the same institution. In a report about a visit of the Free University in Berlin to the Ford Foundation, Killian noted that "in accord with German tradition and practice, TUB as well as the Free University I judge to be a collection of academic Baltic States with high tariff barriers and Checkpoints Charlie effectively separating them."[15]

In 1959, however, when the Study Group on Western Science was created, Killian was not part of it. His name had been mentioned in the preliminary list of study groups members, but in the end the U.S. representative was the Nobel laureate Isidor Rabi. According to Jean-Jacques Solomon, Rabi was anything but a supporter of the integration between natural and social sciences, which was Killian's primary concern. The study group was placed under the leadership of a French policy maker, Louis Armand, former president of the French railways, former president of Euratom, and then president of the council of the École Polytechnique. Several proposals emerged from the first meetings of the group and were discussed, such as

the lack of sufficient scientific manpower and the desirability of establishing an Academy of sciences from the Western countries just as the European Community countries are considering the establishment of a European Community Academy of Science. The study group will probably concentrate on ways in which each country can increase the effectiveness of science within country . . . ; as, for example, using Euratom, as an institution which guides the way to the future; recommendations on an Academy of Science for the Western countries; ways of improving dissemination of information; recommendation on international university; special recommendation for space research.[16]

Rabi indicated that such goals should be reached through the cooperation of research institutions' representatives in the framework of a central body. It was later, at the end of 1959, that the project of creating "an Atlantic University" was developed. This later project was strongly supported by Hendrick Casimir, the director of physics research at the Philips Laboratory, and by NATO's science advisor, F. Seitz. In October 1959, Casimir wrote a report that, while tracing the blueprint for an "Atlantic University," also stressed the obstacles that such an enterprise might encounter, particularly the strong criticism by representatives of existing European universities.[17]

The project to create an Atlantic University was not the only proposal put forward by the study group. It also discussed the possibility of creating "some type of co-ordinating agency . . . supplied with considerable funds and trying to provide in the Western countries some of the beneficial, but not the more dictatorial services, of the USSR Academy of Sciences in Moscow."[18] The French representative, Robert Danjou, presented another proposal. He stated that "it would be preferable to use and support existing institutes, which would thus quickly attain international standing." He cited the Naples Laboratory of Biology as a model of an international type. Similar establishments could perhaps be grouped together in the future and named the Atlantic Institute. He called attention to the likely disadvantages of starting such an institute from scratch, including the breakup of research "teams which had been formed with so much difficulty."[19] Finally, a proposal to create a Western Science Foundation was presented with the strong support of the French; it was, however, rejected, "chiefly for financial reasons."[20]

Moreover, the Atlantic Institute project was not the only international program under discussion at the time. The Euratom project of creating a European University was also in progress. While the French insisted on a rigid interpretation of the Treaty of Rome, affirming that the treaty envisaged only the creation of a center on atomic research and training for scientific and technical personnel of the European Community, the Germans preferred an institution that integrated scientific disciplines as well as the human and social sciences.

This position was also supported by the Ford Foundation, which since 1958 had granted $500,000 to the European Community Institute for University Studies, created in Brussels in 1957 under the leadership of Max Kohnstam and with the support of leading personalities such as Jean Monnet, Etienne Hirsch, and Louis Armand. The institute's main role was to disseminate in European universities a strong interest in inter-national cooperation among European universities and research centers, and between Europe and the United States. The activity of the institute was considered by the Americans a relevant framework to consolidate a network of scholars firmly devoted to the advancement of Western science and scientific cooperation, and to the development of the Atlantic partnership.

According to the Ford Foundation, when it approved the grant to the institute, "The European Community Institute will be in a central position to aid European Universities to overcome parochial interests. The development of a European and Atlantic outlook at the old universities of Europe and the funding of a new university are revolutionary steps in European higher education"[21] In the original recommendation for grant action, the foundation's trustees were assured that "the ECIUS trustees were characterized by political sympathy for the United States and the belief that without the United States even a United Europe would be overrun by Soviet Russia."[22]

Actually, the year 1959 was a period of intense negotiations among different national and international actors. The risk that projects would share similar goals and overlapping issues was rapidly becoming apparent. In October 1959, a memorandum to the officers of the Ford Foundation International Program mentioned that "Mr. Hirsch, Professor Amaldi and Max Kohnstam had dinner to discuss what could be done to strengthen science in the European Community. . . . They all agree that they did not want in any way to compete with the science study that is now being supported by us and NATO," but at the same time "they believe that if the Six came up with some science recommendation, the European Community can implement them, whereas they have some doubts about whether or not the recommendations made brought in by a wider group will really be implemented or simply be a report."[23]

The Ford Foundation's officers encouraged this kind of competitive cooperation, stressing that "there was no reason why the European Community countries should not try to put science together" and inviting Hirsch and Kohnstam to participate in the meeting of the NATO's study group.[24] Their reaction was immediate: Hirsch told Stone that the day after the dinner with Kohnstam and Amaldi, the foreign ministers of the six European countries had decided to establish a committee to investigate and write a report on a European University. "The report," Shepard Stone noted,

is likely to be a recommendation for a post-graduate institution where postgraduates would obtain their Ph.D. This institution will cover the humanities and the natural sciences and is likely to be established in Florence. Both Hirsch and Walter Hallstein, president of the Common Market Commission, are eagerly behind the establishment of this institution. . . . They recognize, of course, that there is a powerful opposition to the establishment of such an institution in many European universities.[25]

A visit to Princeton University made by Hirsch, the president of Euratom, in June 1959 played a crucial role in the general agreement that human and social sciences had "a primordial importance for European integration." According to Hirsch, American pressures were determinant in drawing the blueprint of the proposed European University Institute. It is possible that in 1959 the study group considered developing a kind of institutional division of labor in which the Euratom project would focus on human and social sciences, and an Atlantic University, conceived as a kind of European M.I.T., would focus on the natural sciences and technology. Actually, at the beginning of the sixties both projects entered a phase of stagnation, but with different institutional effects in the long run. The negotiations for the European University Institute were renewed in 1969 and successfully ended with the creation of the institute in Florence. The European M.I.T. project, however, met with grave difficulties and finally ended in failure, at least from the institutional point of view. The "Group Armand" finished its work in March 1960 with the publication of a report stating that if the idea of creating an international M.I.T. was considered worthy of further study, a small and efficient working committee should be appointed to make concrete plans, because the institutional configuration of the center remained vague.[26] The Armand group accepted the principle of a division of labor between the Euratom project, focused on human and social sciences, and a still vague project of creating an Atlantic University focused on the natural sciences and technology. One of the first tasks of the new committee "would be to coordinate its plans with those for the European University." The Armand group also accepted the observation made by Alexander King, who, as a leading member of the Organization for European Economic Cooperation (OEEC), was invited to attend the study group's meetings. King said that

the OEEC felt strongly that before any action was taken an independent inquiry should be carried out on the real needs of Western science. . . . Much work was still necessary in order to persuade governments of the importance of science; very few Western governments had as yet a policy for science and it is unlikely that a European policy could be evolved in these conditions.[27]

Speaking in his capacity as consultant to the secretary general of OEEC, Ambassador Wilgress insisted on the "importance of coordinating the scientific work being carried out by OEEC and NATO. The aim was to ensure that the efforts of the two organizations were complementary and did not result in duplication. . . . He felt that OEEC should be a forum in which national representatives could exchanges views on the possibility of further cooperation."[28]

Significantly, the NATO science advisor's comments on the report were far from enthusiastic. In a letter to Shepard Stone, he wrote:

On the whole, the conservatism of the group is now beginning to appear and many of the recommendations will be made in a somewhat mellower fashion. For example, it now looks as if the Atlantic Institute of Science and Technology will appear in the report as a possibility rather than as a strong positive recommendation. In essence, this means that other groups will have to pick up the issues.[29]

The Killian Group and the European M.I.T. Project

The new working group was soon set up, this time exclusively within the NATO framework, under the prestigious leadership of James Killian. In November 1960, the recommendations of the Armand study group were transmitted to the North Atlantic Council, and its secretary general effected the recommendations by appointing a small high-level working group and establishing an International Institute of Sciences and Technology. Killian was appointed president of this group, which, from the beginning, was characterized by increasing instability and uncertainty. The national representatives in the Killian group were, with a few but relevant exceptions, all from the Armand group.

After the creation of the Killian working group, the NATO science advisor, Eugene B. Skolnikoff, was less pessimistic about their prospects for success than his predecessor had been, but he stressed the high level of uncertainty in the political decision-making. In a letter to Shepard Stone, he wrote:

it is not clear yet what the attitude of various governments will be, but Dr. Killian's presentation was favorably received. In the science committee itself the French representative was quite negative, which is consistent with his previous position. Whether this is the official position of the French government or a very personal reaction remains to be seen.[30]

The working group quickly prepared a new feasibility report in which Killian was particularly careful to avoid any overlap with the European University Institute's project. He accepted at face value the logic of an institutional division of labor based on the separation of the two cultures, humanistic and scientific. But if we look more carefully at the final report, we see that it insisted on recogniz[ing] the growing inter-relationship among different fields of learning and research. In its structure and in all of its programs, the Institute should stress the unity of knowledge and seek to achieve a flexibility, which promotes easy inter-relationships among fields, and which avoids rigidly organized depart-ments The important objective is to achieve interdisciplinary programs, rather than to attempt to limit the institute to the particular formula proposed, even though the Working group strongly believes in it.[31]

Killian insisted on the necessity of improving the understanding of how science and technology impact national public policies:

It is important that the Institute should promote studies in this field. Scientists must be constructively interested in the effects of government policy and orga-nization of the welfare of science; and statesmen and political scientists must in-creasingly deal with the impact of science in the process of making political decisions and governmental organization. For these reasons the interactions be-tween science and the policies of nations have become an area of challenging interest to scientists, politician scientists and politicians alike. The working group feels that these general areas, including the "inexact" sciences (e.g. econo-metrics, communications, psychology, linguistics and other fields) warrant the attention of the Institute and fall naturally within its format of interdisciplinary studies. The whole area of the study of management, known as industrial dy-namics, represents a new opportunity for joint studies by scientists and tech-nologists on the one hand and administrators and social scientists on the other.[32]

The report of the Killian working group was based on the uneven re-sults of a questionnaire filled out by member countries regarding their educational and scientific policies. While France, the United States, and the United Kingdom sent very detailed information, Italy, Germany, and Belgium did not. The report was first presented as a NATO document (CM-61-85) in October 1960 and led to the proposal that "a fully cen-tralized Institute be created in the form of a post-graduate University em-bracing some five centers or divisions covering various fields of science and technology defined in very broad terms."[33]

The project was discussed extensively during the next two years and generated different reactions among the national representatives on the NATO Scientific Committee. The Greek member, with the full agree-ment of his government, presented an enthusiastic declaration of sup-port that included an offer to have the center located in Athens. Agreement came also from the Italian representative; the German and Dutch representatives, while accepting in principle the blueprint of the institute, were more careful and adopted a "wait and see" strategy. Most national representatives agreed on the proposal to declassify the report and make it available for discussion among "non-governmental as well governmental authorities in all member countries and also in non-member countries of Western Europe."[34] This proposal came from the British representative and was "instrumental" in allowing the circulation of the report along with another document prepared by a group of British scientists submitting alternative proposals for accomplishing the purpose of the Killian report.

The British proposal tried to realize a compromise between a positive American position and the position of the French, which was still very negative, particularly at the level of the French Ministry of Defense. Instead of a centralized institution, the British proposal focused on a federation of centers.

A July 1962 common report declared:

In a number of quarters, doubts have been expressed whether the proposal in its present form does in fact represent the best solution in view of the present conditions and long-term needs of Western Europe. Europe has a large number of great national institutions—Universities, technical Universities and colleges—each reflecting in some measure the social and cultural background of its own country. . . . The difficulty of adapting existing long-established institutions to fit new patterns of scientific education is great and . . . the achievement of such adaptation, without added stimulus, might take a longer time than the Western world can afford. But it could equally be argued that such a change might be more rapidly attained by producing a number of centers spread over the Western countries and associated with existing institutions. . . . An international institute which was not centralized but which consisted of a group of dispersed centers each associated by its location with an existing institution would be more appropriate to our needs. . . . All centers would be under the control of the Institute which would give a doctorate degree having international recognition.[35]

The British proposal made the discussion particularly intense and even tense. Although almost all the national representatives agreed that the institute should not be placed exclusively under NATO, opinions on the British proposal to decentralize its organization consistently diverged.

A joint meeting of foreign and defense ministries was held in May 1962 in Athens, with the support of the Greek government, which allowed its representative to present an official document stressing that the value of the institute's interdisciplinary approach was "not purely symbolical since, in the opinion of the Working Group, the Institute should strive to combine scientific research with the spirit of humanism, the high achievements of which may well be jeopardized by the spectacular advance of modern science and technology."[36]

Despite strong support for the European M.I.T. project expressed by the U.S. secretary of state, Dean Rusk, with the full agreement of the Italian foreign minister, Giulio Andreotti, the Athens meeting did not reach a final decision about the creation of the institute. The French minister expressed clearly his opposition to the project, and British Secretary of State Home confirmed the previous position of his government. Then came the famous veto by General de Gaulle, and in 1963, as stated in a report of the Scientific Committee, the European M.I.T. project entered a phase of stagnation: "The project is at the present time rather dormant," B. Coleby declared in October 1963.[37] It would, however, be simplistic to say that the project failed exclusively because of French opposition and General de Gaulle's veto.

The "Long Whimper" of the European M.I.T. Project and Its Effects in the Mid-Sixties

Patterns of resistance were at work even in the earliest phases of the M.I.T. project. As previously stated, ever since the period of the Armand study group there had been an ongoing debate about whether to create an institute or a foundation. The French delegates never abandoned their original position in favor of the creation of a Western foundation. Despite cooperating with the Killian working group in helping to determine the state of scientific research and technical equipment in the European countries,[38] the French maintained an ambivalent position that revealed itself as strong resistance when the British presented their alternate plans.

At that time, the French delegation, represented by Raymond Poignant (member of the Delegation Générale à la Recherche Scientifique et Technique [DGRST]) and M. François Charles-Roux (deputy director of cultural and technical affairs), clearly declared its opposition to creating such an institution within NATO.[39] Poignant was convinced that establishing an international institute such as M.I.T. could increase France's brain drain and "sterilize" the work of European research and educational institutions.[40]

The official representatives of the most important research agencies in France also supported this position. Professor Goetz, member of the DGRST, declared that in Killian's project: "What prevails is the notion of predominance imperialism, not that of competition."[41]

The French foreign and defense ministries were the most hostile. On the French side, the dominant suspicion was based on the idea that

The enormous American progress in technological discoveries cannot conceal the fact that almost all fundamental breakthroughs have been achieved by European researchers . . . out of which comes the desire to keep, by means of the creation of an international institution, a European outpost, in order not to be cut off from European work in fundamental research. . . . It is to be regretted that, contrary to its mandate, the Killian work-group has not really proceeded to the inventory of the potential areas of interest of the Institute. On this point, the group's report sounds more opinionated than convincing. It is even more regrettable because the never-ending tension between the imperatives of international cooperation and national interests cannot be resolved, except through a rigorous examination of each research sector, which would allow each partner to make an assessment of what he will contribute and what he will benefit, if efforts are merged in the context of the alliance.[42]

The basic reasons for French opposition to the Killian project were similar to those that had inspired resistance, by General de Gaulle and others, to the idea of creating a European university that could grant degrees; such an institution, he feared, would have the effect of bypassing each state's institutional prerogative.[43] It should not be forgotten that in July 1960, de Gaulle declared: "What is actually the European reality? . . . indeed that of the states . . . [and] to think that something efficient can be achieved outside or above the states is a self-delusion."[44]

De Gaulle's declaration of July 1960 created the framework in which the famous Plan Fouchet was conceived. It stated that cultural and scientific cooperation should be based on the principle of national sovereignty rather than on the creation of supranational institutions. The project to create a European M.I.T. was clearly against this principle, and moreover, as far as the French were concerned, it interfered in the affairs of the defense ministry.

It is, however, only a partial conclusion that the failure of the M.I.T. project was the result of the long-expected veto by the French government, which finally materialized in 1963, during the final phase of the Killian working group's activity. What remains to be explained is the position of the British scientists, who demanded, with the support of their government, that Killian's project be revised. Perhaps the British position resulted from the challenge that the interdisciplinary orientation of the project represented to the British educational system, which at the beginning of the sixties was still based on the separation between the ministry of education and the ministry of technology—institutions that still considered the training of engineers and managers to be lower on the educational ladder than that dispensed by the "public schools" and universities. Significantly, a few years later, acting as a consultant to the Ford Foundation in Europe, Killian observed that with the Wilson government, things were starting to change, albeit slowly. Despite finding great vigor in British education, Killian stated that

a mistake was made in not following Churchill's advice in the early 50's to undertake an M.I.T. type of institution in Britain—an institution of sufficient scale, comprehensiveness and power, that it could set new standards in the field of technological and scientific education and in management. Instead they have opted to strengthen a group of institutions and to develop universities out of a group of colleges of technology.

Along with the political resistance to the European M.I.T. project, there were other constraints to its development posed by the science and science policies within the national educational system.[45]

Increasing competition among different agencies that promoted international science policies also played a role in the failure of the European M.I.T. This was particularly the case for the Organization for Economic Cooperation and Development (OECD), whose emerging strategy was to enhance the role of Europe in international policies, including underdeveloped countries and the Mediterranean area.

If the Killian project was abandoned, however, its contents and recommendations were not entirely destroyed. To understand the less visible part of the story of the rise and failure of the European M.I.T. project, we need to look at the role of the OECD in shaping scientific diplomacy in the 1960s and 1970s. Significantly, since the beginning of the negotiations surrounding the Killian project, the French position had been much more favorable toward OECD policy: strengthen the internationalization of existing institutions and develop cooperation among scholars, eventually through the support of the National Science Foundation.

"Unlike what happens inside NATO," said a report of October 1961, "where national representatives are associated to the project only after much delay, from the beginning a French representative participated in all the studies of European projects, whether they were performed by the OEEC or by the European Communities."[46]

The Killian project was definitively rejected in 1963, exactly when Pierre A. Piganiol, who was at that time the president of the Consulting

Committee for Scientific Policy of the OECD, published his famous "Report on Science and Government Policy: The Influence of Science and Technology on Domestic and International Policy Making." The report stated that each government should have its own central organization for scientific policies and that the OECD should coordinate the activities of the national representatives of these official agencies in order to stimulate the effectiveness of science policies.[47]

Then, according to many, the OECD inherited the legacy of the Killian project by exploiting the side effects of the debate on the technological gap. First, national reports were produced on the state of scientific research and technological development. Second, the OECD, by creating special committees on the social sciences, strengthened cross-disciplinary programs and large-scale cooperation. Finally, it developed a new project—an international institute—and favored the creation of a European Science Foundation, which had been previously discussed by the Armand study group.

In the intermingling of these legacies, there emerges a common pattern that could be found in many institutional projects during the sixties and early seventies, and which produced a common concern among European policy makers. This pattern was based on their refusal, or at least strong resistance, to the creation of centralized international institutions.[48]

The effects of this complex legacy reversed the rationale of the Killian project. Instead of confirming American supremacy, it became the framework for the "European challenge" in which American educational models were selectively appropriated and adapted within different national contexts. In 1965, referring to the discussion about the creation of an OECD institute, Killian revealed that "such an institute would have a better opportunity than did the international institute of technology, which was studied under the auspices of NATO."[49] He also admitted that grant-making foundations could play a key role in developing and strengthening European education and research.

Conclusion

Aside from the different types of resistance to the project of a European M.I.T.—types that seemed to be the result of national policy making—we can see common patterns in many institutional projects of the 1960s and early 1970s. These projects produced a kind of common concern among European policy makers that could be identified as a refusal or at least a strong resistance to the creation of centralized international institutions.

Their concern was particularly evident when the creation of an International Institute for Computing Technology and Research was proposed, with NATO support. The primary reason to vote against this proposal was (as declared by the DGRST official who found, with few exceptions, support in the French army) that the new center's mission overlapped with that of the International Center of Computing created by UNESCO in Rome.[50] Another example was the creation in Brussels of the EIASM (the European Institute for Advanced Studies in Management), which materialized as a network of institutions rather than the centralized organization the Americans originally proposed.

Significantly, one of the few attempts to create a centralized institution in 1969, within the framework of the OECD's International Institute for Management of Technology (IIMT), whose design was drawn "from the example of the Massachusetts Institute of Technology," rapidly collapsed and failed.

The IIMT's project had its origins in the phase of the debate about the so-called managerial gap and was supported in 1973 by the Ford Foundation with a $100,000 grant. "The motivation for the Institute," an officer of the American foundation wrote, "came from . . . the resulting fears of the Europeans that IBM would ultimately take over the world." Simultaneously, the internationalization of European business schools was accelerating. It is not surprising, then, that among the members of the commission who wrote the preliminary reports on the project sat one of the pioneers of the Institut Européen pour L'administration des Affaires (INSEAD), Olivier Giscard d'Estaing, who did not want the international institute located in France.[51] The "pioneers" of the institute were the British and Germans (King from OECD and Pestel of the University of Hanover, who later became the vice chairman of the governing board of the institute), with Italian support. The design of the IIMT—directed by a German scientist, M. Seetzin, and set to go into operation in 1972—was produced by a young British freelance consultant to the Scientific Affairs Directorate at the OECD, John A. Cade. After a long negotiation process, the IIMT had finally located its headquarters in Milan, in a magnificent building, the Palazzo delle Stelline. This was not a mere accident; indeed, the Italian government had been the most favorable to the idea of a centralized institute. In fact, after the failure of the Killian project in 1965, the Italian government, through its foreign minister Amintore Fanfani, recommended to NATO's scientific committee that it create in Italy an international institute for technology. Fanfani used the rhetoric of the Cold War to call for a new "Marshall Plan for technology." After initial resistance, the Milan Institute was created in 1972, within the OECD framework, when, as J. J. Solomon recalled, most of the European community no longer needed it because they had developed their own management educational institutions, on national, European, and even international levels. The Milan Institute, however, was based on a different rationale. The main goal of its founders was to create

an international body financed by industry (mainly IBM Europe, British Petroleum and Royal Dutch Shell) and the governments of several countries, the purpose of which is to improve the management of highly complex technological systems by strengthening training and research programs. The intergovernmental agreement, which will create the institute, will be open not only to all OECD countries but also to additional ones explicitly invited to join the institute. Corporations and other bodies, which will deposit a yearly amount of at least $10,000 for three years, will be given membership in the general assembly.[52]

This institution was intended by its promoters (particularly Alexander King) to counterbalance the impact of American management education by developing neglected factors such as product innovation and engineering, in hopes of reintegrating the link between productive expertise and management. The core network of the IIMT as formed by a group of German, British, and Italian scholars was intended to strengthen this orientation and to stimulate cross-fertilization between business administration and industrial engineering by developing patterns that were more similar to German and, to some extent, British traditions than they were to the American business administration model.[53]

"A sizable faculty was appointed as well as various support staff. All together about fifty people were assembled, some with relatively long-term contracts, and the institute was started with much fanfare."[54] Despite the prestigious appearance of the institute, its goals and effective performance remained fluid. By 1978, IIMT no longer existed, and according to the Ford Foundation's officer Peter de Janosi, "the closing down of an intergovernmental research and training institute, not for reasons of war, pestilence or other calamity, is a unique event and well worth the attention of a sensitive historian."

It seems paradoxical that an institution with such ambitious goals had been created in the country that the OCDE had identified as the least financially supportive of research and the only nation in Europe that had not developed a long-term plan for research and development.

From many points of view, the failure of the European M.I.T. project was not only the result of the political "bang" produced by de Gaulle's veto. It was also the result of a long whimper characterized by a shift away from the policies of the 1950s, which were based on the idea that American educational models could be transferred to Europe, and on the articulate perception of the 1960s, which was based on enhancing the role of national patterns and their mechanism of resistance, selective appropriation, and competitive cooperation, vis-à-vis American models. This shift was important in shaping the new configuration of scientific diplomacy and in enhancing the role of Europe not only in the West but throughout the world.

NOTES

1. "Report of the Dean of the School of Humanities and Social Studies, 1954–55," pp. 1–2, M.I.T. Archive (Cambridge, Mass., Collection), AC 404, box 8, folder 12.
2. Draft of "Report of the Dean of the School of Humanities and Social Studies, Academic Year 1955–56," pp. 3–4, M.I.T. Archive, AC 404, box 8, folder 12.
3. Ibid., 22 and 28.
4. James R. Killian Jr. (1904–1988) was president of M.I.T. from 1949 to 1959. From November 1957 until July 1959, Killian was presidential science advisor to Dwight D. Eisenhower and the first person to hold such a post.
The main research fields were defense and disarmament studies, government and science, economics and technological change, history and philosophy of science, and linguistics. The committee, "built around an analysis of the interaction of sciences, technology and industry to a modern industrial society, . . . could study the process and institutional devices by which scientific concepts became transformed into industrial and military realities, the interaction of pure and applied science, and the impact of such processes and interaction on economic growth and national defense"; Alfred D. Chandler to Max F. Millikan, memorandum, April 6, 1959, M.I.T. Archive, MC 188, box 3, folder 86.
5. Max Millikan to Julius A. Stratton, memorandum, "Sciences and Economic Progress," September 6, 1957, p. 4, M.I.T. Archive, MC 188, box 3, folder 89.
6. See John Krige, "NATO and the Strengthening of Western Science in the Post-Sputnik Era," *Minerva* 39, 1: 81–108.
7. Ibid., 85.
8. James Killian to Henry Heald, summary, "Statement of a Proposal" (draft), March 12, 1957, pp. 2–3, M.I.T. Archive, AC 4, box 89, folder FF (1957).
9. Peter Haas, "Introduction: Epistemic Communities and International Policy Coordination," *International Organization* 46, 1 (1992): 3.
10. Joseph Weizenbaum, memorandum, "Trip to Berlin," July 29, 1965, p. 2, M.I.T. Archive, MC 423, box 32, folder 14-8.
11. See James Killian to Shepard Stone, memorandum, August 17, 1965, p. 7, M.I.T. Archive, MC 423, box 32, folder 14-8
12. "Report to the Ford Foundation on International Activities at M.I.T.—Center for International Studies," p. 4, M.I.T. Archive, AC 236, box 3, folder 16.

13. S. Stone to J. Willems, letter, July 13, 1959, FFA grant no. 59,506, sec. 4. See also "Proposal for an International Institute of Science and Technology, Report of the Working Group Appointed by the Secretary General of the North Atlantic Treaty Organization, October 1961," p. 51, NATO restricted document C-M (61) 85, FFA grant no. 59,506, sec. 5.

14. Interview with James Killian, November 3, 1960, p. 18, M.I.T. Archive, MC 423, box 41, folder 25-1.

15. James Killian, memorandum, "West Berlin," August 14, 1965, pp. 4–5, FFA reel 1965, log 65–420.

16. Shepard Stone to Waldemar Nielsen and others, memorandum, "Study of Western Science," October 27, 1959, pp. 1–2, FFA grant no. 59,506, sec. 4.

17. Ibid., 2.

18. C. K. Jorgensen to the Study Group, memorandum, November 5, 1959, p. 4, NATO Archive (Brussels), SCOM, 5-3-03. The creation of a Western Foundation for Scientific Research had been discussed by the NATO Scientific Committee before the creation of the Armand study group. See NATO document AC/137–D/11, May 23, 1958, pp. 1–2.

19. Summary record of meetings held at the Palais de Chaillot and the United States embassy, January 12 and 13, 1960, p. 4, NATO Archives, SCOM, 5-3-08(60).

20. Summary record of a meeting held at the Palais de Chaillot, November 19, 1959, p. 12, NATO Archives, SCOM, 5-2-03.

21. Ford Foundation, International Affairs, Recommended Action, p. 4, FFA reel 1167, grant no. 58-137, sec. 3.

22. Crawford D. Goodwin, "Memorandum on Evaluation of the European Community Institute for University Studies," January 13, 1976, FFA reel 1167, grant no. 58-137, sec. 3.

23. Shepard Stone, memorandum, "Review of the Activities of the European Community Institute for University Studies," October 13, 1959, p. 5, FFA reel 1167, grant no. 58-137, sec. 3.

24. Ibid.

25. Shepard Stone, memorandum, "Talk with Etienne Hirsch," October 13, 1959, FFA Reel 1167, grant no. 58-137, sec. 3.

26. "Resumé des reccomandations du Group d'Etude Armand," pp. 140–42, NATO Archive.

27. NATO Archive, SC, AC/137–R/3, p. 12.

28. NATO Archive, SC, AC/137–D/38, Reference AC/137–R/3, pp. 11–12.

29. Frederick Seitz to Shepard Stone, letter, March 5, 1960, FFA reel 10,852, grant no. 54-505.

30. Eugene B. Skolnikoff to S. Stone, letter, October 25, 1961.

31. "Proposal for an International Institute of Science and Technology, Report of the Working Group Appointed by the Secretary General of the North Atlantic Treaty Organization, October 1961," pp. 31–32, NATO restricted document C-M (61) 85, FFA grant no. 59,506, sec. 5.

32. Ibid., 4.

33. "An Alternative Proposal Arising from a Meeting between United States, French and British Representatives on July 16th and 17th 1962," Affaire Project Killian, Institut International de Science et Technologie, French National Archives (Mission des Archives Nationales auprès du Ministère de la Recherche), 920,548 art. 20.

34. "Summary Record of a Meeting of the Council," September 26, 1962, pp. 3–4, NATO Archives, SC C-R (62) 47.

35. "Alternative Proposal Arising from a Meeting between United States, French and British Representatives on July 16th and 17th, 1962," pp. 3–4.

36. "Statement of the Greek Representative to the Science Committee on the Report of the Working Group on the International Institute of Sciences and Technology," summary record of a meeting of the Council, February 15, 1963, p. 33, NATO Archives, SC, AC/137–R/15.

37. Summary record of a meeting of the Council, October 28, 1963, NATO Archives, SC, AC/137–R/17.

38. James Killian to Louis Neel, letter, October 27, 1960; French National Archives, 920,548 art. 20. For details on the questionnaire, see 77,321 art. 320, 1960–61, and Neel responses.

39. Ministère des affaires étrangères, June 29, 1962, "Instructions pour la mission française," French National Archives, 920,548 art. 20.

40. DGRST, Raymond Poignant 124/Cce/D.115, November 28, 1961, p. 3, French National Archives (Paris), 81/401 CCRST dossiers de travail, box 60, folder 147.

41. French National Archives (Fontainebleau), Contemporary sec., 810,401 art. 54/123. My translation.

42. Secret-confidential, Etat-Major Général de la défense nationale, October 31, 1961 (Projet d'état-major de la défense nationale, projet Killian), pp. 5–6 and 11, French National Archives, 920,548 art. 20, 1961–63, and 810,401 art. 60, 1961.

43. Jean-Marie Palayret, *Une université pour l'Europe, préhistoire de l'Institut Universitaire Européen de Florence (1948–1976)* (Florence: E.U.I., 1996).

44. Quoted ibid., 101.

45. James Killian to S. Stone, letter, August 17, 1965, p. 2, FFA reel 1965, log 65-620.

46. Roland Latarjet, "Remarques sur la création d'un institut international (projet Killian)," French National Archives, 810,401, box 54, folder 125. Comité Consultatif de la Recherche Scientifique et technique, 126/CC2/D.117 Annexe du compte rendu de la réunion du 1er décembre 1961.

47. Lorenza Sebesta, "Un nuovo strumento politico per gli anni sessanta. Il technological gap nelle relazioni euro-americane," in *Economia e creatività*, ed. Giuliana Gemelli and L. Sebesta, special issue of *Nuova Civiltà delle macchine* 16, 3 (1999): 11–23; and Jean-Jacques Solomon, "L'OCDE et les politiques scientifiques. Entretien avec Jean-Jacques Salomon, Propos recueillis par Muriel Leroux et Girolamo Ramunni," *Revue pour l'Histoire du CNRS* 3 (2000): 40–59.

48. Giuliana Gemelli, "From Imitation to Competitive-Cooperation: The Ford Foundation and Management Education in Western and Eastern Europe (1950s–1970s)," in Giuliana Gemelli, *The Ford Foundation and Europe: Cross-Fertilization of Learning in Social Sciences and Management* (Brussels: P.I.E., 1998), 267–304.

49. James Killian to Shepard Stone, letter, August 17, 1965, p. 5, FFA reel 1965, L65-620.

50. French National Archives (Fontainebleau), Contemporary sec., 810,244 art. 197, 1969–71; and Mission des Archives Nationales auprès du Ministère de la Recherche, 121 art. 6, Projet de création d'un Institut informatique international, 1967–70.

51. "Ecarts technologiques entre pays membres, Paris OCDE 1968," in Olivier Giscard d'Estaing, Eduard C. Pestel, and Alexander King, *Rapport de la Commisson d'etude sur la création d'un Institut Européen de la science et de la Technologie* (Paris and Hanover, 1968).

52. John A. Cade, "Un centre d'excellence pour le perfectionnement de la gestion: L'institut International de Gestion de la Technologie," *OECD Bulletin* (1972): 43–47.

53. Interview with Alexander King, London, June 9, 1996.

54. Peter de Janosi, "Visit to International Institute for the Management of Technology, Milan, June 5, 1975," FFA reel 1366, grant no. 73,222, sec. 2.

PART THREE

SOCIAL RESPONSES

American Democracy and the Welfare State: The Problem of Its Publics

JAMES T. KLOPPENBERG

Historians distrust the idea of inevitability. Whereas European and American social scientists earlier in the twentieth century advanced various cultural or structural explanations to account for differences between American and European societies and political systems, the recent renaissance in the historical study of politics has emphasized contingent factors that have determined outcomes on both sides of the Atlantic. Specific historical experiences, not a purportedly exceptional "liberal tradition," shaped social policy in the United States in the twentieth century. Those experiences predated the emergence of problems characteristic of urban industrial societies—the problems that welfare states attempt to solve—and more recent patterns have emerged through a series of contingent twentieth-century events that shunted decision makers toward particular outcomes. Instead of blaming the ghosts of John Locke or Thomas Jefferson or the supposedly stateless institutional structure of American government, we should look more closely at the political and cultural history of democracy in America.[1]

The title of this chapter inverts the title of John Dewey's most important book, *The Public and Its Problems* (1927). Written as a response to critics such as H. L. Mencken and Walter Lippmann, who dismissed democracy as foolish, impossible, or both, *The Public and Its Problems* presented Dewey's defense of democracy as a cultural and ethical as well as political project uniquely suited to a scientific, secular, and disenchanted age in which traditional sources of authority were no longer available. Dewey advanced three distinct arguments on behalf of democracy. First, because questions of desire and conceptions of interest are historical rather than timeless, democracy requires that such interests be shaped through interaction with others rather than in isolation from them. Second, community is not something elusive or romantic; it is forged by individuals through the imperfect process of communication and brought to life through their active participation in joint endeavors. That is the meaning of democracy as an ethical project. Third, the democratic project involves widespread participation and critical reflection on the constitution of desires, the communication of ideas, the construction of communities, and the shaping of public policy. That democratic ideal derives, Dewey pointed out, from the experience of individuals in their families, their homes, and their neighborhoods; only if we can find ways to extend those experiences to the broader local, state, and national levels can we create a genuinely democratic culture.

In this chapter I argue that there have been many publics involved in shaping politics in the United States and that the shape of social policy has reflected the fears as well as the aspirations of those diverse components of the American people. The problem of American social policy has been the problem of its publics. Awareness of that problem is as old as the nation itself. The aim of the United States Constitution, at least as it was understood by the individual who played the most important part in its framing, James Madison, was to enlarge the scope of politics so that a broad view of the public interest could emerge from the narrow, factionalized squabbles of local and state politics. Madison was not a twentieth-century interest-group liberal intent on institutionalizing faction. He valued above all the *process* of seeking provisional agreement, which was to be achieved by institutionalizing the means of moderating disagreement. Madison believed that through the presentation of diverse and competing points of view, a broader view would emerge, a more general perspective that would approximate a "public good" or "the true interest of [the] country," as he called it in *Federalist* number 10.[2]

But of course American politics did not live up to Madison's republican ideal, and he soon found himself joining with his friend Jefferson to combat the faction of financiers that they feared would transform national politics into a private club for Alexander Hamilton and his cronies. After a generation of American historians has focused on identifying when the initial American republican ambition gave way to a politics of self-interest, we should now examine the ways in which democratic institutions, which were put in place by the seventeenth- as well as eighteenth-century architects of American government, at the local and state as well as national levels, served to moderate or harden social tensions and initiate a politics of compromise or domination. The American people divided according to religion, race, and ethnicity. With different groups enjoying very different degrees of access to political power, they created a public realm that reflected those divisions and differences. Lacking a unified national authority or a unitary cultural tradition, the United States during the nineteenth century developed as a nation characterized not merely by the obviously distinct cultures of the slave South and the more or less free North but also by a patchwork of diverse political cultures animated by lively local voluntary associations. These institutions descended from earlier, often self-sufficient (if not always harmonious) communities, which created the sphere of civil society Tocqueville judged the distinctive and sustaining feature of democracy in America.

The distinctiveness of the American experience with poverty stems not from that division between the deserving and the nondeserving poor, which was universal in the Atlantic world, but from the absence of a unified national policy to cope with it. Because Americans understood poverty to be a local problem, towns and cities developed a multitude of different strategies to cope with it in the eighteenth and early nineteenth centuries. The first large-scale, nationwide program emerged with the Civil War pension system of the late nineteenth century, arguably the largest government program in the world at that time—a startling and paradoxical achievement for a nation generally characterized as lacking a fully developed state. Whether in the shape of the pension system or in the shape of local systems of care-giving, many Americans wanting or needing assistance came into contact with some agency of government.[3] Because political parties controlled these forms of assistance, however, they were especially vulnerable to criticism in a nation that cut its teeth on the fear of dependency and the belief that nothing threatens civic virtue more directly than the corruption of administration.

Thus before progressive reformers could discover that business corrupts politics, their predecessors the Mugwumps had already discovered that politics corrupts government. That conviction led many (although by no means all) late nineteenth- and early twentieth-century reformers to shy away from administration, which they deemed inherently corrupt, and to seek refuge in nostalgic invocations of a romanticized antistatist tradition. In their quest for social assistance for the poor, most progressives followed John Commons and the Wisconsin school of economists in emphasizing private schemes of social insurance. Only a minority of progressives believed, with Commons's colleague Richard Ely, that a social democratic state, funded by a system of graduated taxes, properly organized and efficiently administered, might provide universal coverage, impossible to achieve through the private sector, without falling victim to Bismarck's autocracy or the corruption of American schemes tainted by patronage.[4]

Progressives who did not dismiss the possibility of state action hoped the experience of federal activism in World War I might lead to permanent expansion of the national government's role in the economy and the provision of social welfare. Across the political spectrum, though, postwar sentiment turned away from the state and toward various private-sector alternatives. Welfare capitalism and industrial democracy attracted more talk than action, but both generated greater enthusiasm than did calls for government planning and social insurance. Although Herbert Hoover's ideal of an "associative state" differed from laissez-faire liberalism, the planning he envisioned was to be done at the instigation of, and on terms agreeable to, the private rather than the public sector.[5] Then came the New Deal.

Designed to mitigate the effects of an underregulated economy that seemed stuck in a downward spiral, the New Deal so clearly reflected what was politically feasible that many commentators have doubted there was any coherence at all to Roosevelt's policies. Roosevelt's administration did inaugurate an enduring national system of contributory old-age pensions, a system initially limited in scope that has gradually expanded enough to raise most retired Americans above poverty. Beyond that achievement, however, the legislation passed during the 1930s and 1940s seemed to contemporaries, as it seems to historians today, haphazard and chaotic. That much of the story is familiar.

Less familiar is Roosevelt's unsuccessful attempt, during the last three years of his life, to establish in the United States a social welfare state as extensive as any established in Europe in the late 1940s. Roosevelt announced that plan in the State of the Union Address on January 11, 1944. He described it in familiar terms as a "second bill of rights" because he wanted Americans to see these plans as securing rather than threatening their freedom. Roosevelt proposed programs ensuring that every American would have access to education, a job with a living wage, adequate housing, universal medical care, and insurance against old age, sickness, accident, and unemployment. This agenda was the culmination of Roosevelt's effort to bring order to the chaos of the New Deal. Global warfare dominated the 1944 presidential election, and it has dominated historical accounts of these years as well. But the proposals of the "second bill of rights" surfaced periodically, especially in an address Roosevelt delivered in Chicago on October 28, 1944, in which he delivered what he called "a well reasoned resume of his political and economic philosophy."[6] At the center of that philosophy were his plans for a decentralized and democratically administered American welfare state. Because the war preoccupied America until Roosevelt died, and because the Cold War transformed American politics afterward, Roosevelt's plan for a second bill of rights, and his successor Harry Truman's plan for what he called a Fair Deal that incorporated some of the same ideas, went nowhere.

But the defeat of this plan was not inevitable—any more than the dissolution of the Soviet Union and the reunification of Germany at the end of the 1980s were inevitable—and the little-known story of the plan's emergence reveals dimensions of American political culture almost as significant as the fact that it failed. Roosevelt's blueprints for postwar social policy originated in the efforts of the National Resources Planning Board (NRPB), an agency Roosevelt created after the Executive Reorganization Act of 1939, and received their most elaborate expression in a report delivered to the president by his uncle Frederic Delano, chairman of the NRPB, on December 4, 1941.

From its inception, the NRPB enjoyed a precarious existence. Its relations with Congress, which distrusted all creatures of the executive branch, were nasty, its funding was poor, its reception by the news media was brutish, and its life was short. It was also immensely productive, of plans if not of policies that eventually came to fruition. During the four years the NRPB existed, from July 1, 1939, to August 24, 1943, the board produced 220 reports on everything from "Post-Defense Economic Development in Alaska" to "A Development Plan for Puerto Rico."[7] Its range extended from microscopic studies of local water problems to all-encompassing plans for national economic and social policy. The most ambitious of its reports was *Security, Work, and Relief Policies,* the comprehensive plan for the future that was submitted to Roosevelt on the eve of America's entry into the war. The NRPB, whose most influential member was the political scientist Charles Merriam, engaged the economist Eveline M. Burns as the director of research for this project. Her training at the London School of Economics and her status as an authority on German as well as British social and economic policy made the board's recommendations especially vulnerable to the predictable shrieks of socialism and fascism that greeted the report when it was finally published—after a lengthy delay that reflected Roosevelt's preoccupation with World War II as much as his perception of the political firestorm it would ignite—in 1943.

The first 362 pages of the report today make rather tedious reading, because they consist of detailed descriptions of existing policies concerning public assistance, health care, social insurance, and federal work programs. The second half of the report, on the other hand, outlines bold strategies for solving the problems previously described. Included in this sweeping program were "Government provision of work for all adults who are willing and able to work," "Assurance of basic minimum security through social insurance," "A comprehensive underpinning general public-assistance system providing aid on the basis of need," and "Expansion of social services which are essential for the health, welfare, and efficiency of the whole population." Programs providing "disability insurance," "unemployment compensation," "old age and survivors insurance," and "a comprehensive general public-assistance program" were to be funded by progressive taxes on income rather than comparatively regressive taxes on consumption. In what proved to be a futile effort to forestall charges of fiscal irresponsibility, the NRPB argued that the nation could more easily afford to implement such programs than to ignore them.

It is not the provision of these basic services that would threaten the security and prosperity of the nation, but it is, on the contrary, the failure to develop the purchasing power implied in these services that drags down our national income. . . . Operating at half capacity, . . . we cannot provide these services, nor can the national economy be operated effectively. On a high level income these services are not only possible but are indicated as indispensable even from a narrow economic point of view. From a broader democratic point of view these guarantees of minimum security are equally indispensable.[8]

A distinctive aspect of the NRPB plan has been overlooked in the literature surrounding its work. Critics at the time focused so much on the centralization of government authority that they believed such a plan would bring that they overlooked one of the principal themes of the report, the need for "increased citizen participation." Particularly in the board's conclusion to its recommendations concerning the administration of social services, the report repeatedly emphasized public involvement. "It is highly important that efforts should be made to secure

greater citizen participation in the programs operated by government."
Some historians see such language as rhetoric designed to stave off
charges of totalitarianism. That judgment neglects the board's persistent
emphasis on combining federal coordination of programs and local
advisory bodies of citizens as the most desirable policy as well as the
most effective strategy to win public support. The NRPB recommended
specifically creating local boards that could report to administrators and
to legislatures "concerning failures to attain the objectives of the program attributable to organizational or administrative defects," and it
emphasized engaging the "lay public with the appeals machinery of the
different programs." Cumbersome as such procedures might be, that
was simply the price of democracy. Such provisions would "add to the
duties of the administrator and may well involve less speedy action. But
the gains through the enlistment of public support and understanding of
the issues faced by the administrator will more than compensate for any
slight delay."[9] Such advantages would flow in both directions, because
the desire for civic involvement that might motivate citizens to join such
advisory bodies would be further bolstered by the experience. The board
members had read their Tocqueville as well as their Madison.

They had also read their Dewey. The NRPB arguments for citizen
participation seem to me less a form of rhetorical self-defense than a
self-conscious endorsement of an ideal of open-ended, deliberative democratic community. In the 1930s, that ideal was most often linked with
the philosopher John Dewey, whose work was well known by Merriam,
who taught at the University of Chicago, and by Burns, who was
Dewey's colleague at Columbia. In fact, the final paragraph of the NRPB
discussion of "The Administration of Public Aid" could be a paraphrase
of Dewey's arguments in not only *The Public and Its Problems* (1927)
but also *Individualism Old and New* (1930) or *Liberalism and Social
Action* (1935):

lay participation will make great demands upon the individual citizens. . . . they
must be prepared to take their duties seriously and to sacrifice time and effort
to public service. The solution of the complex problems of public aid awaits the
concentration of the best thinking of the country upon this aspect of our national life. It calls, too, for a willingness on the part of the population at large
to subordinate cherished illusions and traditional values when they impede the
attainment of our national objectives. Prominent among our postwar objectives
is the assurance to our citizens of that minimum of security which keeps alive
self-respect and initiative, which will permit a higher standard of living and give
the opportunity to participate in the good things of life which our productive

capacity makes possible. We look forward to the day when this objective will come to be regarded as one of the most challenging and significant of all the problems facing a great people.[10]

As the final phrase makes clear, the NRPB realized that day had not yet dawned. They did not know just how far away it was.

Howls of protest greeted the NRPB report when it was published. Critics could not decide which part of the report was most objectionable—the idea of a welfare state, the expansion of the authority of the federal government, or a third dimension of the report that endorsed the idea of a mixed economy and called for government planning. Again Merriam's staff tried to reassure the public that they were democrats rather than autocrats; again they failed.[11] "We recommend," they wrote in another report submitted in 1943, "that governmental *planning programs be decentralized,* as far as administratively practical, to the States, counties, cities and appropriate regional agencies. Only in this way can we keep our post-war planning and action programs close to the public."[12] But how much decentralization is "administratively practical"? How can programs designed to coordinate activities beyond the grasp of local governmental agencies remain "close to the public"? These were questions that might trouble even those sympathetic to the NRPB's Deweyan vision, and they suggest the difficulties that would ultimately bring down the NRPB and its ambitious plans for the postwar world. The references to democracy, decentralization, and citizen participation that run through the NRPB reports indicate both the distinctiveness of the American plan for a welfare state and also suggest, paradoxically enough, the reasons why it failed. Regardless of whether the NRPB intended its democratic pronouncements to be taken as serious indications of its commitment to decentralization or intended them merely as a smokescreen, they testify to the persistent appeal of democratic and community-based approaches to economic and social problems.

Scholars have quarreled for five decades now about the thrust of Roosevelt's policies, and I cannot hope to resolve the controversies here. The tumult will no doubt continue, because it is impossible to determine exactly what Roosevelt intended the New Deal to be. Congress, the Supreme Court, and the ebbs and flows of public support for his programs severely constrained Roosevelt's options. Debates about whether or not he believed in the social democratic programs of the New Deal, however, have begun to seem pointless. Evidence is accumulating that he not only read but helped write the celebrated speech at the Commonwealth Club in the 1932 campaign, that he was an active member of the Brains Trust that framed the New Deal, and that his persistence in the face of mounting opposition during the years from 1934 to his death in 1945 testifies to his commitment to the welfare state. Recent work on the New Deal by Barry Karl, Alan Lawson, and Sidney Milkis in particular indicates that Roosevelt sought far more change than he got. Charges that Roosevelt wanted nothing more coherent than popular support ignore many of the major initiatives of his presidency, all of which were risky and most of which significantly eroded his political base. He embarked on his Supreme Court packing plan, his doomed effort to purge conservative congressmen from the Democratic Party, and, most importantly for my purposes here, his futile attempt to muster support for the policies of social provision recommended by the NRPB, not because such ideas were politically popular but because he considered them necessary. As more recent experience has shown, presidents intent on pleasing the American public learn to avoid such unpopular and expensive initiatives whenever possible.

Roosevelt was committed primarily to widening the door to economic opportunity and rigging the safety net that Harry Hopkins had been talking about since 1931.[13] He was a politician rather than a visionary, but he knew where he wanted the nation to go. He articulated his ideal most clearly in his 1944 State of the Union address. That speech was clearly based on the NRPB report delivered to him two years earlier, three days before the Japanese attack on Pearl Harbor on December 7, 1941, abruptly reordered his priorities. In this 1944 speech, which James MacGregor Burns has accurately termed "the most radical speech of his life," Roosevelt laid out the package of benefits that Congress would deliver in the G.I. Bill for veterans. But as he reiterated throughout the 1944 election campaign, the president wanted to secure those benefits for all citizens, just as the NRPB had urged.

Roosevelt was in good company, just in the wrong country. Whereas in America the NRPB's report led many liberals to disown the board and Congress to dismantle it, the Beveridge Report won solid, bipartisan support for a similarly ambitious scheme in Great Britain. Roosevelt clearly felt cheated by fate. He complained to Frances Perkins that the British version ought properly to be called the Roosevelt Plan, and he very much resented the pressures that forced him first to postpone discussion of the welfare state and then to surrender its most visible proponent, Henry Wallace, as a sacrificial lamb to propitiate Southern Democrats. The mood in Britain was clearly very different.

In June 1941, Beveridge was appointed to direct a committee charged with cleaning up Britain's existing national insurance scheme. Displaying more ambition than respect for the wishes of his superiors in the Treasury, he transformed the committee into a one-man band announcing the need for a wholesale revision of the entire scheme of social services. According to his biographer, Jose Harris, Beveridge almost immediately decided on the principal ideas that would appear in his final report. He aimed to banish from Britain "Five Giant Evils": Want, Disease, Ignorance, Squalor, and Idleness. After he had formulated a tentative plan of attack, Beveridge began calling before the committee witnesses from various groups to discuss his ideas. He discovered a surprising degree of agreement. In his published report, he called for a comprehensive system of social insurance, with benefits guaranteed by right to all citizens, for a national health service, for family allowances, and for policies sustaining full employment.[14]

In striking contrast to the hostile reception from the Left and Right that the recommendations of the NRPB received in America, the Beveridge Report was an immediate hit. Astonishingly, it sold over 600,000 copies. None of the witnesses Beveridge had called from the business community had objected that his ideas violated the inviolable principles of the free market, and none of the conservative press condemned his published report. None of the Labourites called as witnesses had protested the dangers of creeping autocracy, and such fears did not surface in the publications of the Left that discussed his plans. Even the Communist Party lionized him. Although Beveridge himself was a member of the Liberal Party (as was John Maynard Keynes, the other British prophet of the postwar world), both the Conservative and Labour Parties endorsed his proposals. The only discouraging words came from grumpy ministers in the wartime coalition government, who wondered aloud how a nation struggling to survive might afford the lavish programs Beveridge proposed. Churchill warned the Cabinet that "a dangerous optimism is growing about the conditions it will be possible to establish after the war. . . . I do not wish to deceive the people by false hopes and airy visions of Utopia and Eldorado." Churchill was still playing Cassandra. His government by then was rather more interested in hopes and visions, false, airy, or otherwise, than in continuing to confront the bleak features of the present.[15]

How can such near unanimity of opinion in Great Britain be explained? For twenty-five years a popular answer was that offered in 1950 by Richard Titmuss in his official study *Problems of Social Policy.*

Titmuss wrote, "the mood of the people changed and, in sympathetic response, values changed as well. . . . Dunkirk, and all that evokes, was an important event in the wartime history of the social services. It summoned forth a note of self-criticism, of national introspection, and it set in motion ideas and talk of principles and plans."[16] Perhaps, but commentators have become increasingly suspicious of the "war-warmed" glow of Titmuss's own account. Constructing the welfare state in Britain—as elsewhere in Europe—was arduous economically and politically. Any residue of the widespread enthusiasm at first felt for the Beveridge Report quickly sank in the morass of inflation, shortages, and unemployment that ultimately enveloped Atlee's Labour government. Perhaps consensus carried Labour into power, but it could not dissolve the economic and political problems that eventually drove it out.

Several features of the Beveridge Plan deserve consideration because of their contrast with the NRPB report and with FDR's and Truman's plans. As is true of the NRPB report, contemporaries writing about the Beveridge Plan focused on certain themes while all but ignoring others. The first is the extent to which Beveridge's apparently radical scheme was advanced on the basis of familiar premises. "The state in organizing security," he wrote toward the beginning of his report, "should not stifle incentive, opportunity, responsibility; in establishing a national minimum, it should leave room for encouragement for voluntary action by each individual." In his conclusion, Beveridge distinguished his scheme from the social insurance programs of other European nations. Whereas others calibrated benefits to the level of contributions, which varied according to salary level, Beveridge insisted that both benefits and contributions remain uniform. "The flat rate of benefit treating all alike is in accord with British sentiment for equal treatment of all in social insurance, irrespective both of their previous earnings and of the degree of their risk of unemployment or sickness."[17] This provision sounds egalitarian, even altruistic. But Beveridge clinched his argument, on the closing page of his report, by pointing out that equal treatment would be achieved by setting benefits at a level low enough to encourage all citizens to continue contributing to their own supplementary insurance schemes as well. From the outset, then, Beveridge took for granted the precariousness of life for those without resources of their own. The minimum standard was to be austere as much by design as by necessity; the economic constraints, real as they were, mattered less to Beveridge than the moral reasons for encouraging prudence and foresight. Echoes of earlier, and very widespread, concerns, including those of the 1790 Report of the Committee on Begging of the French Constituent Assembly, are easy to identify.[18]

Second, Beveridge felt no need, and made no effort, to defend his program against criticism of its centralized administration. Again, regardless of whether members of the NRPB are judged genuinely democratic or merely cagey, their report crackles with a rhetoric of participatory democracy altogether absent from the Beveridge Report. Beveridge discussed administration in considerable detail, but the question of the bureaucracy's problematical status vis à vis the public evidently concerned him not at all. A unified system would be more efficient and more cost effective, Beveridge contended, and the public would find the programs less confusing. His section "Advice to Citizens" contained no discussion of citizen participation or appeal procedures. Instead Beveridge blithely assured the public that an official would be present in every local office to explain the program to them and answer their questions. Nothing more was deemed necessary, and no objections were raised on this issue.

The Deweyan concern with popular consultation and interaction that marked the reports of the NRPB seems never to have crossed Beveridge's mind. In a later report, *Full Employment in a Free Society,* Beveridge elaborated his conception of British government in a passage illuminating the gulf separating his conception of representative democracy and the more Deweyan conception of the value of participation that animated the NRPB. "The constitution of Britain concentrates in the Government of the day the great power without which the problems of a great society cannot be solved. . . . Britain has a public service central and local, second to none in the world for efficiency, integrity and devotion to duty." Since our civil servants are neither Prussian autocrats nor American crooks, Beveridge reasoned, the British public need fear neither tyranny nor corruption. Even when Beveridge did indulge in a bit of democratic rhetoric, his words revealed an unself-conscious smugness altogether missing from the NRPB report. "The British people can win full employment while remaining free. But they have to win it, not wait for it. . . . It is not a thing to be promised or not promised by a Government, to be given or withheld as from Olympian heights. It is something that the British democracy would direct its Government to secure, at all costs save the surrender of individual liberties."[19] The democratic responsibilities Beveridge envisioned for British citizens would begin and end with the ballot. After representatives have been selected, and programs created, the government would take care of them itself. Administration must be left to a crackerjack corps of civil servants, not muddled by the intrusions of amateurs.

That predisposition likewise surfaced in Beveridge's call for government planning to sustain economic growth. "To look to individual employers for maintenance of demand and full employment is absurd. These things are not within the power of employers. They must therefore be undertaken by the State, under supervision and pressure of democracy, applied through the Parliament men." Once more, citizens are to apply pressure only through their elected representatives, not through direct involvement in the processes of planning or administration.[20]

The British experience with the politics of poverty helps explain Beveridge's approach to these problems just as clearly as American development helps account for the shape of the NRPB report. The world of the workhouse is familiar from the nightmarish accounts in Dickens's novels, but less frightful alternatives emerged during the nineteenth century. An elaborate network of private charitable organizations developed, and mutual societies and union-sponsored programs provided other sources of relief. Although the Charity Organization Society demanded moral reform almost as rigorously as the Poor Law did, the various worker-organized insurance plans offered less punitive solutions to the problems of short-term poverty. Perhaps as much as half the adult male population of England participated in such programs by the middle of the nineteenth century. But such plans survived only by turning away the worst risks. They thus cut adrift those most in need of assistance, who then had recourse only to the tender mercies of private or public Victorian "charity."

The Liberal Government that came to power in 1906 undertook the challenge of replacing the inadequate Poor Law system, and both trade unions and the struggling mutual societies reluctantly endorsed David Lloyd George's plan to provide pensions, public assistance, and insurance against ill health and unemployment. Until World War I shattered the optimism that undergirded the Liberal Party's philosophy of a new liberalism, the Liberals' program of social insurance and other progressive reforms seemed likely to succeed in integrating the working classes into a widening mainstream of British life. Although there were scattered protests concerning the potential intrusions by an alien bureaucracy into the sanctity of private life, by the 1920s the legitimacy of the national insurance program, and the integrity and efficiency of its administration, was well established. When thoughts turned toward expanding the welfare state during World War II, the precedents of government-sponsored and centrally administered insurance programs were already in place. Viewed in this context, the Beveridge Plan can be seen as a logical extension rather than a radical departure, and the widespread support it attracted from across the political spectrum seems no more surprising than the abuse that greeted the NRPB report.

American resistance to further expansion of the welfare state and economic planning stands in stark contrast to the experience of European nations, and it has attracted the attention of a number of historically minded social scientists. The most persuasive of these accounts have recently paid attention to a dimension that has not always figured prominently in social science, the subjective side of social experience. Identifying institutions and structures is essential, but it is equally essential to remember that unless institutions and structures have meaning for individuals, they do not survive. American political, social, and economic institutions have changed over two centuries, and those changes have reflected the efforts of individuals, groups, classes, and the emergence of uncontrollable or at least uncontrolled forces such as urbanization and industrialization. Unless we attend equally to the phenomenology of historical experience and to the structural dimensions of social life, our explanations are bound to be incomplete. Having noted that beneath these general characterizations lie the particular commitments and loyalties of individuals, I will briefly outline some of the features of American political culture that stood in the way of Roosevelt and his plans.

The absence of a tradition of royal absolutism in the United States and the fact that democratization preceded the emergence of the state contributed to the rise and persistence of boisterous, vital, and diverse political cultures at the local and state levels. These jurisdictions have developed vested interests, cherished different aspirations, and exhibited often quite limited administrative competence, all of which have enormously complicated efforts at national reform. Moreover, America's two-party system and tradition of pluralism have meant that parties are coalitions lacking unity of identity and purpose, primitive creatures that rarely generate sufficient ideological loyalty to sustain ambitious political programs. These features of public life invite widespread participation at every level of decision making, and that degree of democratic engagement makes the creation of coherent national policies almost impossible. When Roosevelt tried to reorganize the executive branch of the federal government, pack the Supreme Court, purge the Democratic Party of conservatives who opposed the programs of his New Deal—or extend the federal government's role in social welfare or economic planning—he encountered opposition at every step. The traditions of decentralization, local government, and separation of powers are values that Americans cherish for a variety of high-minded as well as self-interested reasons. If "bringing the state back in" is to mean more than Hegel's revenge, students of American public life must appreciate that the flip side of the narrow-minded parochialism often associated with antistatist positions is the relatively autonomous, local democratic community, whether it offers the warm and nurturing intimacy of Tocqueville's acquaintance or the cold-blooded power politics of urban machines. The American distrust of bureaucracy springs from a long-standing association of virtue with autonomy and of dependency with corruption, and American champions of state activism must continue to contend with the variations on that theme that persist across the political spectrum.

Roosevelt disliked John L. Lewis of the CIO as much as he disliked Sewell Avery of Montgomery Ward, but he nevertheless fancied himself a friend of organized labor as well as, in his own words, the best friend America's capitalists had. Unfortunately for the New Deal, neither group reciprocated. Organized labor continued to migrate into the Democratic Party during the 1930s and 1940s, but beyond workers' votes, Roosevelt received little visible support for his more ambitious social and economic policies during World War II. Labor opted instead for collective bargaining, preferring the autonomy of private negotiations on fringe benefits to the universal programs urged by the NRPB report.[21] Although some self-styled progressives saw the opportunities planning presented for corporate America, most business leaders distrusted Roosevelt's vision of a mixed economy. Farmers' organizations likewise grew cooler about Roosevelt's plans once prosperity returned to American agriculture. Southerners saw lurking behind every national program dangerous threats to the system of racial supremacy that they had no intention of surrendering. Lacking support from labor, business, farmers, or the South, Roosevelt found few to rally behind his "second bill of rights." Even liberal economists, whose support Roosevelt had thought secure by the end of the 1930s, began shifting their allegiance from trust busting or regulation to Keynesian fiscal policy as the most promising strategy for achieving full employment. Pump priming through tax cuts appeared far more palatable—and more effective—than expensive public works projects. As Keynes's stock rose, whatever limited enthusiasm there might have been for the more elaborate plans of the NRPB fell.[22]

As fundamental as any other factor, though, was the economic boom that war brought to America. With prosperity came satisfaction, and satisfaction eroded reformist sentiment. Public sacrifice, at least on the scale that Titmuss and others considered adequate to account for the acceptance of the Beveridge Report in England, was largely absent in the United States. Although the suffering of Americans separated by the war cannot be denied, Americans were required to give up much less in the way of material goods than were the populations of some European nations. In the unsentimental formulation of Mark Leff, the characteristic American response to calls for solidarity was "What? Me Sacrifice?" Confidence in business and commitment to the superiority of the American way of life soared during the war and peaked at the war's end. Roosevelt's (and later Truman's) postwar plans spelled change. Americans were ready to celebrate, not ready to reform.[23]

American political institutions, various economic characteristics, the crucial fact of racism, and the unanticipated return of prosperity all presented obstacles to the Second Bill of Rights. Beyond all of these, though, was another set of factors, the contingent, unpredictable political developments that likewise limited Roosevelt's options. First, both the successes and failures of his own initiatives constrained him. The Social Security system was safe, but its safety was secured by institutionalizing the long-standing division between the deserving and nondeserving poor. The American plan drew a line separating old-age pensions, funded by contributions, from welfare programs, which would remain discretionary, means-tested, and political lightning rods. By contrast, the problems involved in administering both the NRA and the WPA sobered Roosevelt, and his ambivalence about postwar economic planning derived at least in part from his doubts about the compatibility of democratic politics and government by central planning boards—doubts that recent experience with planned economies has shown to be well founded. Other non-institutional, nonstructural developments included the dramatic losses Democrats sustained in the mid-war congressional elections in 1942. Just as the triumph of the Beveridge Plan was confirming a wartime political truce in Britain, the New Deal coalition was losing control of Congress to an alliance of Southern Democrats and conservative Republicans. Whereas Britain's coalition government effectively suspended most partisan squabbling for the duration of the war, Roosevelt was granted no holiday from politics. When the NRPB report appeared, for example, it was quickly branded "socialist, fascist, and medieval," an omnibus charge that indicted the

Roosevelt administration for moving at once too fast, too slow, too far to the left, and too far to the right. Roosevelt had reason to act cautiously in 1944: charges of dictatorship and collectivism were fighting words. Despite the best efforts of Roosevelt and Truman to present their plans in democratic terms and to couch them in the vocabulary of rights, in the supercharged atmosphere of wartime America and during the early days of the Cold War that followed, all change was suspect, all government ominous.

The confidence Americans felt in the free enterprise system was more than matched by the confidence and pride Britain felt in its government's resourcefulness in the face of the Luftwaffe. The Labour Party's participation in Churchill's government enabled Labour ministers to establish their legitimacy and responsibility without identifying them too closely with the war itself. Ministers such as Ernest Bevin, Clement Atlee, Hugh Dalton, and Herbert Morrison succeeded in associating Labour with the Beveridge Plan, and all that it promised, without appearing to be either disloyal or responsible for the hardships of the war. Hysterical protests against government tyranny, of the sort common in America, were mooted by the simple fact that the British government had managed the economy effectively during World War II, nationalizing industries and running the health service to see the nation through the emergency. Condemning such measures as un-British in the same way that they were dubbed un-American was not an option.

Moreover, Conservatives and Liberals had vied with Labour in their enthusiasm for the idea of the welfare state and planning even before the war. The renegade Tory Harold Macmillan favored the nationalization of the coal mines (a measure he opposed after the war). In 1936 he called for a new Centre Party, which would be "a fusion of all that is best in the Left and the Right." Macmillan also wrote a book, *The Middle Way* (1938), in which he argued the case for a national minimum, to be secured by a welfare state and financed through revenues derived from a comprehensive plan for a managed economy. Although Liberals differed on how extensive planning should be, contributors to the Liberal manifesto *The Next Five Years* (1935) agreed that government must broaden its horizons. During the war a royal commission headed by Sir Montague Barlow recommended a plan for allocating resources and locating industrial development, and in 1944 the Conservative minister of health, Henry Willink, proposed a plan for a permanent national health service. At times it seemed Liberals such as Beveridge and Conservatives such as Macmillan were trying to outflank Labour on the left. In the words of

T. H. Marshall, whose postwar writings on the welfare state helped explain its emergence and legitimate its presence, by the end of the war the welfare state "could enjoy a ready-made consensus."[24] What to build on that consensus, not whether to accept it, was at issue in the elections of 1945. Churchill promised to remain rock-solid until Japan was defeated; Labour promised mass housing. Churchill miscalculated the public mood; Labour triumphed. But it is worth noting that both parties endorsed the Beveridge Report. Although they disagreed about nationalization, there was no point in discussing the welfare state and economic planning, which by 1945 had moved beyond controversy. They had become integral parts of the British conception of government, as they remain today despite the spirited efforts of the Conservative Party to dismantle costly social programs.

Just as the New Deal took shape under circumstances strikingly different from those of the Beveridge Plan, so did it leave a strikingly different legacy, a pattern of social welfare programs bifurcated along two separate axes. The public system distinguished between Social Security, with benefits "earned" by contributions, and welfare, with "unearned" and means-tested benefits paid from general tax revenues. An equally split private system of employee benefits packages developed alongside this public system. Millions of workers contributed to company- or union-sponsored insurance plans, while others, usually those in the most marginal positions in the economy and thus most vulnerable, survived without any insurance at all. As such programs became increasingly comprehensive and generous, they cemented the commitment to the private sector of those who stood to benefit from them, while at the same time they eroded public interest in state-sponsored programs designed to assist those who lacked access to such insurance. Not only salaried members of the middle class but also unionized workers achieved levels of insurance that rivaled those of the most elaborate European welfare states. Because these schemes remained private in the United States, however, participation in them remained no more secure than the jobs workers held or the prosperity of the sectors of the economy in which they were employed. As the economy has been transformed in recent decades, the extent of those risks has become increasingly apparent.

Despite, or perhaps, paradoxically, because of this doubly divided system, America's fragmented welfare system has expanded slowly and not surely. The Social Security system has become as generous as any pension plan anywhere; its benefits are indexed to inflation and set at a level that makes retirement for most Americans far less perilous than it once was. Private benefits packages have become increasingly comprehensive. For those excluded from these contributory schemes, however, the situation has remained bleak. Studies of public opinion have found repeatedly that Americans are "operational liberals" and "ideological conservatives." In other words, they want existing programs to continue, although often not to expand, even as they proclaim themselves philosophically opposed to government assistance. Cross-national studies confirm the near universality of such contradictory positions, which underscores the persistence of distinctions long drawn between the deserving and nondeserving poor. To reiterate, the American scheme is unusual—although hardly unique—because it institutionalizes that division by separating contributory from noncontributory programs. Acknowledging that limitation, however, should not blind us to the steady expansion of the American Social Security system, which now covers more than 90 percent of the work force, or to the more recent creation of programs providing food stamps, Medicaid, and Medicare, which have further broadened the benefits available.

Despite its successes, the American welfare state has remained on the defensive, assailed from the Right for wastefulness and from the Left for institutionalizing social control. Despite such criticism, the system survives, sustained by its own bureaucratic momentum and by the general belief that something (usually unspecified) must be done about poverty. To a degree, the perpetuation of the system reflects the accuracy of a prediction offered by one of its many architects, Joseph Harris, at a planning session for the federal Committee on Administrative Management in 1936: "We may assume that the nature of the problems of American economic life are such as not to permit any political party for any length of time to abandon most of the collectivist functions which are now being exercised. This is true even though the details of policy programs may differ and even though the old slogans of opposition to enlargement of governmental activity will survive long after their meaning has been sucked out."[25]

Not only have the "policy programs" of the New Deal and the "old slogans of opposition" both survived, as Harris anticipated, so has the meaning of that opposition. Opposition to welfare, in other words, need not always be rooted in racism, although surely it often is. It can also derive from a legitimate fear that corruption of both parties—the one receiving and the one providing benefits—inevitably results under conditions of dependency. In such conditions, the reciprocity that should undergird democratic culture cannot be secured because of the asymmetry of the relationship.

Philosophers from Hugo Grotius and Thomas Hobbes to Robert Goodin and Jeremy Waldron have argued that everyone has the moral right to do what is necessary to survive. Thus the most solid, if not the most inspiring, defense of the welfare state may be among the most simple: Welfare, Waldron writes, "is a way of ensuring that no one should ever be in such abject need that he would be driven to violate otherwise enforceable rules of property." Beyond that rather modest justification, champions of the welfare state might add Joseph Raz's autonomy principle, which requires, as a cost of freedom, making efforts "to secure the conditions of autonomy for all people." Together these principles provide a rationale for welfare that does not require altruism or a commitment to equality as a higher priority than liberty. In Robert Goodin's words, "If full participation in our societies is conditional upon a person's being a minimally independent agent, then morally we must not only serve the needs of those who are dependent upon us but also do what we can to render those persons independent." Viewed in this light, the welfare state can be defended not as a form of soft-hearted humanitarianism but as nothing more (or less) than a manifestation of a thorough-going commitment to autonomy for all citizens. Until or unless such arguments are made, the welfare state will continue to appear vulnerable to legitimate criticism from the Right as well as the Left.[26]

The problem with America's welfare state, conceived in these terms, is not its degree of generosity but its lack of generality. To quote Goodin again, "what was crucial in the shift from the old poor law state to the modern welfare state was the move (coming in 1911 in Britain, and 1935 in the United States) away from discretionary public charity and toward nondiscretionary entitlement rules. It is these nondiscretionary entitlement rules, more than anything else, that give the welfare state its peculiar moral flavor."[27] Thus it was not, as is often argued, the shift in rhetoric from responsibilities to rights that doomed America's welfare state. Roosevelt's decision to follow the NRPB, and to frame the issue in terms of individual freedom, was not a fatal error but rather a sensible strategy that failed. It failed, moreover, not because it embodied a faulty conception of the purpose of welfare, but for the various political, economic, social, and circumstantial reasons already discussed. Americans were not prepared in the 1930s, and will not be prepared in the twenty-first century, to endorse principles they consider socialist. Michael Walzer has urged partisans of a universalist welfare state, a system that would extend its benefits to all citizens as a matter of right and without means testing, to stop trying to socialize the means of production and concentrate instead on trying to socialize the means of distribution. As socialist states have learned from decades of experience, public ownership is a disappointment. At a time when the buying power of the minimum wage in the United States has dropped below its 1970 level, and when the richest one percent of Americans, approximately 2.7 million people, take home as much after-tax income as the bottom one hundred million put together, the challenge remains to find ways to continue to maximize production while assuring that all citizens have access to the opportunities necessary for autonomous life, access that appears to be slipping further beyond the reach of those stuck on the lower rungs of America's economic ladder as the extent of income inequality has increased in the last two decades.[28]

Equally attractive are the means Roosevelt's planners preferred. In the introduction to his comparative study of the welfare state, *In Care of the State,* Abram de Swaan writes, "it may well be that the collection and distribution of money transfers is handled best by the central state—for reasons of distributive justice—but that the adjudication of cases and the administration of human services is better left to small, self-managing cooperative bodies of citizens."[29] That sensible judgment resembles nothing I have encountered in the literature of the welfare state so closely as it resembles the final recommendations of the NRPB. Principled democrats distrust powerful state bureaucracies for good reasons, which Max Weber explored in his analysis of the elective affinities between the disenchantment of the world and the rise of rationalization: the principles of effective administration require predictable procedures and impersonal rules, whereas the principles of democracy provide for change and innovation in response to public demand. The conflict between bureaucracy and democracy is inescapable, and only to the extent that participation can be built into administration, as the NRPB hoped and Walzer and de Swaan urge, can those conflicts be eased. They can never be eliminated.

It is impossible to explain the results of the American or British efforts to construct a welfare state by concentrating exclusively on social structures, long-term processes, political institutions, or cultural traditions. All of those factors played a part, yet they are necessary but not sufficient elements of an adequate explanation. In addition to such components, we must add—as historians always do—the contingent and unpredictable circumstances within which individuals made choices, the subjective dimension of these policy-making processes that the effort to construct analytical models may cause us to overlook. As studying the construction of welfare states in America and Britain reveals, history without a structural framework is shapeless, but institutional explanations without a phenomenology of historical experience are hollow.

The references to democracy, decentralization, and citizen participation that run through the NRPB reports indicate both the distinctiveness of the American plan for a welfare state and the reasons why it failed. The democratic pronouncements of the NRPB testify to the persistent and powerful appeal in the United States of democratic and community-based approaches to economic and social problems. Yet it was the resistance of certain communities in the United States—notably the communities of white Southerners who successfully blocked any initiatives that might destabilize a social order premised on racism and designed to preserve inequality, but just as crucially the steadfast opposition of midwestern farmers and organized labor to Roosevelt's Second Bill of Rights and Truman's Fair Deal—that eventually defeated these proposals. The wealthy white males who dominated the United States Congress deliberated on these ideas and rejected them because they threatened their own treasured forms of hierarchical community. Roosevelt's and Truman's programs for a generous, extensive, and democratic welfare state foundered for many reasons, but they did not fail simply due to the absence of social democratic ideas similar to those that triumphed in Western Europe after 1945. Without a commitment to the ethic of reciprocity, deliberation within formally democratic institutions does not guarantee egalitarian results.

NOTES

1. This essay extends and elaborates arguments first advanced in James T. Kloppenberg, *The Virtues of Liberalism* (New York: Oxford University Press, 1998); readers interested in fuller discussion of the secondary sources on these issues should consult pages 210–17 of that volume. On the need to focus on democracy rather than earlier quarrels over liberalism and socialism, see James T. Kloppenberg, "From Hartz to Tocqueville: Shifting the Focus from Liberalism to Democracy in America," in *The Democratic Experiment: New Directions in American Political History,* ed. Meg Jacobs, William J. Novak, and Julian Zelizer (Princeton: Princeton University Press, forthcoming).

2. For more extensive discussion of Madison and democracy in early American politics, see Kloppenberg, *Virtues of Liberalism,* 3–70.

3. See William R. Brock, *Investigation and Responsibility: Public Responsibility in the United States, 1865–1900* (Cambridge: Cambridge University Press, 1984); and Theda

Skocpol, *Protecting Soldiers and Mothers: The Political Origins of Social Policy in the United States* (Cambridge: Belknap Press of Harvard University Press, 1992).

4. See Richard L. McCormick, *The Party Period and Public Policy: American Politics from the Age of Jackson to the Progressive Era* (New York: Oxford University Press, 1986), 197–227, 263–88, 311–56; and James T. Kloppenberg, *Uncertain Victory: Social Democracy and Progressivism in European and American Thought, 1870–1920* (New York: Oxford University Press, 1986), 199–297.

5. Barry D. Karl, *The Uneasy State: The United States from 1915 to 1945* (Chicago: University of Chicago Press, 1983), 46–69; Ellis Hawley, "The New Deal State and the Anti-Bureaucratic Tradition," in *The New Deal and Its Legacy: Critique and Appraisal,* ed. Robert Eden (New York: Greenwood Press, 1989), 77–92.

6. For Roosevelt's 1944 State of the Union Address, see *The Public Papers and Addresses of Franklin D. Roosevelt,* ed. Samuel I. Rosenman, vol. 13, 1944–45 (New York: Russell and Russell, 1984), 299. For Roosevelt's campaign speech, see "We Are Not Going to Turn the Clock Back, Campaign Address at Soldiers' Field, Chicago, Illinois," October 28, 1944, in *Public Papers and Addresses,* 13:369–78.

7. Marion Clawson, *New Deal Planning: The National Resources Planning Board* (Baltimore: Johns Hopkins University Press, 1981), 322–47, provides a chronological list of the major reports published by the NRPB. On the NRPB, see also Barry D. Karl, *Charles E. Merriam and the Study of Politics* (Chicago: University of Chicago Press, 1974); Philip W. Warken, *A History of the National Resources Planning Board* (New York: Garland Publishing, 1979); and Alan Brinkley, *The End of Reform: New Deal Liberalism in Recession and War* (New York: Knopf, 1995), 245–64.

8. National Resources Planning Board [NRPB], *Security, Work, and Relief Policies* (Washington, D.C.: U.S. Government Printing Office, 1943), 4, 345–49.

9. Ibid., 400, 405, 410–12, 420, 424.

10. Ibid., 544; emphasis in original. Cf. NRPB, *Report for 1943* (Washington, D.C.: U.S. Government Printing Office, 1943), 81: "Greater efforts must be made by administrators to take the public into their confidence, and all techniques for enlisting lay participation, such as advisory committees and representation of citizens on appeal boards, must be exploited to the full. In this venture, the private social agencies have an important role to play. The sphere of their activities has been changed by the increasing assumption by government of responsibility for maintenance of the needy, but their opportunities for experimentation in the improvement of service and for leadership in evaluation and understanding of policies and programs have been correspondingly increased."

11. Congressman John Rankin of Mississippi called the NRPB's report "the most fantastic conglomeration of bureaucratic stupidity ever sent to Congress. . . . It would wreck this Republic, wipe out the Constitution, destroy our form of government, set up a totalitarian regime, eliminate private enterprise, regiment our people indefinitely, and pile up on their backs a burden of expenditures that no nation on earth could bear." Rankin's editorial from the *New York Times,* March 14, 1943, is quoted in Warken, *National Resources Planning Board,* 233.

12. NRPB, *Report for 1943,* 18.

13. Harry Hopkins, "Beyond Relief: The Larger Task," *New York Times,* August 19, 1931.

14. William Beveridge, *Social Insurance and Allied Services* (London: Macmillan, 1942).

15. Churchill quoted in Derek Fraser, *The Evolution of the British Welfare State: A History of Social Policy since the Industrial Revolution,* 2d ed. (London: Macmillan, 1984), 218.

16. Richard Titmuss, *Problems of Social Policy* (London: Her Majesty's Stationery Office, 1950), 508.

17. Beveridge, *Social Insurance and Allied Services,* 6–7, 293.

18. Ibid.; see also the discussion of Beveridge's earlier manifesto, *Insurance for All and Everything,* published in 1924, in Michael Freeden, *Liberalism Divided: A Study in British Political Thought, 1914–1939* (Oxford: Clarendon Press of Oxford University Press, 1986), 98.

19. William Beveridge, *Full Employment in a Free Society* (New York: Norton, 1945), 257–58.

20. Ibid., 16. See also William Beveridge, *Causes and Cures of Unemployment* (London: Longmans, Green, 1931).

21. In a letter to Felix Frankfurter, written February 9, 1937, Roosevelt wrote, "it is the same old story of those who have property to fail to realize that I am the best friend the profit system ever had, even though I add my denunciation of unconscionable profits." Frankfurter Papers, Library of Congress, Washington, D.C., quoted in Sidney M. Milkis, "The Presidency, Policy Reform, and the Rise of Administrative Politics," in *Remaking American Politics,* ed. Sidney M. Milkis and Richard A. Harris (Boulder, Colo.: Westview Press, 1989), 185; see also Sidney M. Milkis, *Political Parties and Constitutional Government: Remaking American Democracy* (Baltimore: Johns Hopkins University Press, 1999).

22. For the most detailed account of the rise of Keynesian thinking and its effect on social democratic initiatives, see Brinkley, *End of Reform.*

23. Mark Leff, "The Politics of Sacrifice on the American Home Front in World War II," *Journal of American History* 77 (1991): 1296–1318.

24. T. H. Marshall, "The Welfare State: A Sociological Interpretation," quoted in Stein Ringen, *The Possibility of Politics: A Study in the Political Economy of the Welfare State* (Oxford: Oxford University Press, 1987), 35.

25. Joseph Harris, "Outline for the New York Conference," May 9 and 10, 1936, Franklin D. Roosevelt papers, Hyde Park, N.Y., quoted in Sidney M. Milkis, "The New Deal, Administrative Reform, and the Transcendence of Partisan Politics," *Administration and Society* 18 (1987): 445.

26. Jeremy Waldron, "Welfare and the Images of Charity," *Philosophical Quarterly* 36 (1986): 463–82; Joseph Raz, *The Morality of Freedom* (Oxford: Clarendon Press of Oxford University Press, 1986), 409; Robert E. Goodin, *Reasons for Welfare: The Political Theory of the Welfare State* (Princeton: Princeton University Press, 1988), 183.

27. Ibid., 368.

28. Michael Walzer, "Socializing the Welfare State," in *Democracy and the Welfare State,* ed. Amy Gutmann (Princeton: Princeton University Press, 1988), 13–26. On the increasing gap between rich and poor in America since 1980, see Robert B. Reich, "The Great Divide," *American Prospect,* May 8, 2000, 56; Richard B. Freeman, *The New Inequality: Creating Solutions for Poor America* (Boston: Beacon Press, 1999); Theda Skocpol, *The Missing Middle: Working Families and the Future of American Social Policy* (New York: Norton, 2000); and James T. Patterson, *America's Struggle against Poverty,* rev. ed. (Cambridge: Harvard University Press, 2000), esp. chap. 16, "The Amazing 90s."

29. Abram De Swaan, *In Care of the State: Health Care, Education, and Welfare in Europe and the USA in the Modern Era* (New York: Oxford University Press, 1988), 11.

A Checkered History:
The New Deal, Democracy, and Totalitarianism
in Transatlantic Welfare States

MAURIZIO VAUDAGNA

In its special issue of December 31, 1999, *Time* magazine renewed its gratuitous but amusing habit of announcing the Person of the Century. Between Albert Einstein in first place as the embodiment of scientific and technological change, and before Mohandas Gandhi in third as the champion of the end of colonialism, came Franklin D. Roosevelt. The eulogy written by President Bill Clinton cited the "two decisive victories" that Roosevelt managed to win in the twentieth-century battle for freedom: "first over economic depression and then over fascism."[1] In the first instance, Roosevelt realized that "for markets to flourish, government must be devoted to opportunity for all. He understood that the initiative and the responsibilities of community must be woven together."[2] The interdependence of a socially compassionate government and the battle against fascism as two sides of a single defense of democracy is stressed equally by others in the same issue of the magazine. Roosevelt's social and economic program, said Andrew M. Greeley from Chicago, "laid the groundwork . . . for the progress in justice for all Americans."[3] Senator Edward M. Kennedy stressed that during his more than thirty years in Congress, Roosevelt's legacy—be it in foreign policy, national defense, or Social Security—had always been on the agenda: "The genius of his leadership guided us through the Depression and world war."[4]

When, on January 6, 1941, Franklin D. Roosevelt defined the purpose of American participation in the war with his "Four Freedoms" address, he "naturally" mentioned freedoms "of" and "from"—the human, political, and social freedoms of speech and religion, from want and fear—as being part of the same political vision. In his history of freedom in America, Eric Foner has stressed that, in both the Progressive Era and the New Deal, the pursuits of political, personal, and social liberties were one and the same thing.[5] The memory of the welfare state held by both Europeans and Americans in the postwar years, especially by Progressives, has identified the growth of the Social Security system and the progress of democracy as one sociopolitical development. Historically oriented analysts of the welfare state, while well aware that the origins of the social insurance harked back to the paternalist "social monarchy" of the German-speaking world, still played down the challenge to democratic institutions vented by the social criticism of both bolshevism and fascism, and tried instead to analyze regularities between the growth of democracy and the increase in the welfare provision. Peter Flora and Arnold J. Heidenheimer have stressed,

the real beginning of the modern welfare state, however, had to await the transformation of the absolutist state into mass democracy in the last third of the nineteenth century. . . . In thus linking welfare state development with the evolution of mass democracy, one may interpret the welfare state as an answer to increasing demands for socioeconomic equality or as the institutionalization of social rights relative to the development of civil and political rights.[6]

American and European responses to the "social question" as it emerged in the last third of the nineteenth century were very different, and the "social service state" (to use the term preferred by William Beveridge) has been defined by commentators and scholars as a "European specificity." The German social historian Hartmut Kaelble, who recently detected a growing social convergence among European societies in the twentieth century, has stressed that "Europe has been the true bastion of the modern welfare state throughout the twentieth century. Nowhere else did it grow to such proportions, nowhere else was it imbued with such vigor."[7] American leaders, scholars, and public opinion have been very aware of the "European primacy" in the advancement of social protection and rights for a long time. Between 1900 and World War II, public leaders and commentators frequently defined the United States as a "laggard," a latecomer in building social protection, whose coverage was also less generous and comprehensive than that of most European countries because of America's prevalent values of individualism, localism, and privatism. In the first third of the twentieth century, European social-democrat and labor observers joined with American Progressives and New Dealers in expecting the United States to catch up in the building of its social provision. Commentators were confident that the welfare state was inescapable: the fundamental features of modernity would soon Europeanize the United States—that is, make it expand its social protection through new welfare programs that were managed by the federal government and were national in scope. America too, as it seemed during the New Deal, would embrace the European principles of industrial labor and class alignment that would frame and channel welfare policies; it would overcome the federalist tradition of local government and self-help, its opposition to federal social protection, its preference for schemes of privately based social benefits and insurance, and its distaste for public bureaucracies, which were nationwide in scope and legitimized by a public action that was necessary to manage encompassing national programs. The notion that a welfare state was of necessity bound to happen was the public version of the scholarly discussion on whether there had been, in the history of the social provision, a threshold at which capitalist industry and urbanization prevailed so significantly that the onset of social security and services was inevitable.[8] In 1998, Daniel T. Rodgers published a masterful work on the extensive borrowings from the European social experience by an unending stream of American reformers, intellectuals, politicians, social scientists, and journalists in areas such as urban planning, cooperatives, low-cost housing, social insurance, and public education. From the beginning of the century until World War II, these "Atlantic crossings" identified an age in the framing of social policy in America.[9]

If the invention of the welfare state has been mainly a European innovation, then it is surprising that its historians have given little attention to how the social issue was related to the great twentieth-century tragedy of European history and the battle between liberty and dictatorship that raged in the Old World. Did the fact that, until World War II, the idea of an inescapable social provision was held not so much by the liberal democratic orders but mostly by its authoritarian counterparts affect the way in which social rights were framed, expanded or limited, and approved or disapproved of in America during the strategic decades of the 1930s and 1940s? This chapter tries to show that what Volker Berghahn and Charles Maier have called the European "laboratory of political pathology,"[10] within which the European welfare states developed, helps explain some features of the way in which social assistance and the "mixed system" came to emerge in the American New Deal order.

Throughout the 1930s, and peaking in the presidential election of 1936, a ferocious controversy raged in the American political arena: the issue was whether the New Deal was illegitimately importing from Europe and imposing upon the country a series of "foreign isms" (as the language of the time put it)—fascism, communism, socialism—with no roots in American principles. In the mid- and late 1930s, the issue of the New Deal's coherence within a thinly defined American political tradition grew significantly more important, because, among other things, the image of Europe had been changing and European social experiments took place amid increasingly successful totalitarian orders. After 1933 and Hitler's rise to power in Germany, Europe was increasingly identified with the forces of antiliberalism and totalitarianism. By mid-decade, the image of the international scene as one of competitive society-ordering principles potentially at war with one another had made much progress.

How social policy would locate itself in the emerging great divide became a painful and controversial issue. In the early 1930s, the Rooseveltian idea (to be revived during World War II) that liberalism could be made more socially minded and communism more freedom conscious still had credibility. Italian fascism could be seen as responding to local conditions and being part of the Mediterranean political folklore of a second-rate country in the European theater. American democracy seemed so obviously different and Italy such an irrelevant threat to the international order that Franklin D. Roosevelt, Rexford Tugwell, and progressives of many countries could praise the Italian corporative state and be at the same time quite sure that they were not inadvertently catching some authoritarian "germs" of fascism. The distinguished foreign correspondent of the *New York Times,* Anne O'Hare McCormick, could be a supporter, a frequent interviewer of, and personal visitor to both Roosevelt and Mussolini, because of the then often-heard notion that social policy was on the public agenda in every country, differences in the political orders notwithstanding. Her Janus-faced Roosevelt-Mussolini hero remained acceptable to her readers until 1934–35. Then she started publishing reports from Germany, enriched by a personal interview with Hitler, and stressed that, although at odds with democratic values, Nazi success was due to unemployment and social distress; Hitler was fundamentally unthreatening and deserved at least a wait-and-see attitude. At that point, letters from angry readers began pouring in, the editorial board was politically embarrassed, and the parallel between fascism and liberal democracy as framers of social measures started to crumble.[11]

By the mid-1930s, European public interventionism and state-sponsored social programs were appearing in a more sinister light. The interest in the Russian five-year plans had been tainted by the Stalinist purges, which had cancelled the old leadership of the revolution; the stabilizing role of Mussolini's pre-1935 foreign policy, which had been a feature of the European Versailles order, had been lost in the Ethiopian war and in the initial steps of the coming Italian-German alliance; most importantly, the racist, militaristic, revisionist face of German Nazism had come unmistakably to the fore.

Totalitarian orders criticized democracy and vindicated their own leadership in social-protection programs—stained though they were by racist and sexist biases. The class-based criticism of democracy, enhanced by the 1917 Bolshevik victory in Russia, had been around for a long time and was no less virulent. Only a socialist society—recited soviet public discourse—could fulfill human needs. The substance of capitalist social security "lies in the use of pacifiers, in the form of assistance, in order to protect capitalist property against encroachment from the poor."[12] Fascism, the new idea on stage, was essentially the opposite of the spirit of progressive rationalism and popular sovereignty, which were at the root of the notion of democracy. In the fascist rationale, democracy was the reign of the mediocre, a state that never "dressed up," an irresponsible political order bent on compromise and transaction instead of strength and affirmation, which were the foundations of the consensus in a "dictatorship of high morality."[13] Liberal democracy was spineless, impotent, and without any guiding idea. Representation and the derivative claim that the people were the cornerstone of democracy were a sham, which only meant a quantitative regime of numbers. Instead, it was fascism and its leader that were close to and shared the real life and historic experience of the masses, which, instead of being atomized by liberal individualism, were unified in a "crowd of believers."[14] Alfredo Rocco, top ideologue of Italian fascism, said that there was a fundamental contrast between "the principle of organization embodied in the state and the principle of disruption represented by individuals and groups."[15]

Fascism thought that democracy was unable to deal with the social

issue that was central to the twentieth-century governance of mass society and looked at liberalism in terms of what Rimlinger has called the
"liberal break" of the nineteenth century, when the ideas of individual
liberty, autonomy, and self-sufficiency helped break up the old, decentralized institutions of social protection in the ancien régime.[16] The
Duce was instead "the great administrator of social justice," which,
against the social indifference of the atomized and self-centered liberal
economy, was a fundamental condition of the unified, national community of military strength and of the all-encompassing fascist state.
Before it was sacrificed to military priorities, the new network of German highways, more than three thousand kilometers long, had been
intended to be used by the newly conceived "people's car," the Volks-
wagen, which was to symbolize the regime's attention to its people's
needs and welfare. "The social legislation of the fascist regime," said
Mussolini, stressing the important role of social policy in the Fascist
self-image, "is the most advanced in the world."[17] In Italy, the ONMI
(National Agency for Maternity and Infancy) of 1925 was to assist
poor, deserted mothers and children.[18] For Victoria de Grazia, Fascist
social policy had the traits of both modernization and traditionalism
and saw assistance at the workplace as a way to outlaw industrial strife,
while simultaneously stressing the patriarchal hierarchy in the family as
the beneficiary. In the fascist states, social security was enlarged, centralized, and politicized: in Germany, public health was unified in one
organizational body under the auspices of the Nazi ideology, and the
new Social Agency for the German People concentrated and expanded
the different types of social insurance financed by general tax revenue.
The Nazi regime shaped social services along the lines of its demographic and racial principles. The long tradition of "racial purification"
and "social eugenics" in its extreme form permeated German health services, which condemned to death and sterility individuals affected by
mental disease or physical deformation. In 1940 the Robert Ley Plan
embodied the "social promise" for a postwar Nazi Europe: an extensive old-age and invalidity pension system financed by general revenues
and covering all those who had been loyal to the Nazi state and its duties and who did not belong to the "enemies of the state" or an "unso-
cial minority." The same use of social security as an avenue of control,
legitimization, and promotion of political principles was attempted in
the Soviet Union. "Since the early days of the Bolshevik Revolution,"
says Rimlinger, "social security has been hailed as one of the fruits of
the victory of the workers over capitalism." A unified old-age, health,

and disability insurance financed completely by the state, without contributions from the recipients, was created in the 1930s and hailed as a great achievement of socialism. Benefits were dependent on the obligation to work, which helped stabilize the labor force at a time of chaotic immigration of millions of peasants to the new, burgeoning industries. Both Germany and the Soviet Union claimed, albeit in different terms, that social security was the "most primordial duty" of the state, which made it conditional on loyalty to the political regime and its funding accordingly to be drawn from the general revenue. The contributory systems adopted by liberal democracies showed the limited scope of social insurance in these countries: the contractual nature of social security as dictated by the liberal indifference to the general welfare, and the functions of social control and labor market stabilization performed by liberal/capitalist social provision.[19]

While the totalitarian regimes vocally vindicated their social measures as a sign of their higher modernity, it was not impossible to wonder if, between government interventionism, state social assistance, and dictatorial rule, there was an interdependence whereby national social protection could be seen as a way to decrease freedom. Because liberal democracy is such a central component of American national identity, the possibility of an American dictator seizing power via a legal/electoral path, as both Hitler and Mussolini did in different degrees, was never a significant factor in American public life. Roosevelt and American liberals of the 1930s saw the international arena as one of competing sociopolitical orders and growing totalitarianism, which, however, could not come to America. Still, it was in the 1930s that fears of infection were voiced in the United States as European authoritarian orders became more rigidly dictatorial, seemed more successful than liberal democracies in dodging the Depression—or in dealing more efficiently with it through new, radical programs—and rapidly expanded into central, Eastern, and Balkan Europe. Sinclair Lewis's popular novel *It Can't Happen Here* of 1935 was echoed by charges of "government dictation" leveled against Roosevelt by urban and agrarian populists. Anti–New Deal conservatives denounced the new "national regimentation" and freely associated Stalin with Lloyd George, as their notion of socialism encompassed both the Soviet Five Year Plan and the British social insurance of 1906–11. The revival, in the 1930s, of the cries of the Europeanization of America sounded decidedly more sinister than they had before.

The ambiguity in the relationship between federal social protection and democracy goes back to the very origins of social insurance. "What became the welfare state . . . has in fact a chequered history," said British sociologist and public intellectual Anthony Giddens:

Its origins were far removed from the ideas of the left—indeed it was created partly to dispel the socialist menace. The ruling groups who set up the social insurance system in imperial Germany in the late nineteenth century despised laissez-faire economics as much as they did socialism. Yet many countries copied Bismarck's model. Beveridge visited Germany in 1907 in order to study the model.[20]

The modern social provision had a decidedly un-democratic birth in that it was first inaugurated by the German-speaking "social monarchies" of the 1880s, a fact that is somewhat embarrassing for analysts who see it as a function of twentieth-century mass democracy. The stifling of both democratic participation and socialism, together with sustaining social control, were open aims of Bismarckian social innovation: they coincided with an age in which the Center Party, which had roots in religious social doctrine, and then the social democrats, were outlawed. Bismarck had enacted universal male suffrage to bring peasants to the polls to counterbalance the votes of the urban middle and working classes and to support the authoritarian monarchy.

Flora and Alber speak of the tradition of paternalism in constitutional monarchies with limited suffrage, and/or corporative representation by social "states," as being based on the principle that the ruler(s) is responsible for the welfare of needy, obedient subjects. If, as these scholars stress, the development of the nation-state, urban/industrial capitalism, and the political mobilization of the working class are the fundamental historic reasons for the birth of the welfare state, then the German case seemed to renew the legacy of the ancien régime, in which the modern state started taking shape through the nationalizing of the king-figure and the establishment of the national bureaucracy and the national army.[21] This development coincided with the legitimizing of the king as the "father" of the country, a development that was concerned with the fate of the little people against the profit-oriented middle classes. The metaphor of fatherhood in government has traditionally stressed the interdependent duties of discipline and affection by a ruler. The father figure is by definition nonrepresentational, because, just like a real father, he cannot be replaced. The result was an ideology of the centralized state that was in charge of both the discipline and welfare of its subjects; the trade-off for this care was the denial of self-government and participation in policy making. The obligatory, nationwide, and state nature of the German old-age, disability, and health insurance of the 1880s had made Germany the leader of centralized social development in Europe. American institutional economists and social scientists of the 1880s and 1890s flocked to Germany to study the new interaction between government and society, and the German influence loomed large in American Progressive thought.

Competition in democratic and paternalistic social innovation in both Europe and America occurred at the turn of the century, and the social measures of Lloyd George in Britain in 1906–11 were the main liberal response to the German model. Until World War I, however, the paternalistic path to social protection held the limelight, and Germany was still in the lead when, in 1919, social rights were written into the constitution of the Weimar Republic. World War I radicalized the contrast between the prevailing paternalistic and the weaker liberal social protection schemes of the prewar years: the competition between imperial Germany and liberal Britain became, after the war, the struggle between warring principles of political and societal organization. Libraries hosted shelves of analyses of the merits of communism, fascism, and democracy, and the conflict became even more intense when Hitler brought fascism to power in the heart of Europe. Communism had won in Russia and claimed—until the mid-1930s, when Stalin proclaimed the doctrine of "socialism in one country"—that it was the vanguard of world revolution. Admiring observers from Europe and the United States stressed the spirit of sacrifice and commitment, the egalitarianism, and the sense of industrial and social creativity that characterized the country. The Five Year Plan of the thirties seemed to exemplify, better than did timid Western attempts, the ideal of the rational management of the economy as embodied by the popular principle of "national planning," which policy makers and public observers were heatedly discussing in both Europe and America. Mussolini had allegedly brought order to Italy after the turmoil of 1919–22; according to many enthusiastic international observers, incomes and living conditions were improving; the country was industrious, and, until 1934–35, the Duce was considered an important international actor who could bring stability and compromise to the opposing camps fighting over the legacy of the Versailles treaty, and even curb Hitler's initial expansionist pretenses. At the beginning of the 1930s, the fascist corporative state was often viewed with great favor by progressive economists and social engineers as a way to both consciously manage the economy and ensure class compromise and industrial order.

In turn, although a source of concern from the beginning of his rule because of his racist and militaristic overtones, Hitler's huge public works and revived military production quickly brought unemployment down to a level that democracies were unable to match.

Leninist communism, Italian fascism, and German Nazism claimed to embody the social inspiration of the twentieth century, which democracy was unable to deal with. More fundamentally, all of them, while very different, claimed that liberal democracy was basically unjust and unable to meet the issues of modernity. The issue is stressed adamantly in former President Herbert Hoover's *The Challenge to Liberty,* one of the most prominent anti–New Deal manifestoes of the old liberal view against "the vast centralization of power in the Executive" that was brought about by the New Deal.[22] According to Hoover,

The tremendous advances in production technology, the failure to march with a growing sense of justice, the sweeping social forces unleashed by the political and economic dislocations of the World War . . . Today these complexities loom large, and the voices of discouragement join with the voices of other social faiths to assert that an irreconcilable conflict has arisen in which Liberty must be sacrificed upon the altar of the Machine Age.[23]

"Can freedom live in the machine age?" echoed Progressive editor William Allen White at the 1934 University of Kansas commencement, and Lewis Mumford became the leading American espousing the notion that modern technology implied enlarged, centralized political power.[24] Both Russian communism and fascism voiced extreme visions of the "century of the state" and posited the necessity of the authoritarian to manage a just, socially responsible public order. Leninism saw state power as the way to enforce the "dictatorship of the proletariat" as a precondition to "expropriate the expropriators." Fascism aimed at erasing any difference between civil society and the state, the latter being embodied in the personal leadership of the Führer/Duce and his omniscient perception of the national and popular needs. If the eighteenth century had been the century of human rights and the nineteenth that of political rights, the social issue was at center stage in the twentieth; but liberal democracy was allegedly ill equipped for the task. When Mussolini criticized the New Deal as a late, imitative therapy to the ills that were "of," not "in," the democratic order, he referred to the notion that authoritarian state rule was necessarily to govern modernity and respond to its social needs.

Against what appeared to be the innovative march of the dictatorships, which were all characterized by an all-encompassing authoritarian state, liberal democracies had little to claim on the eve of Roosevelt's accession to power. In the United States, Herbert Hoover, the "progressive engineer" so popular in the twenties, was voted out in 1932 for presiding over the country in times of distress and being unable to fix it. France (until the controversial Popular Front of 1936) and Great Britain had reacted to the political difficulties brought about by the economic slump with new governments of little brilliance, while the German democratic experiment of the Weimar Republic had ended in disaster. Totalitarianism was on the ascent, and liberal democracy was on the defensive. When, in his acceptance address of June 27, 1936, in Philadelphia, Roosevelt stressed that America "was waging a great war," and added, "It is not alone a war against want and destitution and economic demoralization. It is a war for the survival of democracy. We are fighting to save a great and precious form of government for ourselves and for the world," he was not just using a rhetorical metaphor. On the contrary, he was reporting the widespread sense that liberal democracies were being cornered by expansive, regimented, and aggressive dictatorships on the march.[25]

Finally, because the social issue was stressed more vocally by enemies of liberal democracy, whose achievements dwarfed those of liberal democratic social protection, even if Roosevelt frequently mentioned Lloyd George in his search for a precursor, it was unclear how personal independence, autonomous civil society, and pluralist order could exist alongside the huge enlargement of the government powers and resources needed to manage the economy and build a network of social protection. Even the Scandinavian "Third Way," frequently praised by New Dealers, offered no complete model because at the time it was still under construction.

When, in 1935, the president introduced in Congress a relief bill of $5 billion, fears that government money would derail the democratic process—what government critics called the "Santa Claus principle of politics"—were vented by, among others, Republican congressman John M. Robsion from Kentucky, who said that as a result of holding such money, Roosevelt would have "more dictatorial power than Hitler in Germany or Mussolini in Italy."[26] In 1935–36, lacking the hindsight of half a century of the democratic welfare state, concern over the relationship between government interventionism, social protection, and liberal rights and institutions was neither a waste of time nor an excuse for partisan criticism only. "I for one," said public intellectual Joseph Wood Krutch, "should prefer to form some definite idea of just what it is that I am in for."[27] *Insecurity* is probably the word most symbolic of Depression America for, among other things, its multiple meanings. Alf Landon, Republican candidate in the presidential elections of 1936, had adopted the rhetorical stratagem of asking the supportive crowds at his electoral gatherings what the consequences would be of the different programs of the New Deal and of the Democratic platform. "No one can be sure!" shouted Republican enthusiasts in ritual response. The purpose was to oblige Roosevelt to openly confront the Republican candidate, but the rhetorical choice was indicative of the puzzling climate.[28]

The impact of the international systemic competition and the ambiguous historical relation between the social issue and liberal democracy impact on the intellectual and political controversy inside the United States of the 1930s was very important. The discussion was centered mainly on the place of the government and the state in American life. The issue, at least among Roosevelt's critics, was frequently assessed in light of the political orders competing in the world arena, which suggested the possibility that a clandestine or open authoritarian rule could make individual and economic freedom subservient to government dictation. Herbert Hoover thought that the threatening growth of the American state was coming close to the anti-American philosophies of socialism, communism, and fascism. To these foreign "isms," Hoover added "National Regimentation" and denounced the New Deal as an unconstitutional growth of government to the detriment of individual liberties (often exemplified by private economic discretion) and governmental management of the economy, currency, and trade.[29] In its effort to create new words for an unprecedented order—"the managed economy," "the collectivized society," "the state capitalism"—the New Deal, or some of its central programs, was compared in derogatory terms with both communism and fascism. The controversy had many facets to it. The communist comparison was more in the tradition of red-baiting, even if in the 1930s the coexistence of apparently opposite regimes with similar features of dictatorial rule innovated that tradition. The protagonists of the "red and pink Communists" comparison,[30] to use the words of the populist and popular radio priest Father Charles Coughlin, were basically of two types: on the one hand, the populists of the Huey Long and Francis Townsend brand, and on the other, Jeffersonian Progressive and laissez-faire, primarily business-inspired liberals. Both pointed to government dictation brought to America from "the garbage cans of Europe." Both, but especially the populists, used a highly stereotypical language that left little ground for analysis. "They are in the Russian primer," governor of Georgia Eugene Talmadge said of the New Dealers in 1935. Populists preferred the moral invective and the fear of conspiracy (although the business-inspired American Liberty League had a very similar approach): communists—and by association New Dealers—were mean, treacherous, two-faced enemies of all that was good and traditional in American society. "It is," Coughlin reiterated, "Christianity or chaos, Americanism or Communism." And the choice between communism and fascism was inevitable, because the election of 1936 would be the last one. Coughlin said decisively, "I take the road of fascism."[31] In extreme right-wing, fundamentalist circles, anti–New Deal, anticommunism, anti-intellectualism, and anti-Semitism all came together. Roosevelt, said Joseph McWilliams of the Christian Mobilizers, "represented the interests of international communism and this to us is synonymous of world Jewry."[32] This strain of opinion would be revived through the Martin Dies House Committee on Un-American Activities of 1938, which, at a time when the New Deal was quickly weakening, would officially voice this line of argument on the congressional floor.

The criticism from the Jeffersonian liberals and conservatives, who frequently directly or indirectly voiced opinions of the business community, was somewhat more thoughtful, even though the shrill cries from the Liberty League on the eve of the 1936 presidential election, or from the National Committee to Uphold Constitutional Government during the judicial reform controversy in 1937, were almost as stereotypical and moralistic as were those of the populist fundamentalists. What conservatives and business circles objected to were the institutional and governmental implications of the social service state, which, according to Flora and Heidenheimer, "implies a basic transformation of the state itself, of its structure, function, and legitimacy." Old, local centers of social support had been destroyed, social life is centralized, and "public bureaucracies take over many of the functions formerly filled by smaller social units."[33] "The gravest and most constant danger to a man's life, liberty and happiness," said playwright Maxwell Anderson, echoing the tenets of Jeffersonian individualism, "is the government under which he lives."[34] After giving Roosevelt significant support in 1933, the business community the following year drastically opposed the administration with the catchphrase "the government must get out of business." Invading business prerogatives, distorting market mechanisms, destroying business confidence, tampering with the currency, shifting control of the economy to huge, suffocating, public bureaucracies—these were the points a group of business writers, including former Roosevelt administration member James P. Warburg, former Secretary of the Treasury Ogden L. Mills, and others voiced in books and magazine articles. In a way they were agreeing with the prominent English welfare-state analyst Asa Briggs, who, in his 1961 definition of the welfare state, called it "a state in which organized power is deliberately used (through politics and administration) in an effort to modify the play of market forces."[35] The outcome was, said Ogden Mills, "state capitalism"—just one of the catchwords, along with "National Regimentation," "Democratic Despotism," "the collective state," and "government by bureaucracy," that business spokesmen coined to discredit the New Deal. The end result, they said, would inevitably be political control to the point of dictatorship of the Italian, German, or Russian brand. "By means of taxation and spending," said the _National Republic,_ "by indefinite extension of bureaucracy and by political control of the courts . . . a Socialistic-Communistic state has the machinery . . . to perpetuate its own political power."[36] These words sounded again like red-baiting, but the fact that the Liberty League, for all its big-business, Wall Street flavor, was able to enlist the support of two former Democratic presidential candidates of the 1920s—Alfred T. Smith and James W. Davis—shows how profound was the sense of established American principles being overturned.

The criticisms that paralleled the New Deal with rampant international fascism were sometimes more thoughtful. In line with the notion that liberal democracy was in trouble trying to govern a complex modernity, for American commentators the meaning of _fascism_ changed, depending on the political vision of the speaker. James Burnham thought that liberal means of government were insufficient to deal with the enormous dislocation brought about by the Depression, and Roosevelt could not help but move toward some sort of dictatorial power.[37] "Capitalism is doomed," proclaimed Joseph Wood Krutch.[38] To radicals and communists on the Left, fascism was the trend adopted by the dominant economic interests and enacted politically by Roosevelt in order to save, at all cost, profits that were being destroyed by the Depression. In 1929–35, when the denunciation of progressive "social-fascists" was the party line, then-communists such as Earl Browder thought that a monopolistic corporate state was the centerpiece of the New Deal program. This stand was not too distant from that of the western Progressives in Congress. The cartels of the National Recovery Administration, with their disturbing resemblance to the fascist corporative state, were most often cited as embodying the "save capitalism at all cost" fascist trend in the government. For others, especially conservatives and many Jeffersonian liberals, fascism was clearly seen as a political dictatorship and an all-encompassing state that prohibited individual initiative or strictly dictated the boundaries within which it was relegated.

On the whole, the international systemic competition dictated some of the fundamental criteria used by critics of the New Deal in both their thoughtful and stereotypical opposition, whereas the administration preferred to focus the merits of its programs in terms of recovery, compassion, and socioeconomic imperatives. A closer look at the theme of the foreign "isms" implied that fascism and communism, while apparently in conflict, were instead similar in the dictatorial dictation of an all-encompassing state. This notion was voiced by conservatives, Jeffersonian liberals, most western Progressives, and some populists, even when some in the latter two groups were more or less sympathetic to Italian fascism. "They have a tacit understanding between themselves," said Eugene Talmadge in reference to fascism and communism, "to fight on the surface."[39] The language of Herbert Hoover, the Liberty League, the spokesmen for business, and the conservative newspapers stressed that Stalin, Hitler, and Mussolini all went together. The word *totalitarianism,* which was coined in intellectual circles in the 1930s, was not explicitly adopted; but the criticism of the total state's attempts to shape all aspects of life and erase the line between political and civil society suggests how the interaction between public controversy and scholarly creativity may have inspired the invention of that "ism."

In American twentieth-century history, conservatives with the language of the limiting of federal government have often fought the battle for private economic power and unregulated income distribution. Still, as Walter Lippmann said, "the so-called liberals of today think that federalism was invented by the Liberty League and is defended only by hirelings of the du Ponts."[40] The controversy was not completely opportunistic: the issue of government power had merits of its own and was of significant concern for many.

What is more interesting for the notion that the coordination between the welfare state and liberal democratic institutions was by no means established in Depression America is that the more thoughtful critics did not state that communism or fascism was already established in the United States as the result of the New Deal, but that the expansion of government implied a potential shift toward them. In the first place, the sense of uncertainty about the country's direction was heard from all quarters: Roosevelt portrayed it in bright colors as "experimentation," while business used the same word in derogatory terms, saying that a bunch of impractical brain-trusters was leading the American economy astray through uncharted ways. Once the old boundaries between public and private, and market and politics, had been abandoned, nobody really knew where they would be redrawn, and on this matter foreign examples were a source of concern. Fascism spoke more of "discipline" than of dictatorship, and the term appeared in Roosevelt's appeals more than once; a fairly widespread international opinion foresaw Roosevelt necessarily tightening his rule if he wanted his program to succeed. State capitalism implied moving either toward fascism as a one-sided defense of profits (which American socialists often stressed) or toward communism because of the need to enforce economic dictation (as Ogden Mills indicated). Either of them would probably come to the United States without the aesthetic paraphernalia they had acquired in Italy, Germany, and Russia, but the substance would be the same. Radical commentators thought Roosevelt was paving the way for the onset of an American fascism, which, according to Mauritz A. Hallgren, editor of *The Nation,*

can unquestionably come without the emotional hoopla of Hitler or the stage maneuvering of Mussolini. . . . in this country it will come gradually, dressed in democratic trappings as not to offend the democratic sensibilities of the great American people. But when it comes it will differ in no essential aspect from the Fascist regimes of Italy and Germany. This is Roosevelt's role: to keep the people convinced that the state capitalism now being set up is entirely democratic and constitutional.[41]

European correspondent Raymond Gram Swing added that fascism was "a reorganization of society to maintain an unequal distribution of wealth by undemocratic means," which is exactly what the United States government was doing as well, the only difference being that "one tolerates the democratic means of operating the country, the other does not."[42] The sense was that the control and management implicit in the governance of the mixed economy and welfare system were redrawing the boundaries between autonomy and conformity, rights and duties, and the individual and the collective; whether or not this was consistent with the exercise of democratic rights was fuzzy and unclear with many commentators.

Another possible reason for the shift into authoritarianism was the ambiguities and multiple meanings of the word *democracy:* dictatorships of the 1930s never relinquished the term. Communism spoke of the "popular democracy" of the soviets and the kolkhoz, which claimed to be the "real democracy" against the liberal illusion, which manipulated representative institutions to favor class interests. Fascism too vindicated a postliberal and antiliberal democracy, attaching such adjectives as organic, organized, authoritarian, hierarchical, and centralized; it criticized the "fetish of the demos." Representative institutions were a cage for the twentieth-century society of the masses. A "democratic dictatorship" was the pretense that the masses were at the center of the regime and the leader's concerns. A disciplined, unified people were the primary force of the regime, which was, in this particular sense, "democratic."[43] The United States could imperceptibly shift into a different meaning of democracy. Progressive senator Burton K. Wheeler stressed that control of Congress and the Supreme Court could lead to "a modern democracy of a Hitler or a Mussolini." Embattled foreign correspondent Dorothy Thompson spoke of the "popular tyrants like Mussolini and Hitler who claimed to be democratic because of the overwhelming popular approval registered on their behalf by their own staged plebiscites."[44] Fascist-style democracy that threatened the United States was a mix of mass demagoguery, a traditional dark side of "mob rule," plebiscite plebeian acclamation, and "dictatorship of the majority." Ideally, the response to these fears came from John Dewey, the public intellectual most committed to framing the intellectual foundations of the joining of the active government to the social service state within a liberal, pluralistic democracy. The threat from attitudes that had given "a victory to external authority, discipline, conformity and dependence upon the Leader in foreign countries"—attitudes far from absent in America as well—could be avoided if Americans were able to think of societal planning not as a set of ultimate truths but as a continuing, pragmatic, pluralistic process of government, because "democratic ends demand democratic methods for their realization."[45]

In stressing the context of the international, alternate orders, the criticism leveled by conservatives, Jeffersonian liberals, and western Progressives against Roosevelt was more than just red-baiting: it was an early attempt to put him on trial in the court of public opinion for un-American activities at a time when the worldwide systemic competition made foreign un-American orders especially visible and threatening. The most important supporter of the critical, traditionalist position was the Supreme Court, whose anti–New Deal judicial reviews were endlessly reported by the conservative press. When the Court struck down in 1934–35 the centerpieces of the New Deal legislation, the action seemed to indicate that the highest-level judiciary in the United States, the one in charge of defending constitutional principles, believed that the core of the Roosevelt program fell outside the legal foundations of the Republic and was charging Roosevelt with the excess delegation of power to, and centralization of, the government. The Supreme Court's rulings opened a major breach between two top powers of the Republic, the executive and the judiciary. When the Court proclaimed that the New Deal legislation violated the Constitution, by implication it substantiated the notion that the government's principles fell outside the national public tradition and lent credibility to the critical argument of the foreign "isms."

Although earlier compromises were found, the conflict was not resolved until the election of 1936, when the great majority of the American voters, after the Social Security Act, the Wagner Labor Act, the huge WPA appropriation for public works, and the "Soak-the-Rich" tax bill, said in unambiguous terms that they liked the welfare programs and did not think they violated the Constitution. The opinion of most New Deal historians is that the constitutional controversy and that involving the foreign "isms" were cases of rabid, ultra-traditionalist partisanship in favor of the vested interests with little substantive interest of their own. Still, Progressive Amos Pinchot said he was "mortally afraid of what Managed Economy will do to us if the Constitution and the Court don't intervene and stop it."[46] The members of the American Civil Liberties Union could not relinquish the notion of liberty being a rein on government discretion in favor of a different definition of freedom as government-enforced. The election of 1936 was actually a sort of constitutional referendum to evaluate the alleged "un-Americanness" of the New Deal. Giving Roosevelt one of the grandest landslides in history, most Americans voted for their homes, their jobs, and their pockets, but also they overwhelmingly agreed that the interventionist, social-minded government of the New Deal was well within the boundaries of the Constitution and that the accusation of "un-Americanness" bringing in foreign "isms" was unfounded. "The constitution of 1787," said Roosevelt at his second inaugural, "did not make our democracy impotent." It was a claim that the secretary of agriculture and leading Progressive Henry Wallace had reiterated in his book of 1936, *Whose Constitution?* in which he said in classic New Deal language that the original constitutional ideal of a democratic political society meant, in the twentieth century, the ideal of a cooperative economic society.[47] The electorate had thrown its support behind this interpretation of American constitutional principles, and, as a result of the multiple, often unwritten ties existing in the United States between the institutions of popular sovereignty and the rule of law, the electoral message was heard by the "nine old men." In 1937, when he launched the famous Court-packing scheme, Roosevelt tried to "tamper" with the structure of the Supreme Court, which among other things, as Stephen Early, the president's press secretary, said, "seems to be the only institution . . . for which there is a popular reverence."[48] Roosevelt overestimated his political clout, revived accusations of political dictation, and lost. But after 1936, the issue of the alleged unconstitutional nature of the New Deal and its "un-Americanness" was put to rest for good. It was a major step in legitimizing the coherence between the interventionist state, social protection, and liberal democracy.

The strong political emotions that characterized the public arena in the 1930s were warranted by the radical departure in policy making that the New Deal represented and, even more, by the intense, widespread perception of the change. In the absence of a well-defined, widely internalized notion of the harmony between the interventionist state and liberal democracy, the systemic competition in the international arena dictated and dramatized some of the terms of the controversy. Policies were analyzed and assessed in light of foreign, unwelcome dictatorial regimes, which claimed to be more advanced in responding to the social issue. The persistence, throughout the thirties, of that particular international scene acted as a significant roadblock to adopting even bolder welfare measures.

Tracing the ambiguous history of the relationship between the welfare state and liberal democracy until the eve of World War II is not another attempt to destroy whatever sense of value and roots we still invest in public life after so many changes in recent years. My personal opinion is that if, among so many pathologies, twentieth-century Europe has left any decent legacy to the future, the "mixed system" and the welfare state are certainly the more humane and compassionate of them.

The issue, however, is that the end of the so-called American New Deal order or the European age of social-democracy in the late 1970s has changed how the historian looks at the history of the welfare state in Europe and America. The smartest attempt at historically interpreting the Roosevelt myth and the New Deal order has been Arthur M. Schlesinger Jr.'s *The Age of Roosevelt,* published at the end of the 1950s.[49] The Harvard historian and public intellectual managed to match the idea of a compassionate, interventionist government necessitated by the imperatives of twentieth-century history with the progressive historiographic tradition of the great American presidents. In Schlesinger's view, Roosevelt's outstanding personality and brilliant leadership gave birth to the new liberalism of the active government that was required by the times. The New Deal was both extraordinary and normal: the latter because government compassion, which had already been inaugurated in other countries, was required to right the imbalances of capitalism and the shortsightedness of big business; the former because only an enlightened leadership could remove the powerful roadblocks that prevented twentieth-century "normalcy" to emerge.

If Roosevelt's program was so deeply imbedded in the overall trends of Western history as much as in American political values, then his political foes were portrayed in Schlesinger's volumes not as the champions of serious alternatives who ended up on the losing side but as outworn remnants of the past, supporters of a bygone age of inhuman business dictation and "cutthroat" competition—if not the fellow travelers of totalitarian dictatorships of different colors but similar purpose. In Schlesinger's reconstruction, Roosevelt and the new liberalism dominated the historical scene, and all alternatives were squeezed to the margin of invisibility and irrelevance.

Because historians of the welfare state living at the peak of the "century of the state" and the "mixed system" seemed to go unchallenged until the midseventies, the "modern liberalism only" interpretation of American welfare was accepted as a matter of course. Then, at the beginning of the eighties, Ronald Reagan, Margaret Thatcher, and a decade of neoconservatism (which still influences public ideas in Western countries) came as a surprise. Slogans that had been considered long dead revived in full force: "Get the government off my back," "Government is the problem," "Let the market run its course." On the other hand, the ongoing "crisis of the welfare state," with, among other things, accusations of excess bureaucracy and centralization, has also redirected the attention back to the tradition of localism and self-government in American welfare. Not surprisingly, the shift of public opinion in the late seventies (which could be seen as the end point of the twentieth century) made historians look at the welfare state in a different way. Ideas advanced in the 1930s by such opponents of the New Deal as the Republican Party, former President Herbert Hoover, and the National Association of Manufacturers were not only opportunistic defenses of selfish interests sugarcoated by nostalgia. They voiced instead a frame of mind that, especially in the United States but in other countries as well, was sometimes in hibernation during the twentieth century, but always alive, and a vision of public life that never stopped being one of the great protagonists of the contemporary historical scene of the industrialized countries. Friedrich von Hayek gave the theme a formidable boost when he published *The Road to Serfdom* in 1944. The liberal criticism of the interventionist state may be disagreed with but was never marginal—"à la Schlesinger" in his history of the Depression years—because, among other things, these ideas were being expressed at a time when the compatibility of social policy, the interventionist state, and liberal democracy was not yet established, and when the strongest voices claiming leadership in social protection came from dictatorial leaders and regimes utterly critical of liberal democracy. The public anti–New Deal debate conducted in terms of the systemic competition, which nowadays is hardly mentioned in the 1930s textbook narrative, cannot be dismissed only because of its opportunistic and openly partisan, derogatory use of such words as *communism* or *fascism*. Such competition characterized the international arena at that time, and there was no certainty that democracy would prevail, because totalitarianism seemed triumphant and on the march.

If the 1930s in the United States are seen as an era when different sets of public principles competed for power and influence, without any one being historically determined, then Roosevelt's leadership looms even larger than it does in the Schlesinger's synthesis, according to which the American president acted, almost in Marxist terms, as the clever obstetrician who brought the new, necessary order to America against powerful obstacles. Such celebration of the Depression president implies, however, a subtle deterministic implication that diminishes his merit.

If, instead, Roosevelt is considered a leader and the New Deal a set of programs that prevailed against equally vital, yet unacceptable, principles of public life, then their achievement is even more important. Roosevelt's merit would amount to not only bringing to America a public life and government more concerned for the poor and weak, but also powerfully helping to unite liberal democracy and social protection, convincing the public that democracy was not socially indifferent. Roosevelt was able to frame a welfare state that could reinforce democracy, that could claim to extend a helping hand to those in need without sacrificing liberty—unlike the other socially oriented political orders of the day. Starting from Lloyd George's social liberalism at the end of the first decade of the twentieth century, peaking during the New Deal and the Scandinavian social-democratic programs in the 1930s, continuing through the social promise of the "Four Freedoms" address and the Atlantic Charter during the war, and coming to full fruition in the British Beveridge Plan of the late forties, the marriage of liberal democracy, social protection, and the interventionist state, for all its limits, shortcomings, continuing poverty and exploitation, was complete. The adoption of the expression "welfare state," coined in Britain during World War II to express the social promise of the democratic nation at war in contrast to the social pretenses of the dictators, signified this newly acquired interdependence. It gave democracy a "social soul," which helped it win the battle against fascism, and then made it competitive and finally victorious against the challenge of communism. More than fifty years after Bismarck's social insurance, the authoritarian model of social protection that prevailed for almost half the century gave way after World War II to a full-blown democratic alternative of social rights. If it came to be known as a "British" model despite the powerful contribution of Americans in the 1930s, it is because the dream of the New Dealers—that social reform had just begun and would continue in the postwar years— was curbed by the recovery of business through wartime production and the conservative turn at the onset of the Cold War: in the late forties, full employment, national health insurance, and government reorganization were turned down or vetoed; New Dealers were marginalized in government circles; and union action was drastically limited. The reasons for this postwar New Deal diminishment lie primarily in the social and political, domestic and international contrasts of the 1930s and 1940s. However, the uncertain nature of the relationship between social protection and liberal democracy throughout the thirties and most of the forties amplified opposition to a larger American welfare state and constantly slowed its progress. Now, at century's end, when the European welfare state is "in crisis" and American social protection is looked at with keen interest for its decentralized and less bureaucratic nature, Franklin D. Roosevelt can be crowned in the pages of *Time* magazine as the champion of the battle for both social compassion and liberal democracy, and their unification.

Notes

All translations from books and essays published in a language other than English and with no English editions are mine.

1. Bill Clinton, "Captain Courageous," *Time*, December 31, 1999, 82.

2. Ibid., 84.

3. Ibid., 10.

4. Ibid.

5. Eric Foner, *The Story of American Freedom* (New York: Norton, 1998), esp. chaps. 7–10.

6. Peter Flora and Arnold J. Heidenheimer, eds., *The Development of Welfare States in Europe and America* (New Brunswick, N.J.: Transaction Books, 1981), 22. See also George Reid Andrews and Herrick Chapman, *The Social Construction of Democracy, 1870–1990* (New York: New York University Press, 1995), esp. 1–28.

7. Hartmut Kaelble, *A Social History of Western Europe, 1880–1980,* trans. David Bird (Savage, Md.: Barnes and Noble, 1990), 74.

8. Peter Flora and Jens Alber, "Modernization, Democratization, and the Development of Welfare States in Western Europe" in Flora and Heidenheimer, eds., *Development of Welfare States,* 63–70. According to Theda Skocpol, the different features of the American social provision (the term is hers) would make of the United States not a latecomer in social policy but just a nation that followed a path different than that of Europe. See Theda Skocpol, *Protecting Soldiers and Mothers: The Political Origins of Social Policy in the United States* (Cambridge: Harvard University Press, 1992).

9. Daniel T. Rodgers, *Atlantic Crossings: Social Policy in a Progressive Age* (Cambridge: Harvard University Press, 1998).

10. Volker Berghahn and Charles Maier, "Modern Europe in American Historical Writing," in *Imagined Histories: American Historians Interpret the Past,* ed. Anthony Molho and Gordon S. Wood (Princeton: Princeton University Press, 1998), 402.

11. Federica Pinelli and Marco Mariano, *Europa e Stati Uniti secondo il "New York Times." La corrispondenza estera di Ann O'Hare McCormick* (Turin: Otto, 2000).

12. Gaston Rimlinger, *Welfare Policy and Industrialization in Europe, America, and Russia* (New York: Wiley, 1971), 252.

13. Piergiorgio Zunino, *L'ideologia del fascismo. Miti, credenze e valori nella stabilizzazione del regime* (Bologna: Il Mulino, 1985), 181.

14. Ibid., 201.

15. Ibid., 188.

16. Rimlinger, *Welfare Policy and Industrialization,* 35–86.

17. Lorenzo Gaeta and Antonio Visconti, "L'Italia e lo stato sociale," in Gerhard Ritter, *Storia dello stato sociale* (Rome: Laterza, 1996), 238.

18. Victoria de Grazia, *How Fascism Ruled Italian Women, 1922–1945* (Los Angeles: University of California Press, 1992), 59–68.

19. Rimlinger, *Welfare Policy and Industrialization,* 134, 252. Ritter, *Storia dello stato sociale,* 129–36.

20. Anthony Giddens, *The Third Way: The Renewal of Social Democracy* (Malden, Mass.: Polity Press, 1999), 111.

21. Flora and Alber, "Modernization, Democratization, and the Development of the Welfare States," 40, 48.

22. Herbert Hoover, *The Challenge to Liberty* (1934; reprint, New York: Da Capo, 1973), 76.

23. Ibid., 5, 1.

24. Arthur A. Ekirch Jr., *Ideologies and Utopias: The Impact of the New Deal on American Thought* (Chicago: Quadrangle, 1969), 195.

25. Roosevelt's address is reproduced in William Allen White, *What It's All About: Being a Reporter's Story of the Early Campaign of 1936* (New York: Macmillan, 1936), 146.

26. George Wolfskill and John A. Hudson, *All But the People: Franklin D. Roosevelt and His Critics* (New York: Macmillan, 1969), 222.

27. Ekirch, *Ideologies and Utopias,* 196–97.

28. Donald R. McCoy, *Landon of Kansas* (Lincoln: University of Nebraska Press, 1966), 334–35.

29. *The Memoirs of Herbert Hoover,* vol. 3, *The Great Depression, 1929–1941* (New York: Macmillan, 1952), 369–464; Gary Dean Best, *Herbert Hoover: The Postpresidential Years, 1933–1964,* vol.1, *1933–1945* (Stanford, Calif.: Hoover Institution Press, 1983), 37–73.

30. Woolfskill and Hudson, *All But the People,* 107.

31. Quotations are ibid., 104, 107, 112.

32. Ibid., 114.

33. Flora and Heidenheimer, *Development of Welfare States,* 23–24.

34. Ekirch, *Ideologies and Utopias,* 203.

35. Flora and Heidenheimer, *Development of Welfare States,* 29.

36. Wolfskill and Hudson, *All But the People,* 154.

37. Richard H. Pells, *Radical Visions and American Dreams: Culture and Social Thought in the Depression Years* (New York: Harper and Row, 1973), 84.

38. Ekirch, *Ideologies and Utopias,* 196.

39. Wolfskill and Hudson, *All But the People,* 104.

40. Ekirch, *Ideologies and Utopias,* 201.

41. Ibid., 188–89.

42. Ibid., 189.

43. Zunino, *Ideologia del fascismo,* 181–85, 203.

44. Both quotations are in Ekirch, *Ideologies and Utopias,* 199–200.

45. Ibid., 205.

46. Ibid., 195.

47. Ibid., 198.

48. Ibid., 197.

49. Arthur M. Schlesinger Jr., *The Age of Roosevelt,* 3 vols. (Boston: Houghton Mifflin, 1957–60).

Consuming America, Producing Gender

Mary Nolan

American mass consumption and mass culture have been at the center of European debates about national identity and modernity, culture and gender throughout the twentieth century. Did cheap cars and refrigerators, vacuum cleaners and television sets, Coke and blue jeans carry with them distinctly American attitudes toward consumption and leisure, domesticity and family, femininity and masculinity? Or were these commodities and their meanings transformed through their incorporation into distinctive cultural contexts, their deployment in emphatically national ways? Did American music and movies, TV shows and fast food chains transform not only the more mundane practices of everyday life from eating to shopping to sociability but also European values about gender and generations, about sexuality and style? Or were the images of America free-floating signifiers that could be appropriated and re-presented to convey meanings that were markedly different from the American originals? Is the master narrative of the American Century one of hegemony or hybridity? Of Coca-colonization or creolization? Of Americanized modernity, now marching under the banner of globalization, or of multiple modernities, in which America as myth and reality, as material practice and discourse, features prominently but not hegemonically?

The varied and often contradictory answers to these questions have been shaped by the political, class, and geographic location of any given analyst/polemicist as well as by her/his gender and generation. They

243

have varied depending on the country and period being discussed and the perceived power and seductiveness of American commodities and cultural forms. Rather than rehearse the many variants of Americanism and anti-Americanism that have proliferated in the last century, this chapter explores possible links between American commodities and images on the one hand and European experiences of domesticity, mass consumption, and conceptions of femininity and masculinity on the other hand. It does so not by examining the gender implications of post-war youth culture, a theme to which much excellent scholarship has been devoted, but rather by exploring the varied forms of the modern housewife and domesticity, and speculating about "the new man" who has been markedly absent in discussions of Americanization.

The focus is on the American Century classically defined, on the post–World War II decades when American goods and American mass culture entered Europe on a massive scale and without the mediating and limiting influence of fascist regimes and depression economies. The chapter examines the fantasies and fears about Americanization in the 1950s and early 1960s by looking at appliances, housework, and domestic spaces, by sketching the varieties of modernity—more or less explicitly coded as American—that were offered to adults striving to reconstruct and transform home and family, and by suggesting the forces that structured the lived experiences of those spaces and goods.

Whether it is celebrated or condemned, Americanization is all too frequently discussed in hyperbolic rhetoric and binary extremes. What follows suggests the contours of a complex narrative of both strong American influences on European mass consumption and domesticity and quite distinct national lived experiences of gender and family. This chapter explores how Europeans selectively appropriated American mass culture and mass consumption, negotiating with and transforming goods, institutions, and cultural practices, even as they were altered in the process. It insists that gender ideologies and gendered welfare states help explain how this selective appropriation operated.

This chapter makes two other points, less often heard in debates about Americanization. First, there were European sources of the efforts to create modern individuals, with modern subjectivities and modern ways of living at home and outside. These were in dialogue with American models but had indigenous roots and were harnessed to national projects of becoming modern. After World War II there were also quite varied national efforts to protect, stabilize, and reform the family by transforming domesticity. Although these may have looked similar to those undertaken in post–World War II America, they were part of distinctively national political concerns and reflected nationally specific cultural anxieties. Second, the flow of ideas was not just from America to a receptive or resisting Europe. There was a movement of ideas, cultural products, and consumer goods from Europe to America, in the pre–World War I and interwar periods and especially from the 1960s on, and of equal importance, there were flows of ideas, goods, gender ideologies, and people among European countries. European nations engaged with the ways in which other European societies, and not just the United States, appropriated and interpreted an international modernism. To understand the transformations of both individual European countries and the United States, it is necessary to recapture the complexity of these multidirectional exchanges of products, people, cultural values, and gender regimes. A more transatlantic and less America-centric approach to the American Century is needed.[1]

The New Woman as Modern Housewife

From the early twentieth century there were vigorous debates on both sides of the Atlantic about how to transform the home, housework, and family life. The modern housewife and the modern family, living in a new apartment or single-family dwelling, filled with new household technology, evolved more slowly, emerging in the United States during the interwar era and in Western Europe from the late 1950s on. During the fifties and early sixties, European teenage girls were exposed to unclear and contradictory images of where they fit into Americanized leisure and popular culture, but their adult counterparts were offered the sharply focused, highly modern, and seductive but limiting representations of the new woman as modern housewife. Teenage girls and women of the 1950s, like their predecessors in the 1920s, were offered the ambiguously emancipatory promises of both Americanized mass culture and Americanized forms of domesticity, marriage, and motherhood. Yet, unlike the interwar era the 1950s saw European homes and conceptions of domesticity transformed by the arrival of consumer economies. Did the propagation of similar ideologies of domesticity and the consumption of similar consumer durables on both sides of the Atlantic reflect the hegemony of American conceptions and produce Americanized versions of femininity and masculinity?

One possible narrative stresses the spread of American consumer durables, forms of family life, and discourses of domesticity. A focus on

Americanization captures a part of what many Europeans hoped or feared was happening as a result of the market, advertising, magazines, and movies. It also reflects the continued use of Americanism as a language in which to debate modernity. But Americanization is only one part of a much more complex story. Homes, families, and conceptions of gender became more modern but in distinctly national ways and by particular national paths. Images of and goods for the modern home came not only from the United States but also from other European countries, and above all from Sweden. New consumer durables and new forms of housework, leisure, and family life were adopted differently in different countries. What was selected and when depended not only on income and class, on the technical characteristics of particular goods, and on the household infrastructure of plumbing and electricity but also on women's conceptions of how to cook, clean, and wash properly—and these differed from country to country.[2] Throughout Western and Eastern Europe, images of the modern housewife and home were mobilized for Cold War political purposes and cultural agendas by conservative national elites and built on both long-standing and postwar national projects for becoming modern that were shared by the Left and Right. Finally, the modern home and modern housewife were contextualized within different understandings of female citizenship, different attitudes toward female employment, and different welfare state structures and assumptions.

The modern housewife, performing her domestic tasks in her modern home and fulfilling her responsibilities toward her modern small family, had existed as image and in certain classes and countries as embryonic reality since the 1920s. She marked a significant departure from both earlier visions of model domesticity and the prior experiences of housewives. Throughout the nineteenth century, bourgeois reformers on both sides of the Atlantic produced innumerable household manuals for middle-class and working-class women. A sharp separation of home and work was the organizing principle and underlying value of these advice books. Reformers made no claims about the economic import or scientific character of housework; nor did they speak the emerging language of efficiency. Household help was expected from servants or children, not from plumbing, electricity, and appliances. It was not until the interwar years that both the attributes and the accoutrements of a distinctly modern vision of housewifery, maternity, and femininity emerged.

What precisely was new? First, the modern home, like the modern factory, was considered to be an integral part of the national economy, and the home, like any business, was to be organized along the lines of efficiency and productivity, of planning and the rational calculation of money, materials, time, energy, and attention. The housewife was ideally to arrange her home and perform her multiple tasks in the scientific manner prescribed by the discipline of home economics and propagated by schools, government agencies, and the manufacturers of appliances and housewares. Interwar versions of the modern housewife were part of an international movement to reform both the spaces and practices of the home. America pioneered home economics and led in both the quantity and quality of household technology, while Europe did more to advance the design of the modern home. Think of the Frankfurt kitchen and Bauhaus projects or the functionalist furniture and homes displayed at the 1930 Stockholm Exhibition. Europe was key to the creation of an international modernism, but a modernism that was always given distinctive national inflections. Germany, faced with the cost of postwar recovery and lacking high wages and vibrant domestic markets, developed an austere version of the modern home that stressed Taylorizing the housewife without transforming the home through consumer durables or radically altering domestic architecture. In Sweden, interwar Social Democrats made modernity a Swedish project that linked transforming domesticity to democratization and the renegotiation of conceptions of citizenship.[3]

By the 1950s, many Europeans were promoting the American equation of modern domesticity with consumer durables and packaged food. Consumption joined rationalization and efficiency as the hallmarks of modernity in the home. Indeed, modernity was to be produced by means of the housewife's rational purchase and use of consumer durables to promote efficient housewifery. The vision of the modern home and the housewife promised a transformation of masculinity, femininity, and family life. It promised to redraw the line between public and private and to contain history and memory. In the United States, this vision was seen as exclusively and proudly American; in Europe it was simultaneously and confusingly coded as international, American, and Swedish, or British or German. In different national contexts it produced quite distinctive national projects of domestic modernity, quite different lived experiences.

But before we can explore what the gender implications of these visions and projects might be, we need to trace the slow evolution of the modern home from icon of modernity and object of desire to material reality. Images of household technology—efficient, elegant, almost erotic—flooded Europe from the early 1950s on in women's magazines, newspaper ads, trade fairs, and the impassioned pro-consumerist speeches of politicians. But acquiring the savings to purchase electric stoves and vacuum cleaners, refrigerators and washing machines proved to be a slower and more arduous task, because the late 1940s was a time of austerity across Europe and the 1950s a decade of only slowly expanding consumption. Postwar wages were low in most countries, and recovery strategies emphasized producers' goods over consumer ones in the early years. Food bulked large in the family budget, even if the quality and diversity improved, and the radio, which entertained the entire family, was likely to be purchased before appliances, which saved the housewife labor. The technologically modern home and the consuming housewife were legitimated in the eyes of business and politics before they were realized in practice. In the 1950s, the United States purchased three-quarters of the appliances produced in the world. Electric stoves and vacuums were ceasing to be luxury items in West Germany, and many families there had purchased new furniture, but only one in twenty households had a refrigerator as opposed to one in two in the United States and Switzerland. In 1963 nearly two-thirds of Dutch and Belgium households had washing machines, while nearly half of Swiss and British households and roughly one-third of West German, French, and Austrian ones did. Only a scant 8 percent of Italian households had one, indicating the delayed onset of a consumer society there. The Dutch had the highest percentage of vacuums as well, exceeding the level in the United States of 79 percent, while West Germany and Britain came close to it. West Germany led in refrigerators, with 58 percent of households owning one. This was a marked increase from the previous decade and put Germany well ahead of France, Britain, and Italy in the competition for that much-coveted item.[4]

It was not only what was consumed but also where and how that were altered in the postwar decades. The local small shop, whose owner and employees dispensed advice and gave credit, did not vanish by any means, but from the 1960s on, the self-service store gradually gained a foothold in places like Italy, and spread rapidly in West Germany and Britain. From 1950 to 1960, the number of self-service stores in Europe increased from 1,200 to 45,500, and 600 of these were supermarkets. Old and new stores alike carried an increasing number of canned goods and ready-made products. In Victoria de Grazia's suggestive formulation, Europe experienced the transition from a bourgeois to a Fordist mode of distribution. Yet the result, as Frank Mort reminds us, was not uniform Americanization. Rather "the pace of transformation was often extremely uneven," the "paths to mass consumption were plural and diverse," and "compromise patterns of commercial modernization" came in several national varieties. In the case of Britain, national chains both borrowed mass production and standardization and relied heavily on local advertising and marketing. Advertisers and retailers avoided the American "hard-sell" and remained as attuned to the Commonwealth and the former colonies as to the United States.[5]

Consumption of the household technology considered essential to the modern home was bolstered, indeed sometimes first made possible, by the postwar housing boom. Whether a response to wartime destruction, a Keynesian economic measure, a social program to promote modernization, or all three, postwar housing programs took a variety of forms: vast apartment projects in France, New Towns in Britain, and a mix of apartment buildings and single-family houses in West Germany. Modern postwar houses and apartments were designed with either a small working kitchen or a modern variant of the eat-in kitchen and were equipped with the electricity and modern plumbing necessary for the new forms of housewifery. Architects, advertisers, and social policy experts urged residents to eliminate clutter and gloom by acquiring slim and functional furniture, made from wood, plastic, and metal.[6]

Modernizing the home was an international project in the postwar decades, one in which America considered itself a leader and model but in which the national and the international also played major roles. Take America itself. As Gwendolyn Wright has shown in her analysis of the forces shaping American domestic architecture, American modernism was built on pre–World War II borrowings from Europe—Germany, France, and the Netherlands above all. During the 1950s, the American home and its furnishings continued to be shaped by ideas and products from Italy and Scandinavia. But the final product was marketed as "built in the USA," to borrow the title of two international exhibitions of American domestic architecture.[7] Its international origins and hybrid character were masked by the triumphalism of the American Century. America's specifically national form of modern domestic life—combining the dominance of the single-family suburban home, advanced household infrastructure and abundant appliances, and an emphasis on informality—was admired but only partially imitated across the Atlantic and then in distinctly national ways.

Germany led in building single-family homes, for example; yet, although they had at least a modicum of modern furnishings and appliances, they scarcely resembled those in Levittown. The kitchen was in the front of the house, not the back, and the spatial arrangements were "hierarchically compartmentalized within and closed to the world without." Reflecting the postwar persistence of Nazi attitudes, open floor plans and interaction with the outside were associated with Bolshevik collectivism, not Americanism. The French postwar housing boom at times provoked acrimonious public debates about the proper placement of the dining area in relation to the kitchen, debates that reflected French customs and culinary preoccupations that had no American counterparts. "During the 1950s and 1960s Sweden was labeled the most Americanized nation in Europe," according to Orvar Löfgren, "but visiting Americans found that the American styles, goods and rituals mostly had been Swedified beyond recognition." The use of appliances, the preferred color schemes of homes and offices, the shape of brooms, even the smell of multinational disinfectant, in short, everyday modernity, was at once American, international, and profoundly if often elusively national.[8]

The arrival of new consumer goods and new consumption venues did not automatically produce the modern housewife. Indeed, women had to be encouraged to adopt new practices—or so corporations, market researchers, educators, and politicians assumed. In feature articles and innumerable ads, the many women's magazines instructed their readers about particular appliances, defining them first as luxuries to which to aspire and then as necessities without which the modern housewife could not live. These widely read magazines inculcated new standards of cleanliness and style and propagated enticing images of easy comfort, elegant simplicity, and cheerful efficiency. Consumer research, which was an American export (whose leading proponents, however, were European émigrés), engaged women to help produce knowledge about their consumption habits and thereby participate in changing them. On both sides of the Atlantic, women were to be motivated to embrace domestic modernity in the proper spirit. Like their American counterparts, European women were to take pride in exercising consumer choice, but only after experts from politics and business had outlined the parameters of those choices and explained their centrality to both the modern family and modern gendered conceptions of citizenship.[9]

In Europe, changing patterns of consumption were accompanied by changing attitudes toward consumption. The interwar attacks on mass consumption as economically impossible, morally dangerous, culturally corrosive, or politically divisive and diverting gave way to a recognition that economic recovery would require a combination of Fordist production and mass consumption and to a confidence that consumer culture could be disciplined and adapted to national cultural and political agendas. Household appliances, model kitchens, indeed, entire model homes became regular features of trade fairs as well as of the special exhibitions that proliferated in the 1950s. The 1951 Festival of Britain, a celebration of victory and a promise of prosperity to come, drew heavily on the 1930 Stockholm exhibition and energetically promoted modern functional furnishings and architecture. U.S. officials and intellectuals, who in the late 1940s had apologized for American consumerism and insisted that America had high culture as well as homogeneous goods to offer Europe, soon came to celebrate consumer goods and consumer choice as proof of America's cultural and political as well as economic superiority. At the Brussels World's Fair of 1958, for example, the United States countered the Soviet celebration of Sputnik with lavish displays of refrigerators and televisions, washing machines and sporting goods. Photos and scale models depicted the homes and towns in which these new goods were used, and daily fashion shows with models who strolled among this plethora of consumer goods suggested the relaxed and at times elegant life the American housewife, aided by consumer abundance, could lead. The following year the United States exhibited a $250,000 RCA "miracle" kitchen (similar to one previously displayed in Brussels and Milan) in Moscow's Sokolniki Park. There, amid robot floor cleaners and a high-tech dishwasher that came to the table to collect dishes, Khrushchev and Nixon debated the virtues and vices of consumer choice and planned obsolescence and disputed the proper roles for women in family and society. The "kitchen debate" was not merely a verbal dual between Cold War rivals about political ideology but equally importantly a symbol of the growing tendency on both sides of the Atlantic, in Eastern as well as in Western Europe, to make the modern home the measure of civilization.[10]

The arrival, albeit at very differential rates, of the consumer durables and consumption venues associated with the United States was accompanied and further encouraged by new images of femininity and domesticity, of family and leisure that resembled American ones. Women's magazines and advertising both in them and in general publications not only conveyed detailed information about specific appliances but also purveyed broad definitions of modernity and women's place in it. They depicted "a way of life characterized by comfort, hygiene, time-saving and a both practical and charming way of tackling everyday tasks," to quote from one Swedish ad. The housewife took her work with the requisite seriousness but was equally dedicated to making her work and thus her family's life easier by a judicious choice of products. With the right technology, the same Swedish ad for refrigerators promised, "you will be able to take care of household tasks as easily and elegantly as the American wife." Frequently the old-style interwar housewife, shabbily dressed and looking stressed, was contrasted with the modern housewife, easily recognizable by her youth, fashionable clothing, modish haircut, and excessive cheerfulness. Whether depicted alone in her modern home, with women friends showing off her whiter than white laundry, or with the male expert or helpful husband, the modern housewife was represented as relentlessly optimistic and proud of her domestic accomplishments. In Europe as in America she embodied a carefree modernity, one in which technology was benign and progressive, not threatening or destructive as it appeared in its military and to a lesser extent industrial guises. The modern housewife was an individual but seldom alone; although she exercised consumer choice and decorated her home in her own but distinctly modern style, she was never depicted outside the home or away from the family in and through which she was to find fulfillment.[11]

Efforts to construct the modern home and represent the modern housewife as new women were integral to the projects undertaken on both sides of the Atlantic to normalize gender relations after the enormous disruptions of World War II. Despite fascist determination to restore traditional gender relations and prevent the potentially emancipatory wartime mobilization of women, despite British and American insistence that such mobilization was for the duration only, and despite the wartime rhetorical blitz against women among all belligerents, World War II created a crisis of masculinity. War, and especially defeat, gave women a taste of economic and emotional independence, weakened male power, and presented conservative politicians with the challenge of simultaneously democratizing politics, restructuring the economy, and restabilizing the male-headed family while granting women expanded political and social citizenship. Although the causes of marital and familial instability varied from country to country, everywhere there existed a strong belief that the modern home offered women an enticement to resume more traditional gender roles. Elaine Tyler May's study of American families in the Cold War era suggests that white, middle-class women found the new ideology of gender traditionalism packaged in the modern home appealing and that even if modern marriage and domesticity failed to satisfy them as promised, few regretted their life choices or were able to imagine an alternative. For such Western European countries as Britain and West Germany, the legal and social pressures on women to retreat into the home were enormous, and the social policy supports for alternate choices meager, but the prospects of actually being a consumer-oriented modern housewife were slow in coming. European women in the 1950s did not seem to embrace the new domesticity with the same genuine or desperate enthusiasm of their American counterparts; rather, they displayed a more sober determination to work for the future of their children and, in some cases, to build for the more modern future of their society.[12]

With or without extensive consumption, the modern home represented a space in which family life could be not only reconsolidated but also reconfigured. On both sides of the Atlantic, there was a continuation of the demographic transition toward smaller families, which became the focus of intensified emotional investment and the locus of a variety of new shared activities. In Britain and West Germany, as in the United States, there was a renewed emphasis on improved mothering as central to the development of children and the well-being of society. The family became a unit of consumption more than of wage pooling or production. Indeed, it was precisely the shared project of consumption, the creation of modern homes and lifestyles, that would unite and redefine the family. The association of consumption with housework was thus accompanied by the growing and pleasurable family consumption of leisure in the form of movies—and by the 1960s television programs—recreational sports, and vacations and travel.[13]

Did European women find meaning in the modern home and mass consumption? What sorts of identities did they develop and how did the lived experiences of modern domesticity vary from nation to nation, as well as by class and generation? Such questions can be partially answered by the analytic strategies pursued so far, namely, by contextualizing the modern housewife and the modern home in the cultures of consumption in different countries and examining the goods and images, the values and practices that prevailed. But it is equally important to relate domesticity, consumption, and gender to the state and nation in two rather different ways. First, the new woman and the new home, as ideology and practice, were mobilized for different partisan, national, and international political projects, and these need to be analyzed and compared if we are to understand the discourses and politics from which or against which women could construct identities. Second, gendered welfare states and the gendered cultures of production they encouraged played a formative role in shaping how the modern housewife defined herself and experienced the modern home and family.

The retreat *into* the home in the 1950s and 1960s was a retreat *from* nationally and culturally specific problematic pasts and threatening presents. In the United States it represented a search for security in jobs, marriage, and politics in the wake of depression and war and in the face of continued industrialization and urbanization. The idealized American family—patriotic, prosperous, and religious, with a breadwinner husband, a stay-at-home mother, and obedient children—was both a refuge from the Cold War and the home front of that multifaceted struggle. Domestic and geopolitical containment, as May argues, were two sides of the same coin of anxiety and identity.[14]

In Europe, the Cold War was only one source of anxiety, and containment only one political project among many. For West Germans, the retreat into the home and the restoration of sharply demarcated definitions of femininity and masculinity offered a means to restore the material and emotional damage of fascism and war without confronting the Nazi past personally or politically. The consuming woman as housewife was a key agent in the construction of the social market economy and the new postnational identity that emerged from the economic miracle. She was central to the project of living in the present and for the future with no articulated nostalgia for the past. If that project was first and foremost one that originated in and benefited Christian Democracy, it met little opposition from Social Democrats, for it brought the kind of mass consumption for which they had fought in vain in the 1920s. In France the Americanization of home and gender was mediated or triangulated by decolonization, Kristin Ross has argued. The new couple living in a modern and highly privatized home, where the woman followed a new regime of cleanliness, personal and domestic, was part and parcel of a French modernization that was a form of internal colonization. It represented an alternative to the colonial past and an escape from the decolonizing present. One suspects this reconfiguration of domestic roles and practices and the accompanying vast project of building social housing in major cities were also ways of focusing on mastering the problems of the present and forgetting accommodationist and collaborationist pasts. The 1951 Festival of Britain with its celebration of and plea for modern products and model homes offered a diversion from both austerity and the loss of empire as it sought to direct attention away from the anxiety and drabness of the war and postwar years and onto the promise of a bright new future. For the Labour Party in Britain as for the Social Democrats in Sweden, modernizing the home was part of a broader project of political and social transformation.[15]

In Eastern Europe, state attempts—belated and inadequate—to produce consumption on a comparable scale to that of Western Europe were integral to Communist efforts to achieve legitimacy. The popular retreat into the home, usually one with inadequate household technology and consumer goods, or by the 1970s the building of a weekend cottage, represented an escape from the claims and intrusions of the regime. The family was a refuge, much as it was in Cold War America, but from a different set of political forces and fears, and both men and women valued public and private differently than they did in Western Europe or the United States.[16]

The place that modern domesticity occupied in people's lives, the meanings they assigned to household consumer durables, and the gendered identities they developed around home and family varied not only because of different pasts and national memories of them but also because of postwar differences in women's work and social citizenship. The distinctive welfare state regimes that developed in post–World War II Europe significantly shaped the lived experiences of modern families and modern housewives.

Whether housewife and mother were exclusive identities or could be combined with waged or salaried work was significantly determined by the forms sex segregation took in different European countries, on the one hand, and by attitudes toward married women's work on the other. Certain jobs were coded as "women's work" across countries and economic systems—factory jobs in textiles, the garment trades, and the electro-technical industry, clerical positions, elementary school teaching, and domestic service. In East Central Europe and Russia, however, many professions that were masculine preserves in the West, such as medicine and engineering, had a significant proportion of women, and barriers to women's employment in skilled industrial jobs and manual labor were much lower as a result of the acute postwar labor shortages.

In the first postwar decade, women's work force participation was significantly greater in Eastern Europe than in Western Europe, where the male breadwinner/housewife model of work and family predominated. In most Western European countries and in the United States, women's participation in the labor force rose steadily in the 1950s, much of it involving part-time work, most of it regarded as a necessary but undesirable deviation from the societal norm of the stay-at-home wife and mother. By the early 1960s, however, women's participation in the labor force began to develop the divergent national patterns that would persist throughout subsequent decades. The Scandinavian countries, especially Sweden, moved toward very high participation of women in the labor force, including that of married women; in France and Britain the working woman, including the working mother, became much more prevalent, but in Germany, Italy, and the Netherlands, labor force participation by women, especially mothers, remained low. In Communist Eastern Europe the working mother remained the socially sanctioned norm. The substantial increases in women's participation in the labor force that occurred in both capitalist and socialist economies resulted from economic necessity, labor shortages, slow population growth, and pronatalism more than from a concern for women's equality or a critique of the constraints of full-time housework and childcare.[17]

In each country, women's participation in the labor force was thus complexly shaped by the structure of the economy, the preferences of employers, the platforms of politicians, and the prevailing attitudes toward work, motherhood, and family. Most important to shaping women's work opportunities and the new identities that could be built around them, however, was the nature of the social citizenship granted to women and men in the vastly expanded postwar welfare states. If social policy endorsed and reinforced the male breadwinner family, as it did in the conservative West German and Italian welfare states, in the liberal British variant, and in the social democratic Netherlands one, women were not only encouraged but actively constrained to remain in the home, especially when they had children. Benefits derived from their status as dependent wives and mothers, child support went to fathers not mothers, state-run childcare facilities or childcare subsidies were minimal or nonexistent, school days were short, and after-school programs and summer camps were rare. In France, by contrast, although benefits went to families, not directly to women, a variety of childcare facilities, family allowances, and maternity benefits made it much more possible for mothers to work. In social democratic Scandinavian welfare states, payment went to individuals rather than families, support services for parents or single-mothers with children were abundant, and high participation by women in the labor force was both possible and socially valued. Indeed, by the 1970s, northern Europe combined mass consumption, domestic modernity, waged labor, and welfare programs in a distinctive and, many believed, highly progressive manner. Eastern European countries were more successful in supporting childcare, subsidizing single mothers, providing health care, and extending the school day than in producing the household technology and consumer goods that were equally essential to making the working mother a viable and desirable norm.[18]

The complex combination of social citizenship, work opportunities, attitudes toward working mothers, and the availability of household technology and consumer goods defined modernity differently for different women. They influenced whether stay-at-home wives and mothers believed the rewards of their situation outweighed the drawbacks or indeed, whether they could conceive of any alternative. They helped determine whether working housewives and mothers felt themselves to be pariahs, unwilling bearers of the double burden, or pioneers of an expanded if contradictory definition of the modern woman as housewife, mother, and worker. Sometimes the modern European woman in her modern home looked a great deal like her American counterpart in the 1950s and 1960s, but often her options and attitudes were very different, despite her vacuum cleaners, refrigerators, and women's magazines.

In Search of the New Man?

Throughout the twentieth century, European discourses about Americanization have been couched in the language of feminization, and the new Americanized woman in her many incarnations was held to be emblematic of the promise or threat of Americanism. In the postwar decades, the modern woman as housewife was featured prominently, but her husband remained an elusive figure. The 1950s European youth culture and studies of it raise the issue of masculinity, at least in the form of juvenile delinquents, sexy rock stars, and youth rebels on the road. But what happened to teenage boys when they became young and not so young men who worked in offices and factories that used increasingly Americanized business practices, lived in modern, at least partially Americanized homes, and enjoyed that distinctly male icon of consumption, the car.[19] How, if at all, were career and job, fatherhood and sexuality rethought? Was there a "new man" of an Americanized sort, as there was a new woman—always, if not always accurately, imagined as modern in an American way?

Europeans had long critiqued the American man as a singularly superficial and economically obsessed creature; clever, efficient, and able to make a fast buck but lacking in culture and sensitivity, indiscriminately friendly, and dangerously egalitarian. From the interwar fascist

Right, he was viewed as undisciplined, insufficiently militaristic, and excessively materialistic; from the socialist and communist Left, he was viewed as politically uncommitted or naïve but capable of either reforming capitalism or providing techniques and technology useful to socialism.[20] Those were the views from afar or the impressions of travelers.

After 1945, European men encountered American males in a direct, intense, and unequal manner. As occupying soldiers, Marshall Plan officials, private businessmen, and culture brokers they were everywhere, dispensing funds, reorganizing political systems, restructuring firms and entire economies, and profoundly shaping postwar popular culture for the vanquished and the victors alike. Tens of thousands of Europeans went to the United States to study, work, and travel. We know something of what these encounters produced in terms of political ideas, cultural proclivities, and knowledge about technology and industrial relations. We know virtually nothing about their impact on conceptions of masculinity, save that in defeated Germany the relations between German women and GIs, who had energy, confidence, and consumer goods, fed into the postwar crisis of German masculinity and aroused intense anger that German woman did not "resist" the enemy as their men had. We know virtually nothing about what the experience of the modern home and marriage to the modern housewife meant for men. Did they retreat into the home and seek meaning in family and leisure, as their American counterparts were said to have done? Or did economic and social reconstruction and a more partisan and ideological political order save them from the privatization that occurred across the Atlantic? Did their participation in Americanization occur at work, where American business practices and organizational forms carried weight, but not in the home? And did the Americanization of business produce European variants of the lonely crowd and the organization man, concepts familiar to the many Europeans who had read David Riesman and William Whyte? Did men feel excluded from or marginal to the consumer culture in which the new woman played such a prominent role or did they proudly see themselves as the essential earner without whom consumption would not have been possible?[21]

One could enumerate further questions, but the point is clear. Just as we know all too little about how the Americanization of popular culture spoke to and was received by teenage girls, we know all too little about how the modern home and modern domesticity spoke to and were received by adult men. We know too little about the gendering of modernity from a male perspective, perhaps because producing Americanized goods with Americanized methods seemed less threatening than consuming Americanism. If women—consuming, movie going, eroticized—represent the dangerous side of modernity in the American century, then men—producing, engaging in constructive leisure, concerned with politics, and all together less Americanized—represented its promise.

Conclusion

In the two decades after 1945, mass consumption and modern domesticity came to Europe, but the resulting modernity was not a replication of America, real or imagined. There was simultaneously Americanization and nationalization, increased homogeneity and rich hybridity. Modernity, whether in architecture, culture, consumption, or domesticity, was always at once international and national; it aspired to universalized images, goods, and practices, but these were always embodied in an everyday that was national, and that was classed and gendered in distinctly national ways. The pursuit of modernity at home, at work, or in leisure time was simultaneously the practice of imitating and negotiating with America, of pursuing distinctive national projects of becoming modern, and of defining a European identity in a bipolar and decolonizing world.

NOTES

1. Orvar Löfgren, "Materializing the Nation in Sweden and America," *Ethnos* 58, 3–4 (1993): 161–96; Richard Pells, *Not Like Us: How Europeans Have Loved, Hated, and Transformed American Culture since World War II* (New York: Basic Books, 1997), 1–36, 278–324.
2. Joy Parr, *Domestic Goods: The Material, the Moral, and the Economic in the Postwar Years* (Toronto: University of Toronto Press, 1999), 165–266.
3. Allan Pred, *Recognizing European Modernities: A Montage of the Present* (London: Routledge, 1995), 99–173; Mary Nolan, "Housework Made Easy," *Feminist Studies* (fall 1990): 549–78; Löfgren, "Materializing the Nation," 181–83.
4. Adrian Forty, *Objects of Desire* (New York: Pantheon, 1986), 207–21; Christina Hardyment, *Slice of Life: The British Way of Eating since 1945* (London: Penguin, 1995); Michael Wildt, *Am Beginn der 'Konsumgesellschaft': Mangelerfahrung, Lebenshaltung, Wohlstandshoffnung in Westdeutschland in den fünfziger Jahren* (Hamburg: Ergebnisse, 1994); Erica Carter, *How German Is She? Postwar German Reconstruction and the Consuming Woman* (Ann Arbor: University of Michigan Press, 1996), 4–9, 45–59; Karel Ann Marling, *As Seen on TV: The Visual Culture of Everyday Life in the 1950s* (Cambridge: Harvard University Press, 1994), 255; Jennifer A. Loehlin, *From Rugs to Riches: Housework, Consumption and Modernity in Germany* (Oxford: Berg, 1999), 70.
5. Victoria de Grazia, "Changing Consumption Regimes in Europe, 1930–1970:

Comparative Perspectives on the Distribution Problem," in *Getting and Spending: European and American Consumer Societies in the Twentieth Century*, ed. Susan Strasser, Charles McGovern, and Matthias Judt (New York: Cambridge University Press, 1998), 79; Frank Mort, "The Commercial Domain: Advertising and the Cultural Management of Demand," in *Moments of Modernity: Reconstructing Britain 1945–1964*, ed. Becky Conekin, Frank Mort, and Chris Waters (London: Rivers Oram Press, 1999), 59–62, 66–67.

6. Adam Arvidsson, "The Discovery of Subjectivity: Motivation Research in Italy, 1958–1968," in *Across the Atlantic: Cultural Exchanges between Europe and the United States*, ed. Luisa Passerini (Brussels: P.I.E.-Peter Lang, 2000), 285–87; Orvar Löfgren, "Consuming Interests," *Culture and History* 7 (1990): 24–27; Marling, *As Seen on TV*, 253–67.

7. Gwendolyn Wright, "Good Design and 'The Good Life': Cultural Exchange in Post–World War II American Domestic Architecture," in Passerini, *Across the Atlantic*, 269–78.

8. Alexandra Staub, "The All-American Dream Moves to Germany: Housing after World War II," 1999, http://www.ghi-dc.org/conpotweb/; Nicole Rudolph, *La cuisine, cellule de base de la modernisation française: L'architecture, la modernisation et le genre dans la France des Trente Glorieuses* (Paris: Mémoire de Diplôme, Ecolé Normale Superieur, 1999); Löfgren, "Materializing the Nation," 190.

9. See Löfgren, "Consuming Interests," 13–17; Daniel Horowitz, "The Émigré as Celebrant of American Consumer Culture: George Katona and Ernest Dichter," in Strasser, McGovern, and Judt, *Getting and Spending*; Arvidsson, "Discovery of Subjectivity," 279–93; Carter, *How German Is She?* 77–106; Marling, *As Seen on TV*, 203–40.

10. Becky Conekin, "'Here Is the Modern World Itself': The Festival of Britain's Representations of the Future," in Conekin, Mort, and Waters, *Moments of Modernity*, 230–38; Volker Berghahn, *America and the Intellectual Cold Wars in Europe* (Princeton: Princeton University Press, 2001), 96–107, 133–36; Frances Stoner Saunders, *The Cultural Cold War: The CIA and the World of Arts and Letters* (New York: New Press, 1999), 19–24; Robert H. Haddow, *Pavilions of Plenty: Exhibiting American Culture Abroad in the 1950s* (Washington, D.C.: Smithsonian Institution Press, 1997), 106–11, 201–29; Marling, *As Seen on TV*, 242–83.

11. Löfgren, "Consuming Interests," 25. Elaine Tyler May, *Homeward Bound: American Families in the Cold War Era* (New York: Basic Books, 1988), 23.

12. Margaret Higonnet, Jane Jenson, Sonya Michel, and Margaret Weitz, eds., *Behind the Lines: Gender and the Two World Wars* (New Haven: Yale University Press, 1987); May, *Homeward Bound*, 58–91; Robert Moeller, *Protecting Motherhood: Women and Family in the Politics of Postwar West Germany* (Berkeley: University of California Press, 1993), 1–38; Denise Riley, *War in the Nursery: Theories of Mother and Child* (London: Virago, 1983); May, *Homeward Bound*, 183–207.

13. Orvar Löfgren, *On Holiday: A History of Vacations* (Berkeley: University of California Press, 1999).

14. May, *Homeward Bound*, 10–15.

15. Frank Biess, "Survivors of Totalitarianism: Returning POWs and the Reconstruction of Masculine Citizenship in West Germany, 1945–1955," in *The Miracle Years: A Cultural History of West Germany, 1949–1968*, ed. Hanna Schissler (Princeton: Princeton University Press, 2001), 57–82; Carter, *How German Is She?* 20–43, 109–13; Kristin Ross, *Fast Cars, Clean Bodies: Decolonization and Reordering of French Culture* (Cambridge: M.I.T. Press, 1996), 4–10, 71–78; Conekin, "Here Is the Modern World Itself," 228–33.

16. Barbara Einhorn, *Cinderella Goes to Market: Citizenship, Gender and the Wom-*

en's Movement in East Central Europe (London: Verso, 1993); Susan Gil and Gail Kligman, *The Politics of Gender after Socialism* (Princeton: Princeton University Press, 2000).

17. Hans-Peter Blossfeld and Catherine Hakim, eds., *Between Equalization and Marginalization: Women Working Part-Time in Europe and the United States of America* (New York: Oxford University Press, 1987); Jane Lewis, ed., *Women and Social Policies in Europe: Work, Family and the State* (Brookfield, Vt.: Edward Elgar, 1993), 25–48, 116–37.

18. Diane Sainsbury, ed., *Gendering Welfare States* (London: Sage, 1994).

19. Volker Berghahn, *The Americanization of West German Business* (Cambridge: Cambridge University Press, 1986); Nick Tiratsoo, "Limits of Americanization: The United States Productivity Gospel in Britain," in Conekin, Mort, and Waters, *Moments of Modernity*, 96–113.

20. Mary Nolan, *Visions of Modernity* (New York: Oxford University Press, 1994), 109–20.

21. Berghahn, *America and the Intellectual Cold Wars in Europe*; Berghahn, *Americanization of West German Business*; Elizabeth Heineman, "The Hour of the Woman: Memories of Germany's 'Crisis Years' and West German National Identity," in Schissler, *Miracle Years*, 38; May, *Homeward Bound*, 87–90; Pells, *Not Like Us*, 173–75.

The Right to Have Rights: Citizens, Aliens, and the Law in Modern America

RICHARD POLENBERG

"The right to have rights"—the title of this chapter—is taken from a Supreme Court opinion written by Chief Justice Earl Warren in 1958 for *Perez v. Brownell*. The Court in *Perez* narrowly upheld an order stripping a man of United States citizenship. Warren wrote an impassioned dissent, however, which over the next thirty years provided a basis for the Supreme Court to shield native-born citizens from the government's efforts to denationalize them and also to protect naturalized citizens against efforts to denaturalize them. I begin this chapter by evaluating the new post-*Perez* jurisprudence, the substance of which was essentially complete by 1988; next, I examine changing patterns of immigration and naturalization in the 1990s; and then I discuss the meaning of both developments for the current controversy over the question of dual citizenship. That controversy, in fact, has profound implications for America's changing role in the new era of globalization.

THE facts of *Perez v. Brownell* are relatively straightforward. Clemente Martinez Perez was born near El Paso, Texas, in 1909 and so by virtue of the U.S. policy of *jus soli*—literally, the right of the soil—he was a United States citizen although his parents were Mexican nationals. (The son of Clemente Martinez and Maria Perez, his name should have appeared in the record as Martinez Perez, or Martinez, but instead was rendered Perez.) In 1919 or 1920, when he was ten years old, his parents returned to Mexico, naturally taking their son with them. During World

War II, Perez twice entered the United States as a railroad worker, on each occasion claiming to be a Mexican citizen. In 1947 he again sought admission, this time as a United States citizen. At a hearing he admitted that he had wanted to avoid the wartime draft, and he also said that he had voted in a Mexican election in 1946. The government, citing a provision of the Naturalization Act of 1940, ordered his exclusion on the grounds that he had expatriated himself by voting in Mexico. In 1953, after Perez had gained entry to the United States as an alien farm worker, the government moved to deport him for lacking a proper visa.

So the constitutional question before the Supreme Court in 1958 was whether Congress could make the casting of a vote in a foreign election grounds for the loss of citizenship. The majority opinion, written by Justice Felix Frankfurter, upheld the statute. Because Congress had the power to regulate foreign affairs, Frankfurter declared, the only issue was whether the withdrawal of citizenship had a reasonable relationship to the effective exercise of that power. Such a relationship existed, he asserted, because a vote cast by a United States citizen in a foreign election is "potentially embarrassing to the American Government and pregnant with the possibility of embroiling this country in disputes with other nations." Frankfurter explicitly rejected the notion that "the power of Congress to terminate citizenship depends upon the citizen's assent."

Earl Warren's dissenting opinion, joined by Justices Hugo Black and William O. Douglas, is remarkable because it is grounded not only in the Constitution (especially the citizenship provisions of the Fourteenth Amendment) but also in the Declaration of Independence. "What is this Government, whose power is here being asserted? And what is the source of that power?" Warren asked, and he continued: "The answers are the foundation of our Republic. To secure the inalienable rights of the individual, 'Governments are instituted among Men, deriving their just powers from the consent of the governed.'" Warren took those words to mean that "This Government was born of its citizens, it maintains itself in a continuing relationship with them, and . . . it is without power to sever the relationship that gives rise to its existence." Conceding that Congress has broad power over foreign affairs, Warren nevertheless maintained that "citizenship is not subject to the general powers of the government."

To be sure, Warren added, one could voluntarily relinquish one's citizenship by deciding, for example, to adopt a foreign nationality. But the "fatal defect" of the Naturalization Act of 1940 was that it did not confine itself to situations in which persons elected to abandon their citizenship. To cast a vote abroad, Warren concluded, signified no such decision, for "the basic right of American citizenship has been too dearly won to be so lightly lost." His broader argument, which would later carry the day, was that "the Government is without power to take citizenship away from a native-born or lawfully naturalized American."[1]

In 1960, two years after *Perez* was handed down, Ephraim Bait-Ephraim, a naturalized American citizen then residing in Israel, applied to have his passport renewed. Like Perez, he had voted in a foreign election and the State Department therefore turned down his application, asserting he had relinquished his citizenship. Unlike Perez, however, he was not a native-born but a naturalized citizen. He had immigrated to the United States from Poland in 1912 at the age of nineteen and had been naturalized in 1926. In 1950 he moved to Israel, settling in Safad, where he worked as an artist. He voted in three Knesset elections during the 1950s, and in 1960 he found himself unable to renew his American passport. He took his case to the U.S. Supreme Court, which decided in his favor in 1967. His name, Anglicized and rendered phonetically, appears in the Court records as Beys Afroyim. In *Afroyim v. Rusk,* as in *Perez,* the justices were divided five to four, but now the majority sided with the appellant.

The opinion, written by Justice Hugo Black, expressly overturned *Perez.* Although Warren naturally supported it, Black's opinion went considerably further in protecting the rights of citizenship than had the chief justice in his earlier dissent. To be sure, Black followed Warren when he explained his view of the meaning of the Fourteenth Amendment: "In our country the people are sovereign and the Government cannot sever its relationship to the people by taking away their citizenship." But where Warren in *Perez* granted Congress the power to decide that certain "actions in derogation of undivided allegiance to this country"— although not simply the casting of a vote—should lead to a loss of citizenship, Black now significantly placed more stringent restrictions on that power. "The very nature of our free government," he wrote, "makes it completely incongruous to have a rule of law under which a group of citizens temporarily in office can deprive another group of citizens of their citizenship." His inspired definition of the government—"a group of citizens temporarily in office"—served both to demystify those who made the laws and to justify restrictions on the kinds of laws they could make.

Writing for the dissenters, Justice John Marshall Harlan complained that the decision rested "simply on the Court's ipse dixit, evincing little more, it is quite apparent, than the present majority's own distaste for the expatriation power."[2] Perhaps so, yet that distaste, although Harlan failed to appreciate the fact, derived from the majority's conception of the people-as-sovereign that gave citizenship a privileged status. That same conception not only led the Court to restrict the power of Congress to denationalize citizens, either native-born or naturalized, but it also led it to restrict the government's power to denaturalize some individuals who had admittedly lied when they had become citizens. Two cases, different in nature and decided years apart, illustrate this trend: *Chaunt v. United States* (1960) and *Kungys v. United States* (1988).

Peter Chaunt—his given name was Ladislaus Leitner—was born in Budapest, Hungary, in 1899; he immigrated to the United States in 1921 and became a naturalized citizen in 1940. On his application he failed to admit that he was a member of the Communist Party, much less a district organizer, although he did state that he was employed by the International Workers' Order. More importantly, he lied by claiming he had never been arrested. In fact, he had been arrested three times in 1929 and 1930 for distributing handbills, for making a speech on New Haven Green, and for a "general breach of the peace." The government therefore endeavored to denaturalize him on the grounds that he had obtained his citizenship fraudulently. But the Supreme Court, in an opinion by William O. Douglas, would have none of it.

True, Chaunt had lied, Douglas agreed, but "naturalization decrees are not lightly to be set aside." The three arrests "were not reflections on the character of the man seeking citizenship" for they did not involve either moral turpitude or fraudulent conduct. "The totality of the circumstances surrounding the offenses charged makes them of extremely slight consequence," Douglas continued: "Had they involved moral turpitude or acts directed at the Government, had they involved conduct which even peripherally touched types of activity which might disqualify one from citizenship, a different case would be presented." Chaunt may have had any number of reasons not to disclose the three arrests, Douglas concluded, but the government had failed to prove that the truth, if disclosed, would have warranted a denial of citizenship or would have been useful in an investigation possibly leading to the discovery of other facts warranting denial.[3]

In his dissenting opinion (joined by Justices Potter Stewart and Charles Whittaker) Justice Tom Clark maintained that the Court, by rewarding Chaunt for his dishonesty, was in effect inviting others who were seeking naturalization to behave in a similarly fraudulent fashion.

Whether or not truthful answers on his citizenship application would have prevented Chaunt's naturalization, Clark asserted, the government was entitled to such answers, and he added: "We should exact the highest standards of probity and fitness from all applicants."

A considerably more complex, not to say disturbing, case came the Court's way in 1988. Juozas Kungys had immigrated to the United States from Germany in 1948 and had been naturalized in 1954. In 1982, the Office of Special Investigations of the Department of Justice, whose business it is to track down Nazi war criminals, moved to denaturalize him. The OSI attempted to show three things: first, that Kungys, as a member of a Lithuanian paramilitary organization, had participated in the massacre of 2,076 Jewish men, women, and children in August 1941; second, "that in applying for his visa and in his naturalization petition, Kungys had made false statements with respect to his date and place of birth, wartime occupations, and wartime residence" (stating, for example, that he had resided in another city rather than in Kedainiai at the time the atrocities occurred); and third, "that Kungys' citizenship had been 'illegally procured' . . . because when he was naturalized he lacked the good moral character required of applicants for citizenship."

Relying largely on *Chaunt* and other precedents, the justices overturned a Circuit Court of Appeals ruling that had remanded Kungys for deportation. Speaking through Justice Antonin Scalia, the majority held that the three videotaped depositions which asserted that Kungys was a war criminal (taken from survivors living in the Soviet Union) were inadmissible, and that the lies he told to obtain a visa and to become naturalized were not "material" because they would not have warranted denying a visa or withholding citizenship, or have led to an investigation that would have produced those results.[4] Justice Byron White, who dissented in *Kungys,* might well have quoted the dissenting opinion in *Chaunt:* "The Swiss philosopher Amiel tells us that 'character is an historical fruit and is the result of a man's biography.' Petitioner's past, if truthfully told in his application, would have been an odorous one. So bad that he dared not reveal it. For the Court to reward his dishonesty is nothing short of an open invitation to false swearing to all who seek the high privilege of American citizenship."[5]

In the thirty years from 1958 to 1988, then, Supreme Court jurisprudence regarding denationalization and denaturalization had undergone a startling change. Some constitutional scholars have criticized the Court's reasoning, especially Earl Warren's reliance on the Declaration of Independence in his *Perez* dissent. My own view is that Warren was exactly right. I agree with Charles L. Black Jr., who has argued that the Declaration of Independence should be recognized as a source of law, that its doctrines "should be taken to have the force of *law*—the force *in law* of general commitments from which *particular* law can be derived." The Declaration, he asserts, "is the root of all political authority among us, of all legitimate exercise of power."[6] That was rather like the view Warren took when he laid the foundations of a new jurisprudence of American citizenship.

Nothing better typified the new approach than a 1980 decision, *Vance v. Tarrazas*, in which Justice Byron White affirmed the *Afroyim* rule that a loss of citizenship could not occur without proof by the government that an "expatriating act was accompanied by an intent to terminate United States citizenship." Laurence J. Terrazas had been born in the United States, the son of a Mexican citizen, and therefore a citizen of both nations. But in 1970, at the age of twenty-two, he applied for a certificate of Mexican nationality and renounced his United States citizenship. The justices only disagreed over whether, as the majority thought, the necessary intent had to be demonstrated by "a preponderance of the evidence" or whether, as Justice Thurgood Marshall maintained, it required the still higher standard of "clear and convincing evidence."[7]

In 1988, the same year *Kungys* was decided, Congress followed the Court's lead by liberalizing the Immigration and Naturalization Act. An individual would lose his or her citizenship, the statute declared, only "by voluntarily performing [an expatriating act] with the intention of relinquishing United States nationality."[8] And in 1995 the State Department removed the last remaining doubts by reminding all diplomatic posts: "It is no longer possible to terminate an American's citizenship without the citizen's cooperation."[9]

By the mid-1990s, it was abundantly clear that the United States was undergoing the greatest boom in immigration since the turn of the century. The influx began in the decade of the 1980s, when 7.3 million immigrants entered the country, nearly as many as in the two previous decades, the 1960s and 1970s, combined. Then, in 1990, Congress passed the most expansive immigration law in American history. It increased immigration levels by nearly 40 percent, setting the maximum number of annual entries at 700,000 from 1992 to 1994, and 675,000 beginning in 1995. But the act also permitted various exceptions so that the number of persons entering the country often exceeded those levels. (I am speaking here only of legal immigrants; the government estimates that about 275,000 illegal, or "undocumented," immigrants enter the country each year.) More than 900,000 people arrived in the United States in 1992, 1993, and again in 1996. "This annual influx," a scholar has noted, probably exceeds the legal admissions totals of the rest of the world combined."[10]

By the year 2000, the foreign-born, numbering 28.4 million, comprised more than 10 percent of the nation's population, the highest proportion since the 1930s. The sources of the recent immigration, however, are as significant as its size. Before World War II, virtually all immigrants came from European countries: Germany, Italy, Ireland, Great Britain, Austria-Hungary, Poland, Russia, and Greece. Now, 50 percent come from Latin America and another 25 percent from Asia. In the last twenty years, ten nations—Mexico, the Philippines, India, Vietnam, China, the Dominican Republic, Cuba, Korea, El Salvador, and Jamaica—have accounted for nearly 60 percent of all immigrants (Mexico alone for more than 25 percent). Moreover, the vast majority of the newcomers—perhaps three-fourths in all—have settled in only six states: California, New York, Florida, Texas, New Jersey, and Illinois.

The 1990s not only witnessed immigration on a formidable scale but also saw a greater desire on the part of newcomers to become naturalized citizens. This represents a notable break with the past. Immigrants have traditionally been slow to seek American citizenship because there have been relatively few incentives to do so. Children born in the United States are automatically citizens whatever their parents' status. Basic constitutional guarantees—due process of law, freedom of speech and religion, the right against self-incrimination, protection against unreasonable searches and seizures—apply to all persons, to aliens, that is, as well as to citizens. The Supreme Court has invalidated most state laws that prohibit aliens from working in certain professions (for example, as engineers and lawyers) or that deprive them of welfare benefits. To be sure, noncitizens cannot vote, or serve on juries, or hold high elective or appointive office, but these disadvantages, generally speaking, are not considered very onerous.

Since the mid-1990s, however, this pattern has changed. In the 1970s and 1980s only about 100,000 to 225,000 immigrants became naturalized citizens each year. But in the period from 1990 to 1995, the annual number fluctuated from between 250,000 to 500,000. Since 1995 there has been a veritable explosion in the numbers of immigrants applying for, and obtaining, naturalization. The recent figures are highly revealing: 1996, 1.3 million; 1997, 1.4 million; 1998, 475,000; and 1999, 872,500. Four million newly naturalized citizens in just four years—the number, both absolutely and relatively speaking, is unprecedented in American history.

The reasons for the change are readily discernible. In part, it reflects the impact of the 1986 Immigration Reform and Control Act (IRCA), which offered an amnesty to approximately three million "undocumented" aliens who had entered the country illegally but who now became eligible to apply for citizenship. In addition, the impulse toward naturalization is understandable as a defensive, protective reaction by noncitizens to a groundswell of anti-immigrant sentiment that was increasingly evident by the mid-1990s. That sentiment revealed itself in many ways: in polls showing that the public generally favored curbing immigration; in the efforts of organizations such as English First and U.S. English to make English the nation's official language; in the 1994 passage by California voters of Proposition 187, designed to bar illegal aliens from receiving welfare and educational benefits; and in the publication of a steady stream of books whose titles spoke for themselves: *The Immigration Invasion, The Path to National Suicide, The Immigration Time Bomb, Immigration Out of Control,* and *Alien Nation,* a work that purported to offer "Common Sense about America's Immigration Disaster."[11]

The new nativism, however, found its most concrete expression in the Welfare Reform Act of 1996, which represented, as several scholars have said, a radical shift in the nation's thinking about the difference citizenship should make in the way the government treats individuals.[12] The act sharply restricted noncitizens' access to the social safety net. Permanent resident aliens became ineligible for federal means-tested benefit programs, including disability payments under Supplemental Social Insurance and, of greater significance, food stamps. The act also gave the states broad authority to set eligibility rules for immigrants who applied for welfare and Medicaid. Although the statute affected citizens as well as immigrants, the Congressional Budget Office estimated that 44 percent of the expected $54 billion in savings would come from restricting the eligibility of immigrants (who, in fact, make up only 5 percent of welfare recipients).

Many of the harshest provisions of the 1996 act limiting immigrant eligibility were later repealed or modified, but the act nevertheless was properly construed as an attack on the long-standing practice of placing immigrants and citizens on an equal footing when it came to the enjoyment of government benefits. The act lowered the civic status of the great majority of immigrants, signifying, thereby, a "fundamental redefinition of their membership in the society."[13] By making citizenship the gateway to medical benefits, childcare services, and food stamp programs, the measure represented the most important reconsideration of the importance of citizenship since passage of the Fourteenth Amendment in 1868.

Moreover, the Welfare Reform Act had another powerfully—albeit unintentionally—discriminatory effect on American citizens. Families in the United States are not composed only of citizens or only of noncitizens. There are many "mixed status" families in which, typically, one or both of the adults are noncitizens (either legal immigrants or undocumented aliens), and one or more of the children are citizens. Indeed, one in every ten families with children in the United States falls into this category. In large cities, destination points for newly arrived immigrants, the figure is dramatically higher: one in every four families in New York City is mixed status, and one in every two in Los Angeles. The limitations on noncitizen adults' use of public benefits naturally has a spillover effect on the availability of benefits to their citizen children. Because food stamps are allocated on a household basis, welfare reform sharply differentiates between children who are citizens and whose parents are too, and children who are citizens but whose parents are not.[14]

THE combined effect of these two broad trends—a series of Supreme Court rulings sharply restricting denationalization and denaturalization, and an extraordinary increase in the number of immigrants now seeking citizenship in response to nativist sentiment in the 1990s—has been to increase the likelihood that large numbers of people will wish to hold dual citizenship and will in fact be able to do so. True, to become a naturalized United States citizen, immigrants must "renounce and abjure absolutely and entirely all allegiance and fidelity to any foreign prince, potentate, state, or sovereignty."[15] In fact, however, this pledge is not legally binding and does not require individuals to give up their former citizenship or extinguish their prior nationality.

There are, therefore, no longer any significant practical limits on participation by United States citizens in the political life of other nations. American citizens have served as the foreign ministers of Armenia and Bosnia, and as the commander of the Estonian army. Milan Panic, a Serbian-born naturalized citizen, even served as the prime minister of Yugoslavia in 1992, after obtaining assurances that holding that office would not lead to his expatriation. Jesus R. Galvis, a naturalized citizen who was elected to the city council in Hackensack, New Jersey, where he ran a travel agency, ran for the Senate—in his native land, Colombia—but lost. "I was going to travel back and forth," he said, "I saw this as a good opportunity keep some ties to the homeland there."[16]

Many nations, including Great Britain, Ireland, Switzerland, Greece, El Salvador, and Israel, have long permitted their citizens to retain their citizenship after becoming naturalized in a foreign state. Other countries—including Italy, Turkey, Colombia, and the Dominican Republic—have now joined that list. In 1996, according to one study, of the 17 Latin American nations, 7 permitted some form of dual citizenship; by 2000 the number had risen to 14, and more were considering such a change. In all, 89 nations permit their nationals to hold dual citizenship. As a July 15, 2001, headline in the *New York Times* declared: "As Rules Ease, More Citizens Choose to Fly 2 Flags."[17]

The most populous Latin American land to accept a policy of dual citizenship is Mexico, the source of more than one-quarter of all immigrants to the United States, and a nation that saw more than a quarter of a million of its residents become naturalized United States citizens in 1996. On March 20, 1997, Mexico adopted a new provision to its constitution, which went into effect a year later. Mexicans who become naturalized United States citizens may now maintain their Mexican nationality, and Mexicans who have already acquired United States citizenship may apply to reacquire their Mexican nationality. Such dual nationals can continue to use their Mexican passports, own lands normally forbidden to aliens, and take advantage of certain inheritance and property rules. Moreover, their children who are born in the United States would also acquire their parents' Mexican nationality along with United States citizenship.[18]

The emergence of dual citizenship has provoked sharp disagreement among legal scholars. For example, Yale Law School professor Peter Schuck emphasizes the disadvantages, indeed the dangers, implicit in such a development. But Professor Peter J. Spiro of Hofstra University Law School maintains that the development is to be welcomed, especially in view of the end of the Cold War and the diminished fear of disloyalty or subversion.[19] In my view, Spiro is right. I do not believe there is anything to fear from dual citizenship; on the contrary, it can serve as the basis for a transnational model of citizenship that is entirely appropriate for the twenty-first century. One way to demonstrate this is by examining Schuck's arguments in his 1998 volume, *Citizens, Strangers, and In-Betweens: Essays on Immigration and Citizenship.*

Schuck, one of the most perceptive writers on the subject, certainly recognizes the many advantages of dual nationality. It provides individuals who hold such status "with additional options—an alternative country in which to live, work, and invest, an additional locus and source of rights, obligations, and communal ties." United States–based business firms, moreover, benefit from having employees who can travel and work abroad easily, who can build transnational market networks, and who can contribute to "the international flow of human, financial, and technological capital." Finally, insofar as the policy encourages immigrants to acquire United States citizenship, it has the beneficial effect of hastening assimilation.[20]

Having conceded this much, Schuck then attempts to assess the drawbacks of dual citizenship. He claims, for example, that individuals who are entitled to vote in elections in the United States and in another country may face a conflict of interest "in the sense that the other state's election may shape that state's policies—on trade or foreign policy, for example—in ways that either benefit or adversely affect the U.S." Yet Schuck also acknowledges that feelings of attachment to another country may affect voters' preferences whether or not they hold dual citizenship, that such feelings have influenced voters' behavior throughout American history, and that they are entirely legitimate. He approvingly quotes Spiro's comment: "A dual Mexican-American who advocates policies that benefit Mexico is little different from a Catholic who advocates policies endorsed by the church."[21] Irish Americans, German Americans, Italian Americans, Cuban Americans, Chinese Americans—all of these groups, and others like them, are always inclined to vote in ways they think will be advantageous to their own ethnic groups, their own religious communities, and their own ancestral roots, and the inclination would be no stronger if they were to possess dual citizenship.

In the end, then, Schuck claims we must look beyond electoral conflicts "to more transcendent concerns having to do with political unity, identity, community, and loyalty."[22] Yet because he cannot show that dual citizenship tangibly threatens any of those concerns, he falls back on the assertion that citizenship is analogous to marriage, the oath of loyalty to a nuptial vow. "If we think that naturalizing citizens are entering into a kind of marital relationship with the polity, it might seem natural and morally compelling to insist that they make a firm choice of one polity or another," he writes; "We must choose one U.S. state of residence, one political party, one name, and one marriage at a time. Why not require us to choose one national citizenship?" "In marriage," Schuck continues, "we expect a certain exclusivity or (where not exclusive) at least a clear priority of commitment." Conceding that the analogy of citizenship to marriage is "far from perfect," he nevertheless maintains that "marriage probably comes closer than any other common relationship to capturing the quality of enduring loyalty and priority of affection and concern that most American expect from those who apply to become their fellow citizens."[23]

The analogy between marriage and citizenship, however, is not only imperfect; it is also inaccurate and misleading. To be sure, a nation, like a spouse, may inspire feelings of loyalty, commitment, and even love. But the depth and intensity of the feelings between marital partners are in no sense equivalent to the emotions associated with patriotism. The "close and intimate" relationship that marriages are ideally supposed to nurture generates, according to a knowledgeable author, "a commitment to respond to the feelings and needs of the other . . . so strong that the other becomes a part of one's own self-definition." Spouses retain their autonomy, in this view, but it is "an autonomy in which the relationship framework is fundamental to one's self-understanding."[24]

An individual who holds dual citizenship and is therefore entitled to vote in two countries, or to carry two passports, is not analogous to an unfaithful spouse. As T. Alexander Aleinikoff has said: "While some see dual citizenship as membership bigamy, it is probably more appropriate to recognize it as the relationship that one has with one's family and one's in-laws. Such relationships at times produce conflict and need negotiation, but one can still be a functioning member of two families, loyal to both."[25] Whatever one thinks of it, the trend in the United States toward the acceptance of dual citizenship is the product of a half century of legal, political, and demographic change, as well as of a reconsideration of relevant policies by other countries, such as Mexico. There is no indication that the trend is likely to be reversed, and no good reason why it should be.

Indeed, as we enter a new era of globalization, as the Internet overcomes conventional barriers to communication, and as long-standing political, economic, and even geographical boundaries diminish in significance, a transnational model of citizenship may be the most appropriate model for the twenty-first century.

NOTES

1. 356 US 44 (1958).
2. 387 US 253 (1967).
3. 364 US 350 (1960).

4. 485 US 759 (1988).

5. 364 US 350 (1960).

6. Charles L. Black Jr., *A New Birth of Freedom: Human Rights, Named and Unnamed* (New York: Grosset/Putnam, 1997), 8–9. For a critique of Warren's dissent, see T. Alexander Aleinikoff, "Theories of Loss of Citizenship," *Michigan Law Review* 84 (1986): 1480.

7. 444 US 252 (1980).

8. T. Alexander Aleinikoff, *Between Principles and Politics: The Direction of U.S. Citizenship Policy* (Washington, D.C.: Carnegie Endowment for International Peace, 1998), 24.

9. Peter J. Spiro, "Dual Nationality and the Meaning of Citizenship," *Emory Law Journal* 46 (fall 1997): 1454.

10. Peter H. Schuck, *Citizens, Strangers, and In-Betweens: Essays on Immigration and Citizenship* (Boulder, Colo.: Westview Press, 1998), 176.

11. See David M. Reimers, *Unwelcome Strangers: American Identity and the Turn against Immigration* (New York: Columbia University Press, 1998).

12. Michael Fix and Wendy Zimmerman, "Welfare Reform: A New Immigrant Policy for the United States," in *In Defense of the Alien,* ed. Lydio F. Tomasi (New York: Center for Migration Studies, 1997), 19:59.

13. Ibid., 67.

14. See Michael Fix and Wendy Zimmerman, *All under One Roof: Mixed-Status Families in an Era of Reform* (New York: Urban Institute, 1999).

15. Aleinikoff, *Between Principles and Politics,* 37.

16. Mark Fritz, "Pledging Multiple Allegiances," *Los Angeles Times,* April 6, 1998.

17. Amy Cortese, "As Rules Ease, More Citizens Choose to Fly 2 Flags," *New York Times,* July 15, 2001.

18. See Jorge Durand, Douglas S. Massey, and Emilio A. Parrado, "The New Era of Mexican Migration to the United States," *Journal of American History* 86 (September 1999): 518–36; and Carlos Gonzalez Gutierrez, "Fostering Identities: Mexico's Relations with Its Diaspora," ibid., 545–67.

19. Spiro, "Dual Nationality," passim.

20. Schuck, *Citizens, Strangers, and In-Betweens,* 230–32.

21. Ibid., 234.

22. Ibid., 236.

23. Ibid., 240–41.

24. David Hartman, *The Living Covenant: The Innovative Spirit in Traditional Judaism* (New York: Macmillan, 1985), 5, as cited in Sanford Levinson, *Constitutional Faith* (Princeton: Princeton University Press, 1988), 107–11.

25. Aleinikoff, *Between Principles and Politics,* 39.

Contributors

VOLKER R. BERGHAHN is the Seth Low Professor of History at Columbia University. His book *America and the Intellectual Cold Wars in Europe* was published in 2001. He is currently preparing a study of German American business relations in the twentieth century.

ALAN BRINKLEY is the Allan Nevins Professor of History at Columbia University and author, most recently, of *Liberalism and Its Discontents*. He is currently writing a biography of Henry Luce.

DAVID W. ELLWOOD is Professor of International Relations at the University of Bologna. He is author of *Europe Reconstructed, 1945–1950*.

GIULIANA GEMELLI is Professor of European Contemporary History at the University of Bologna. Most recently she has written *American Foundation and Large Research: Construction and Transfer of Knowledge*.

DETLEF JUNKER teaches American history at the University of Heidelberg. Among his books is *The Manichaean Trap: American Perceptions of the German Empire, 1871–1945*.

JAMES T. KLOPPENBERG is Professor of History at Harvard University. Interested in American and Euopean democratic theory and practice, he is author most recently of *Virtues of Liberalism*.

WALTER LAFEBER is the Mary Underhall Noll Professor of American History at Cornell University. He has written many books about American foreign policy. The ninth edition of his *America, Russia, and the Cold War* has recently been published.

R. LAURENCE MOORE is the Howard A. Newman Professor of American Studies at Cornell University. He is currently writing a book about American religion and American culture.

MARY NOLAN is Professor of History at New York University. Her most recent book is *Visions of Modernity: American Business and the Modernization of Germany.*

RICHARD POLENBERG is the Goldwin Smith Professor of American History at Cornell University. His most recent book is *In the Matter of J. Robert Oppenheimer.*

FEDERICO ROMERO is Professor of American History at the University of Florence. He is author of *The United States and the European Trade Union Movement, 1944–1951.*

MASSIMO L. SALVADORI is Professor of History of Political Thought at the University of Turin. The most recent of his many books is *The Political Left in Italian History.*

RONALD STEEL is Professor of International Relations at the University of Southern California. He is the author of *Temptation of a Superpower* and, more recently, *In Love with the Night: The American Romance with Robert Kennedy.*

MAURIZIO VAUDAGNA teaches contemporary history at the University of Eastern Piedmont. He is currently editing *Public and Private in Twentieth-Century American History.*

Index